Side by Sid

Side by Side in Eternity

*The Lives Behind Adjacent
American Military Graves*

JAMES ROBERT MCNEAL *and*
J. ERIC SMITH

McFarland & Company, Inc., Publishers
Jefferson, North Carolina

LIBRARY OF CONGRESS CATALOGUING-IN-PUBLICATION DATA

Names: McNeal, James R., author. | Smith, J. Eric, 1965– author.
Title: Side by side in eternity : the lives behind adjacent American military graves /
James Robert McNeal, and J. Eric Smith.
Description: Jefferson, North Carolina : McFarland & Company, Inc., Publishers,
2023 | Includes bibliographical references and index.
Identifiers: LCCN 2023001709 | ISBN 9781476687926 (paperback : acid free paper) ∞
ISBN 9781476648507 (ebook)
Subjects: LCSH: National cemeteries—United States—History. | Soldiers' bodies,
Disposition of—United States—History. | Military funerals—United States—
History. | Cemeteries—United States—History. | Funeral rites and ceremonies—
United States—History. | Veterans—United States—Biography. | Burial—
United States—History.
Classification: LCC UB393 .M36 2023 | DDC 363.7/5—dc23/eng/20230113
LC record available at https://lccn.loc.gov/2023001709

BRITISH LIBRARY CATALOGUING DATA ARE AVAILABLE

ISBN (print) 978-1-4766-8792-6
ISBN (ebook) 978-1-4766-4850-7

Front cover image: World War II graves
© MyImages—Micha/Shutterstock

Printed in the United States of America

*McFarland & Company, Inc., Publishers
Box 611, Jefferson, North Carolina 28640
www.mcfarlandpub.com*

*To Marcia Brom Smith, Esq., and Dr. Peggy Mansfield McNeal,
for patiently humoring us as we enthused at length about the
stories that follow and for providing advice, wisdom, sanity checks,
and support for this project, among countless other things.*

Acknowledgments

The authors would like to acknowledge and thank the following individuals for providing guidance, interviews, images, maps, editorial assistance, or other indispensable "without which" support for this project: Colonel Adrian T. Bogart III, Petty Officer Thomas Bonaparte, Jr., Annie Britton-Nice, Chief Warrant Officer Aleithia A. Castro, Rose Clark, John Cross, Brigadier General W. Blake Crowe, Elizabeth Cruz, Sam Dorrance, E. Paige Smith Duft, Rachel Essig, Colonel Keith Gibson, Captain Mike Jefferson, Marcus Lee, Charlie Perdue, Sarah Byrn Rickman, Katelin Smith, Linda Waters Smith, Paul Stillwell, Jim Stockdale, Sid Stockdale, Taylor Stockdale, Nancy Tomasheski, Carol Tyler, Franklin Van Valkenberg, and Edward White III.

Table of Contents

Table of Contents

Prologue:
Personal Perspectives on Perpetual Proximity

BY JAMES ROBERT MCNEAL

"The cemetery is an open space among the ruins, covered in winter with violets and daisies. It might make one in love with death, to think that one should be buried in so sweet a place."
— Percy Bysshe Shelley

"I tell ya, golf courses and cemeteries are the biggest wastes of prime real estate."
— Al Czervik (from the film *Caddyshack*)

If you are reading this prologue, I will assume that you plan on reading our book, and for that, thank you! I make this assumption based on my own personal book-buying experience. I don't recall perusing a book for potential purchase by flipping to the prologue; typically, the process entails a glance at the front and back cover, then the table of contents, and if there are pictures, those as well.

So why did my coauthor and I decide to write this book? We are not (or at least I am not) all that enamored with graveyards and cemeteries (what's the difference between the two?), although I do find them interesting. We are not "cemetery tourists," which is in fact a thing. What birthed this book was an epiphany I had after I spent the day selecting photographs for my first book, *The Herndon Climb: A History of the United States Naval Academy's Greatest Tradition*, with apologies for that shameless plug. I was walking down the hill from the offices of the Naval Institute Press (who published the Herndon book) when I passed by the United States Naval Academy (USNA) Cemetery. No, I wasn't whistling; I never got that saying. Out of the corner of my eye, I saw a grave that had some recent flowers laid there and, looking to my right, I saw it was the final resting place of Senator John McCain (USNA '58), who had been buried the previous year. Lying next to Senator McCain was his best friend, Admiral Charles R. Larson, also from the USNA Class of 1958. Best friends since their time as midshipmen, they chose (along with their spouses) to rest together forever.

Admiral Larson was the Superintendent at the Naval Academy the last three years that my coauthor, J. Eric Smith, and I attended USNA. Larson rose to the rank of four-star admiral after his time as our "Supe," then after a major cheating scandal at the Academy, he was (unprecedently) brought back for a second tour as Superintendent in 1994 to "right the ship." He retired in 1998 and passed away at the age of 77 in 2014.

Senator McCain served for 31 years in the United States Senate, but he first became known to the American public through his experience in the prisons of North Vietnam, most notably the Hỏa Lò prison, or, as the prisoners derisively called it, the Hanoi Hilton. Lieutenant Commander McCain was injured when he ejected from his A-4 Skyhawk on October 26, 1967, and upon capture, he was beaten severely by his captors. When he arrived in Hanoi, the North Vietnamese denied him medical treatment until they discovered that his father was a navy admiral. In mid–1968, his father was named the commander of all U.S. Navy forces in Vietnam. The

The "perpetual proximity" graves of Senator John McCain and Admiral Chuck Larson at the U.S. Naval Academy Cemetery, the image that inspired this book (James R. McNeal).

2

Prologue by James Robert McNeal

North Vietnamese, who were always looking for propaganda opportunities (see Vice Admiral Stockdale's story in Chapter Ten for more on that front), offered McCain the chance to go home early, a demonstration of their benevolence. However, by this time, McCain was in communication with his fellow POWs, and although they were in prison, there was a strict chain of command and a standing order stated that no one went home early. (In fact, the order was that releases must be in order of captures.) McCain turned down the offer of early release, virtually guaranteeing that he would not only be denied substantive medical treatment for his injuries but also that he would be subjected to torture that was being administered on a regular basis. He was released as a POW in Operation Homecoming in March 1973 and passed away after a hard-fought and public battle with brain cancer in 2018.

Two very accomplished men, best friends, who chose to lie side by side in perpetuity, is a nice story but certainly not unique. What is unique (at least to me) is that whereas Admiral Larson was at the top of his class and served as the brigade commander his senior year at the Academy, his best friend, John McCain, finished a lowly fifth from the bottom of their class, and as McCain himself described it, "my four years [at USNA] were not notable for individual academic achievement but, rather, for the impressive catalogue of demerits which I managed to accumulate." My epiphany was simply "Wouldn't their friendship make an interesting book?" I have been a fervent admirer of Eric's writing for a long time and was thrilled when he agreed to work with me on this project.

As Eric and I worked to flesh out a book pitch, I had lunch with a friend, and when I told him about the Larson-McCain book idea, he said something that had been lurking in both of our minds: "Do you think that this subject matter is enough for a whole book?" Rather than present a critique with no solution, he followed that up with what became the central theme of our book: "You know there are a lot of other stories like that? For example, Admiral Crowe and Admiral Stockdale, who are buried side by side in the Naval Academy Cemetery, were best friends as well." Their story became our sample chapter and its strength is what set the bar for our subsequent stories, which ironically do not include Larson-McCain in this final version of our book, as we sensed that their story had already been told frequently and well in recent years.

Although there are many other stories that we could have used, we are pleased with both the depth and breadth of our selected chapters, and we hope you agree.

Introduction:
Perpetual Proximity

*Why Care About Adjacent Interments
and the Stories They Tell?*

*"When among the graves of thy fellows, walk with
circumspection; thine own is open at thy feet."*
—Ambrose Bierce

*"The grave is a common treasury, to which we must all be
taken."*
—Edmund Burke

There are approximately 7.5 billion human beings going about the
business of life on Earth today. We speak about 7,000 different languages and have organized ourselves into nearly 200 high-level political
units, governing virtually every inhabitable acre of earth and the seas
surrounding them, around the globe and from pole to pole. We thrive in
great cities packed with more than 100,000 people per square mile and
in sparsely populated regions where individuals or small communities
may be the sole representatives of our species for as far as they can see,
walk, sail, or ride, over many days in many cases.

We experience divinity via at least 4,000 formally organized faiths,
and our secular selves are ruled (willingly or not) by leaders representing thousands of sociopolitical parties and ideologies. We continually
process the world around us through an unquantifiable and distinctly
personal mixture of cultural cues, received wisdom, educational opportunities, physical experiences, interpersonal relationships, and emotional states, often interpreted and codified through artistic and
scientific pursuits and shared across an ever-more-connected global
information network that can exacerbate differences and forge com-
monalities with equal effectiveness and ease.

Introduction

The differences between us, profound and subtle, sensible and non-sensical alike, are often the sources of the great tumults that wrack our species and lead us into homicidal, genocidal, and collectively suicidal behaviors, taking thousands of other species and perhaps eventually the planet at large along a tragic descent into chaos and destruction for destruction's sake, or for profit, or for political point-making and score-settling. Although saner hearts and minds may embrace and celebrate the vast panorama of human diversity and the ways in which it can collectively inspire and enhance our understanding and appreciation of the world in which we live, love, work, and play, the objective fact remains that the ways in which all humans have shared specific motivations and experiences across time and place are fairly reductive and are most often tied to the basic functions of being living organisms within a system where entropy always wins in the end and the fight against decay and disorganization is a constant and unrelenting one.

On a macro basis, where limited individual exceptions define rather than undermine the rule, human beings always have, currently do, and always will eat and breathe, metabolizing the materials that are necessary to our survival, excreting the wastes that are not, and then deploying the life-building energy culled from air, water, and food so that we may grow, locomote, respond to stimuli, communicate, and reproduce. When some crucial combinations of those basic functions fail, so too do we as individuals, our physical beings snuffed out (regardless of any metaphysical journeys on which any eternal essences may embark), and the chemicals and compounds that compose us are liberated for reconstitution into any number of organisms and objects over millennia yet to come.

For each and every human alive today, science's best current estimate is that 14 additional humans have lived, thrived, and died before us, for a staggering total of about 110 billion people having trod the soil and sailed the seas of our planet since our species' emergence in East Africa some 200,000 years ago. Although the vast majority of those fallen human beings' remains were truly and irrevocably dispersed, destroyed, consumed, or compromised, often where they fell, a sizable percentage over a significant time span across the seven continents were accorded a different treatment, indicative of a most unique and unusual shared global human experience: the ritualized, organized disposal of decedents' remains in grave sites, which are often marked, maintained, and serve as points of visitation and veneration for subsequent generations.

Introduction: Perpetual Proximity

Although evidence exists that other species recognize, dispose of, and perhaps even mourn and remember their own dead, human beings are certainly without parallel in the efforts we exert to create specific places of honor and memory for our fallen. And those efforts obviously go well beyond the simple need to free ourselves from any sense of disgust and unease caused by the presence of the dead about us. Bodies can be buried, burned, deposited at sea, or left for predators with relative ease, thereby facilitating the basic disposal-of-the-dead function. But preparing or preserving bodies, conducting rites and rituals of passage or release, relegating valuable assets to lie with the dead, erecting lasting monuments over or around the deceased, and creating literal cities of the dead arranged in grid patterns that mirror our municipal spaces are activities that go above and beyond the call of physical necessity.

Whatever emotional, spiritual, or physiological needs guide and drive the very human desire to formally dispose of mortal remains, they certainly emerged deep in our collective history, perhaps even before *Homo sapiens* became the dominant hominid species on the planet. There is ongoing debate in archaeological circles as to whether 70,000-year-old Neanderthal remains in the Shanidar Cave system of Iraqi Kurdistan reflect evidence of some ritual mortuary practice, with individuals purposefully buried together, perhaps even with grave-site markers, and items of personal significance or totemic power laid to rest alongside the bodies.

Groß Fredenwalde, Germany, is home to the world's oldest confirmable organized human burial grounds, dating from the Mesolithic Era, approximately 8,500 years before the present time. The Kerameikos site in Athens, Greece, has been used as a burial ground for at least 5,000 years, and at various times in its ancient history, it also included a variety of private residences and public structures, allowing the dead and the living to coexist as close neighbors for hundreds, if not thousands, of years. The Mount of Olives Jewish Cemetery in Jerusalem has been used as a burial ground for nearly 3,000 years, and estimates of the number of bodies interred there since its sanctification and establishment as a pilgrimage site range from 90,000 to 300,000.

Two of the Seven Wonders of the Ancient World as documented by Herodotus (the Great Pyramid of Giza, completed c. 2600 BC and the Mausoleum at Helicarnassus, c. 350 BC) were explicitly designed as funerary edifices, and it's reasonable that others could have incorporated burial sites within their grounds or structures. Those two monumental grave sites were actually the longest lasting of the Seven

Introduction

Kerameikos Cemetery, Athens, Greece (George E. Koronaios, via Wikimedia, Creative Commons License CC BY-SA 4.0).

Wonders roster by far, with the Great Pyramid still standing and the mausoleum enduring in earthquake-damaged form until the 15th century. Given that the Seven Wonders list was essentially intended as a guide for cosmopolitan Hellenic citizens traveling the known world, it's clear that cemetery tourism was an ancient custom that remains popular to this day, when over three million people per year visit Arlington National Cemetery, among many other high-profile grave sites and cemeteries around the world. The "built to last" nature of the Great Pyramid and Mausoleum of Helicarnassus also indicates that the concept of "perpetual care" for graves and burial grounds is also of ancient origin, even though their histories prove that "perpetual" doesn't actually last forever, for anyone or anything.

The oldest maintained cemetery in the United States, the Myles Standish Burial Ground in Duxbury, Massachusetts, predates the birth of the republic by nearly a century and half, with its earliest graves dated to the late 1630s. That seems old by generally received American history standards, but when the descendants and followers of those first European settlers worked their way westward into the Great Lakes and Ohio and Mississippi River Valley regions, they encountered massive ceremonial burial mounds built by large and accomplished indigenous civilizations, now known to date back as far as 3500 BC. Today, there are an estimated 144,000 graveyards and cemeteries in the United States, ranging from remote desert sites, where small numbers of bodies lie covered with stones near the surface to protect them from scavenger depredation, up through massive municipal cemeteries filled with elaborate memorials and shaded by ancient trees, served and serviced by large professional maintenance and sales teams.

The variety of approaches to burial and grave markers ranges widely between those poles, reflecting the full spectrum of local climate and surface conditions, prevailing cultural traditions, religious affiliations, economic attainment, and the defining societal roles that buried individuals held during their lives. Although customs and traditions vary around the world, most of what we recognize as "typical" modern American funerary practice dates from the Civil War era, when the nation faced, for the first time, massive numbers of its citizens dying far from home, robbing families of the long-held traditions associated with wakes and visitations at home or in the local church, and burials in personal plots filled with family members and fellow congregants over generations. Embalming, body transport, entombment, scheduling, and grave-marking norms, still recognizable to this day, emerged during and after the Civil War to facilitate the bringing home of fallen loved ones, at least for those families who could afford such services. The less fortunate, then and now, had fewer options, with mass burials and pauper cemeteries meeting the urgent physical demands associated with the disposal of human remains, if not the emotional, psychological, and spiritual ones experienced by the survivors.

Many human beings embrace faiths that guarantee eternal life, reincarnation, or some other form of metaphysical transformation of a soul independent of its physical body. Many others do not, viewing the end of physical life as the inviolable and inarguable end of an individual's existence. In either case, the dead are not likely actively concerned with or impacted by the ways in which their remains are disposed, be it in the ground, at sea, in a crematorium, or even on a high rock frequented by avian carnivores. So formalized cemeteries and other burial sites with markers of memorial exist for the living and those yet to live, and not for the dearly departed, from recent days or from years and centuries long gone by. It takes time, effort, and money to prepare, fill, and mark a grave, and in a world of finite resources, this means that millions of people every year make personal economic decisions to create tangible, lasting memorials to their dead, at reasonably high opportunity costs in some cases, eschewing other more essential goods and services in so doing. Why is this the case? And what is achieved through this practice?

The answers to those questions are obviously widely divergent across different cultures, times, countries, and faith traditions. For the purposes of this book's purview, which is focused on American stories of fallen figures, famous and otherwise, they may be best addressed by simply considering why so many Americans regularly visit graveyards, and what they might experience and carry forward with them after they leave. The most obvious visitation opportunity at a graveyard is to attend an actual burial of a family member, a friend, a colleague, a neighbor, or a valued member of a community. Such visitations mark points of transition, the formal farewell to the fallen, the affirmation of love and support for their closest survivors, and a point of reflection on the value of a life recently ended, perhaps as a way of making sense of its closure through communal experience, rather than by an isolated process of grieving and loss. Experiencing a burial (or a cremation, or any other related funerary rite involving the disposition of human remains) may be an important part of creating emotional closure following a death, demonstrating a tangible, visible first manifestation of a new reality, absent the funeral's most important figure. We leave the fresh grave site of a loved, respected, or admired one facing a different order in our lives, even as we affirm the relationships that make such a new order livable.

Maybe days, or months, or years, or decades later, many of us will often return to the grave sites where we watched our departed interred, alone or with others, for brief stays or long periods of reflection. We bring flowers or other gifts, we wipe dirt and dust from headstones, we pick up blown trash or fallen leaves above the bodies, all acts of respect for those no longer capable of fulfilling such simple tasks for themselves. We may sit in silence, or we may speak to the departed. We may meditate or pray, we may feel a sense of peace, or we may lash and gnash through griefs reawakened by renewed proximity to their source. At the very least, the emotional experience of being drawn to revisit a known grave, and then actions taken to resolve that emotional experience, reflect formal acts of remembrance, keeping alive the memories of the departed, using the grave site as a sort of temporal and physical nexus for bridging the "then" and the "now." And, perhaps also reflecting on the "yet to be," when each and every one of us will face our own mortality and the ways in which those we leave behind will mark our own passing.

Introduction: Perpetual Proximity

But what about the vastly larger number of grave sites where we did not experience a burial, and have limited or no personal contacts and connections? Why do so many people make conscious choices to visit such sites, at the risk of being judged ghoulish or morbid by others or even by themselves on careful self-reflection? To some extent, we can again attribute such cemetery tourism as a tangible recognition of the fact that death is one of the very few things that every single human being who has ever lived, is living, and ever will live has or is going to experience. Some of us will face our own mortality sooner, some later, some suddenly, some after terrible lingering illness, some surrounded by loved ones, some alone, some welcoming the final curtain with a graceful bow, some raging against the dying of the light. We all experience birth (though none of us remember it, so we can't reflect on it), and we all experience death. In between those points, the only things that we all will share are again those basics of being a living organism: breathing, eating, drinking, excreting, sleeping, and aging. Everything else is noise on some plane. Or vanity, to cite the more eloquent words of the preacher Solomon, the son of David: "*I have seen everything that is done under the sun, and behold, all is vanity and a striving after wind.*"

King Solomon went on in his Old Testament Book of Ecclesiastes to lay out a rubric designed to give meaning to our experiences between birth and death, beyond the basics of biological function. His crowning instruction was "*Fear God and keep his commandments, for this is the whole duty of man.*" But before that, he exhorted us to (among other things) enjoy life with the ones we love, seek wisdom instead of folly, cast our bread on the waters, and share our riches with those less fortunate. But even if we follow all of the preacher's instructions, eventually "*the silver cord is snapped, or the golden bowl is broken, or the pitcher is shattered at the fountain, or the wheel broken at the cistern, and the dust returns to the earth as it was, and the spirit returns to God who gave it,*" and "*forever [the dead] have no more share in all that is done under the sun.*"

We cite Ecclesiastes here simply because it's a relevant text in the most common American faith tradition, but we just as easily could have picked any other culture in the world, at any point in history, and found texts related to death and dying and how to prepare ourselves for that imminent eventuality. The universality of mortality means that death must be among the most discussed and debated topics in human experience, and as each of us wrestle with its inevitability individually, so too do we seek to find shared senses of meanings about it, through practices designed to postpone or mitigate our fear of death, through rituals related to the disposition of our bodies, and through spiritual traditions designed to inspire or frighten us as to what we might experience after our final exhalations. So what better place to reflect on such universal matters than in the veritable land of the dead, the sanctified spaces where our cultures collect the physical remains of their former residents? Are there any more tangible, readily accessible sites where such reflections may be manifested meaningfully in a local, personal fashion than in our neighborhood graveyards?

Such big-picture considerations notwithstanding, many people may choose to visit cemeteries and graveyards for more prosaic reasons: they are often exquisite, peaceful sites, green, shaded, well maintained, lined with easily walkable paths, dotted with benches where we might rest our weary feet, and filled with beautiful works of art, much of it from dying or dead creative disciplines. In a plasticine era where chemical manufacturing allows for widespread and cheap production of various elaborate, endlessly replicable objects with neither emotional nor physical heft about them, seeing, touching and experiencing the unique and lasting handwork of long-departed masons, woodworkers, bricklayers, and stone carvers may provide a meaningful connection to aspects of life and living that are mostly long since lost in a world of planned product obsolescence and endless cycles of recycling or landfilling for materials that lend themselves to one process or the other. We may be moved by the variety and breadth and complexity of the graves surrounding us, or we may be equally inspired by their simplicity and uniformity, most especially in many veterans or national cemeteries, where row upon row of identical headstones may cement the extent and toll of military service in ways that textbooks and newspapers never can. Although military figures possess and self-organize by varying ranks and roles in their professional lives, the equality of their funerary markers hammers home the fact that all of their service may be considered to have had equally profound value, significance, and meaning in the eyes of those they served and who remember and honor their sacrifice.

Graveyards are also exquisite primary source repositories for historical perspective and understanding, within and across families and communities. When ambling through a single-family plot or cemetery, it is relatively easy to trace connections and linkages: husbands buried with wives, mothers next to sons, daughters near fathers, children and grandchildren, great-nieces and -nephews and in-law additions of many generations radiating outward from the oldest markers, a tangible embodiment of the multigenerational reach and legacy of a family's forebears. Church cemeteries or other graveyards restricted to specific religious communities may also provide insight into the ways in which those groups interacted with or secluded themselves from the greater world around them. And then, of course, there are celebrity graves to which fans and devotees may make significant pilgrimages, hoping in some way to cement a personal affinity with those who inspired them or outraged them, or some combination of the two. There are telling narratives to be cultivated by flamboyant public figures buried in simple circumstances or by seemingly modest folk resting perpetually beneath or within gigantic, elaborate funerary edifices.

Every grave can frame a story on its own individual merits for those interested in exploring narratives beyond the obligatory birth and death dates found on most headstones. But those individual stories do not exist in vacuums: they represent the terminal points of broad, complex, and interwoven tales involving many players, any of whom may have moved through and altered history in publicly profound or subtly subversive fashions. A visit to a cemetery may provide telling leads on such stories, through the simple placement of markers adjacent to one another, beyond any familial, religious, community-based, or chronological coincidences. Side-by-side burials of seemingly unrelated figures may be purely random occurrences based on a given cemetery's space allotment policies or by the preferences of those who purchased their own plots before they actually needed them. Grave proximity may also be the result of circumstances that took the lives of multiple people through a single fatal event, such as a battle, a plague, or an industrial disaster or fire.

In some arguably special cases, the placement of two graves side by side may be the result of lives entwined so closely, for so many reasons, that individuals or their families consciously chose to situate their final resting places together, demonstrating and preserving those deep bonds for all those who may visit in the future, for whatever personal reasons drew them there. We intuitively understand why spouses are buried together, as a final affirmation of the vows and commitments they made in life. But other side-by-side grave placements may seem to not carry such emotional heft until we understand the lives of the fallen, how they interlaced, and why circumstance or conscious choice led them to their final adjacency.

Introduction

This book intends to explore an assortment of unique examples of such side-by-side burials over the course of U.S. history. To some extent in every story, we must begin at the end: we know that the protagonists are deceased, we know that they lie in repose as neighbors, and we know that their individual experiences in life carry some level of cultural or historic significance, such that we are aware of their achievements. Those points are obvious, but the tales of the actual journeys to those end points may be far less so. By exploring the relationships forged along those journeys, we hope to provide a distinct perspective on the ways that these lives evolved and linked and how the posthumous acclaim accruing to these individuals' narratives stems in some strong ways from the relationships now honored through perpetual proximity. And although true stories do not always present the same sorts of clearly elucidated morals and lessons that their fictional counterparts do, we hope to tease such clarity from the knotted skeins of these intertwined lives and deaths.

We see value in telling these particular stories, of course, but we also see value in encouraging explorations into the causes and effects associated with the placement of other graves you may encounter, through active pursuit or through observation in passing. We live in a time when genealogical and historical research can be readily pursued from the comfort of our own homes, and we believe that your own experiences of visiting or revisiting any cemetery, mausoleum, columbarium, or memorial marker may be enhanced by understanding not only the stories with connections to our own personal narratives but also the stories of those who lie with or near your loved ones, or near the celebrities you admire, or near the departed members of your extended faith or secular communities.

Few of us live our lives isolated in personal vacuums. Few of us will be buried or interred in solitary sites alone. By embracing and exploring the bonds codified posthumously by the placement of graves, we might open ourselves to a deeper understanding of the roles that our living relationships can play as we march collectively forward toward the shared endings of our own stories within our physically perceivable planes. We hope you might find these stories inspiring, thought provoking, and actionable. None of us know what tomorrow may bring. And none of us know how we will be remembered should we not make it until tomorrow. But all of us can consider the relationships that define our days and contemplate codas to our lives that may point those who follow in directions of deepest meaning for us. In so doing, we may create a legacy story not built on self-definition but rather in celebration of the ways in which we worked with, played with, fought with, loved, respected, honored, and uplifted the most important people in our own lives.

The subjects of the stories that follow walked side by side in life, before lying side by side in death. We note the latter fact to celebrate the former. We hope you will appreciate the celebration and the respectful spirits of curiosity and admiration that frame it.

CHAPTER ONE

Robert Gould Shaw (1837–1863) and the Soldiers of the 54th Massachusetts Infantry Regiment (Various Dates–1863)

Beaufort National Cemetery, Beaufort, South Carolina

"Of all the pulpits from which the human voice is ever sent forth, there is none from which it reaches so far as from the grave."

—John Ruskin

"True glory takes root, and even spreads; all false pretenses, like flowers, fall to the ground; nor can any counterfeit last long."

—Marcus Tullius Cicero

As the stars, wannabes, paparazzi, and scene scribblers swarmed along the red carpet into Los Angeles's Dorothy Chandler Pavilion for the 62nd Academy Awards ceremony on March 26, 1990, the lasting cultural and critical narratives surrounding the event ahead of them had already begun to cohere in the film community's collective consciousness. Bruce Beresford's *Driving Miss Daisy* had received the most nominations (with nine), while Oliver Stone's anti-war polemic *Born on the Fourth of July* was positioned in second place among the year's favorite films, with eight nominations. Third place among the nominees (with five each) was shared by Jim Sheridan's literary biopic *My Left Foot* and Edward Frick's Civil War drama *Glory*. In a then-rare feat, African American actors Morgan Freeman (*Driving Miss Daisy*) and Denzel Washington (*Glory*) had received nominations for Best Actor and Best Supporting Actor, respectively.

17

Side by Side in Eternity

Although the Academy of Motion Picture Arts and Sciences may have applauded itself at the time for that small, overdue step toward fair and accurate representation of people of color among their annual honorees, other nominations and other missing nominations belied that narrative. *Driving Miss Daisy* had been (fairly) criticized for largely glossing over the institutional racism embodied in its narrative, with critic Candice Russell of the *South Florida Sun-Sentinel* expressing the widely held sentiment that the film was "one scene after another of a pompous old lady issuing orders and a servant trying to comply by saying 'yassum'"; she further described Freeman's character as having a "toadying manner ... which was painful to see." The influential political hip-hop collective Public Enemy (with equally famous guests Ice Cube and Big Daddy Kane) specifically cited that film as an example of everything that was wrong with the American filmmaking industry in their outstanding and inflammatory 1990 track "Burn Hollywood Burn" from their seminal *Fear of a Black Planet* album, released a month after the *Driving Miss Daisy*–dominated 1990 Oscars ceremony.

Meanwhile, Spike Lee's trenchant (then and now) *Do the Right Thing* was ignored for Best Picture and Best Director nods, though Lee did capture a Best Screenplay nomination. The only on-screen performer from that film's incredible ensemble cast (which included Spike Lee himself, Samuel L. Jackson, Ossie Davis, Ruby Dee, Giancarlo Esposito, Rosie Perez, Bill Nunn, Robin Harris, Martin Lawrence, and John Turturro, among others) recognized by the Academy for his work was the (White) Italian American character actor Danny Aiello. The unjust on-screen death in *Do the Right Thing* of the character Radio Raheem (played by Nunn) from a choke hold at the hands of local beat policemen was such an extraordinarily potent cinematic experience that generations of young creators, artists, activists, and cultural commentators have since come to essentially frame the Radio Raheem narrative as a nigh-unto-historic fact, with that one powerful fictional character serving as a prototype and shorthand stand-in for the legions of people of color who have been killed throughout our nation's history in acts of racially motivated institutional violence. To cite but one of many examples, in June 2020, mere days after George Floyd was struck down in a very real-world example by police violence perpetrated on an unarmed Black man, award-winning hip-hop duo Run the Jewels issued the song "Walking in the Snow," which contained the boom-box-referencing couplet "Word to the old school tape decks / I get Radio Raheem respect" just moments after rapper Killer Mike had sung "And you so numb, you watch the cops choke out a man like me / Until my voice goes from a shriek to whisper 'I can't breathe.'"

Cultural tone deafness in Hollywood being what it was, there's probably little surprise in reporting that *Driving Miss Daisy* took home the most Oscars at that 1990 Academy Awards ceremony, winning Best Picture, Best Actress (Jessica Tandy), Best Adapted Screenplay, and Best Makeup. Spike Lee and Morgan Freeman were both sent home without statues in 1990, while Denzel Washington deservedly won his first Oscar for his brilliant supporting role in *Glory*, which also received Best Sound and Best Cinematography honors. At the time, Washington was only the fourth African American actor (joining Hattie McDaniel, Sidney Poitier, and Louis Gossett, Jr.) to win an acting Oscar since the Academy Awards' inception in 1929; he won a second Oscar in 2001 for *Training Day*, while 15 additional Oscars have been awarded to African American actors and actresses since 1990. Despite progress on the problematic "#OscarSoWhite" front in recent years, many of the same tone-deaf tropes behind *Driving Miss Daisy* remain in force in today's Hollywood, as evidenced by the similarly reductive "White savior" and "magical Negro" (the latter phrase coined by Spike Lee to describe the supporting Black characters in countless Hollywood films who come to the aid of their films' White protagonists, often possessing special insights or mystical wisdom) tokens and tropes that were so deeply embedded in *Green Book*, which won the Best Picture Oscar in 2019, defeating (among other nominees) the highly popular and more racially attuned *Black Panther* and Spike Lee's then-latest film, *BlacKkKlansman*.

Glory, for its own part, was a rousing and popular Civil War drama telling the story of the 54th Massachusetts Infantry Regiment, often cited as the first African American regiment to fight for the Union army in the nation's greatest schismatic tumult, though the First Kansas Colored Volunteer Infantry Regiment was in fact organized before the 54th Massachusetts; the Kansas soldiers, though, were not "professional" military men, paid by the federal government for their service. In the film, Matthew Broderick played Colonel Robert Gould Shaw, the Massachusetts unit's White commanding officer, the scion of a prominent Boston abolitionist family, and a very well-documented, largely historically accurate figure. Denzel Washington played an infantryman named Private Trip, who was a fictional composite character written to reflect various facets of the Black soldiers' experience, without actually celebrating or acknowledging the unique individuality of any of the men who served nobly and bravely under Colonel Shaw. Morgan Freeman also appeared in *Glory* as one of Washington's fellow soldiers, named Sergeant Major John Rawlins, another fictional composite character embodying various real feats of various real soldiers.

For all intents and purposes, Private Trip and Sergeant Major Rawlins were presented as Civil War–era Radio Raheems, fictional film characters crafted to represent certain truths and traits in a palatable and dramatic fashion, without viewers ever learning about the specific personhood of any of the real men who fought for those truths, bore those traits, and often died horribly, anonymously as the reward for their efforts. The great film critic Roger Ebert, writing for the *Chicago Sun-Times*, captured another difficult aspect of the film's storytelling in his contemporaneous review, noting that "watching *Glory*, I had one recurring problem. I didn't understand why it had to be told so often from the point of view of the 54th's white commanding officer. Why did we see the Black troops through his eyes, instead of seeing him through theirs? To put it another way, why does the top billing in this movie go to a white actor?"

We cite these cultural conflicts in a spirit of amity, recognizing that criticism comes easier than craftsmanship. Regardless of the historical accuracy of his character, Denzel Washington's performance in *Glory* is astounding, and Kevin Jarre's generally thoughtful screenplay was based on Colonel Shaw's personal correspondence as well as facts documented in the books *Lay This Laurel* by Lincoln Kirstein (1973) and *One Gallant Rush* by Peter Burchard (1965). Sharp-eyed readers will also note, of course, that we've similarly privileged the White commanding officer in the title of this chapter, recognizing him as an individual, and his men as an otherwise nameless regimental grouping. Sadly, to some extent, such an aggregated biographical or cinematic approach is unavoidable in the 21st century in large part due to the ways in which record keepers disregarded the individuality or mislabeled the identities, personal backgrounds, and achievements of African American Union soldiers during the Civil War (we will touch on that theme again in this book's epilogue) and in the ways that Confederate commanders treated the mortal remains of Black soldiers who fell in combat on battlefields across the American South.

So who, really, were the men of the 54th Massachusetts Infantry Regiment, and how did they come to find themselves as iconic fictional embodiments of the roles that African Americans played in fighting for the freedom of their brothers and sisters in the Deep South? The answer to that question is deeply interwoven with federal actions taken during the Civil War to address the structural, social, economic, historical, and even constitutional inequities that haunted and daunted all people of color in American in the latter half of the 19th century.

In September 1862, President Abraham Lincoln's Emancipation Proclamation declared, "On the first day of January in the year of our Lord, one thousand eight hundred and sixty-three, all persons held as slaves within any State, or designated part of a State, the people whereof shall then be in rebellion against the United States shall be then, thenceforward, and forever free; and the executive government of the United States, including the military and naval authority thereof, will recognize and maintain the freedom of such persons, and will do no act or acts to repress such persons, or any of them, in any efforts they may make for their actual freedom." Explicit in this order through its reference to "the military and naval authority thereof" was the opportunity for formerly enslaved African Americans and their free-born descendants to serve in the U.S. military, as heretical a thought and concept as that was in its time for many of the nation's citizens.

Massachusetts governor John Albion Andrew had long been a champion for providing Black Americans the opportunity to serve their country as soldiers and sailors, regularly petitioning the U.S. Department of War and its secretary, Edwin M. Stanton, to begin recruiting African Americans for the armed forces, even before the Emancipation Proclamation made that possible through executive fiat. His proposal was, unfortunately and wrongly, not a popular one, as many believed and stated openly that African American troops would lack discipline, be difficult to train, and would break ranks and flee once thrust into battlefield situations. But beyond the racial tensions and undertones associated with the mustering and deployment of willing Black troops, the fact of the matter was that the skills and manpower they gladly offered were of significant strategic importance, as Union forces were ever more frequently faltering on the battlefield by 1863. In the early days of the Civil War, Northern pundits and politicians had predicted a swift victory fueled by the Union's superior industrial capacity and manpower advantage. The benefits of those advantages, however, had failed to materialize over the first two years of the carnage-heavy conflict. Enlistments were in decline in the early days of 1863, and a proposed draft program (which would have further entrenched socioeconomic inequities, as deferments would have been available to those who could afford to pay for them) was fostering discontent among the citizenry.

Common sense and military necessity, empowered by the dual forces of Governor Andrew's interests in social justice and equity and by the enactment of the Emancipation Proclamation, prevailed in this case, and the 54th Massachusetts Infantry Regiment began recruiting in February 1863 after Secretary Stanton specifically directed Governor Andrew to begin mobilizing regiments including "persons of African descent, organized into special corps" on January 26, 1863. The initiative earned ardent support from prominent abolitionists within the Commonwealth's boundaries and beyond. Frederick Douglass was a devoted and vocal supporter of the recruitment efforts, and two of his sons were among the first soldiers to join the 54th Massachusetts Infantry Regiment, along with one of Sojourner Truth's grandsons, who relocated from Michigan to join the unit. Boston's free African American community was also instrumental in recruiting soldiers for the newly formed regiment, drawing Massachusetts residents as well as would-be soldiers from other Northern states, and from the population of freed or escaped slaves originally resident in the Confederate states.

The newly organized unit trained at Camp Meigs in the outer suburbs of Boston and marched off for their initial deployment after a celebratory parade down Boston's Beacon Street on May 28, 1863. It was a grand day, even though many prominent Boston merchants barricaded themselves within the confines of the posh Somerset Club, drawing the blinds over their windows to block the sight of Black troops being sent to fight a war that would likely cost them profits earned from their roles in the international cotton trade. Boston's police also had to separate the proud soldiers from mobs of dockworkers, who tossed bricks at the troops as an expression of their misguided belief that the deployment of freed slaves was ultimately intended as an effort to undercut their own earning potential. But those unfortunate side stories aside, the city of Boston and the Commonwealth of Massachusetts did their soldiers proud by seeing them off in fine and felicitous style, with over 20,000 people lining the streets to celebrate the army's newest regiment.

Even though the ability of Black soldiers to enlist in the U.S. Army was certainly a transformational shift in our nation's racial relations, the norms of the day meant that promotional opportunities for those same Black soldiers were limited: most served as privates, with small numbers eventually promoted to sergeant or (in even more limited cases) sergeant major, the highest rank that Black soldiers were allowed to achieve and hold at the time. The restrictions on Black soldiers serving as officers necessitated the recruitment and commissioning

Chapter One. Robert Gould Shaw and Soldiers

Robert Gould Shaw in uniform, photo by John Adams Whipple, circa 1863 (Library of Congress).

of White officers in their stead, and so when the 54th Massachusetts Infantry Regiment made its memorable march down Boston's Beacon Street, they were led by Colonel Robert Gould Shaw.

Shaw was but 25 years old when he took charge of the 54th Massachusetts, commanding a cohort of soldiers ranging in age from 16 to 60 years old. Although he was the son of prominent Boston abolitionists Francis George Shaw and Sarah Blake Sturgis Shaw, he was a somewhat counterintuitive leader for his unit, based both on his prior personal experience and his reluctance to pursue the cause of abolition as fervently as did his parents. Born in 1837, Shaw's childhood and adolescence did not foreshadow the glory that would eventually come to accrue to his name. He was a diffident, bordering on dissolute, student, shuttled between various boarding schools in Massachusetts, New York, Switzerland, and Germany. During his time in Europe, he read and was admittedly moved by Harriet Beecher Stowe's seminal antislavery novel *Uncle Tom's Cabin* (first published in 1852), and he also wrote to his parents informing them that his patriotism for his home country had been inflamed by his experiences of anti-Americanism among his European colleagues and cohorts.

Shaw further expressed a desire to his parents to attend the U.S. Military Academy at West Point, New York, though his parents viewed this ambition with some skepticism, given his proven difficulties in respecting and following orders from authority figures. He returned to

23

the United States in 1856, opting to continue his education as a member of the Class of 1860 at Harvard College, quickly eschewing his dreams of becoming a West Point cadet. His studies and experiences at Harvard were just as distasteful to Shaw as his earlier boarding school experiences had been, and he left the school in 1859, without a degree, moving to Staten Island to work in an office job at his uncle's mercantile firm. Perhaps not surprisingly, his letters home to his parents indicate he found this situation just as disagreeable as all those that had come before it.

As Shaw stewed with ennui in his uncle's Staten Island office, South Carolina became the first of the Southern states to secede from the United States in December 1860, followed by Mississippi, Florida, Alabama, Georgia, Louisiana, and Texas in the early days of 1861. The Confederate States of America were formally constituted on February 9, 1861. (Other states and territories either joined the Confederacy through the remainder of 1861 or voted to do so but were denied by U.S. federal response or other extenuating circumstances.) The conflict between the North and South escalated from a legislative to a military conflict when the Battle of Fort Sumter in Charleston, South Carolina, erupted on April 12, 1861.

One week later, Private Robert Gould Shaw marched down Broadway in Lower Manhattan as a member of the Seventh New York Militia, having volunteered to serve the month prior. Shaw's initial commitment (along with his fellow volunteer soldiers) was for a 90-day service stint, but before he could complete his obligation, the Seventh New York Militia was dissolved, after Shaw and his fellow soldiers served as part of the defensive garrison protecting Washington, D.C. Although his service with that unit was brief, as is often the case for young men struggling to find their way in the world, Shaw was fundamentally moved and changed through his commitment to military service, and he quickly joined a new regiment in his home state, the Second Massachusetts Infantry, to proudly continue his service to his nation as a soldier.

His commitment to his duties and to his unit (likely enhanced and reinforced by his educational background and family connections) led his commanders to commission Shaw as a second lieutenant in late May 1861. The Second Massachusetts Infantry spent the next two years fighting in some of the more heinous campaigns of the Civil War, with Shaw seeing action at the First Battle of Winchester, the Battle of Cedar Mountain, and the Battle of Antietam, the last contested on September 17, 1862, a day that still stands as the bloodiest in American history,

24

with nearly 23,000 battlefield and civilian casualties. Shaw was twice wounded in combat, but he fought on and was promoted to the rank of captain in late 1862.

As Captain Shaw was finding his way and his place in the world through his military service, Massachusetts governor Andrew was moving forward with his now federally ratified plans to raise, train, and deploy an African American army unit. He was personally active in and engaged with the search for (White) officers to lead his new unit, seeking (in his own words) "young men of military experience, of firm anti-slavery principles, ambitious, superior to a vulgar contempt for color, and having faith in the capacity of colored men for military service." Andrew's connections with Shaw's parents in regional and national abolitionist circles quickly moved the younger Shaw to the top of Andrew's candidate list, and the governor wrote to Francis Shaw (Robert's father) in early 1863 to enlist the father in the recruitment of the son; Andrew's letter to the senior Shaw contained the official documentation commissioning Robert to take command of the 54th Massachusetts, pending his would-be senior officer's acceptance of the same.

Francis Shaw traveled to Virginia to meet with Robert and make the case for his son's service in the cause of racial military integration. Captain Shaw was initially reluctant to accept the commission, believing that his superior officers would never actually send the 54th Massachusetts Regiment into combat, relegating them instead to behind-the-scenes logistics and support roles. His father returned to Massachusetts without a commitment from his son, but on February 6, 1863, the younger Shaw telegraphed his father that he would accept the commission. Later that month, in a letter to his fiancée of two months, Annie Kneeland Haggerty (the pair had met in 1861 at an opera party thrown by Shaw's sister), the commander in waiting frankly explained his emotions as he considered the opportunity to lead the 54th Massachusetts thusly: "You know how many eminent men consider a Negro army of the greatest importance to our country at this time. If it turns out to be so, how fully repaid the pioneers in the movement will be, for what they may have to go through. I feel convinced I shall never regret having taken this step, as far as I myself am concerned; for while I was undecided, I felt ashamed of myself, as if I were cowardly."

Shaw spent the remainder of the spring of 1863 organizing, training, and drilling his new unit. He was promoted to major in late March 1863, and to colonel a mere two weeks later. Despite his initial reluctance to take on the role of commanding officer of the 54th

Massachusetts, Shaw found himself deeply impressed by his men as their training continued, writing to his father, "Everything goes on prosperously. The intelligence of the men is a great surprise to me. They learn all the details of guard duty and camp service infinitely more readily than most of the Irish that I have had under my command. There is not the least doubt that we will leave the State with as good a regiment as any that has marched." (Yes, racial justice and equity, and the language used to communicate their underlying tenets, certainly move forward in fits and starts, then and now.)

Colonel Shaw and Annie Haggerty were married in New York City on May 2, 1863, despite misgivings from their families about Robert's upcoming deployment and service. The couple spent a brief honeymoon together in the Berkshire Mountains of western Massachusetts before Shaw returned to his duties training his men and preparing for their deployment into the heart of the Confederacy. Annie was with Shaw's parents and two sisters at Shaw's mother's family's house on Beacon Street for the pre-deployment parade of the 54th Massachusetts Infantry Regiment. As he passed the family home, Colonel Shaw looked up at his loved ones and raised his sword to his lips in acknowledgment. His sister Ellen, then 17 years old, later wrote that "his face was as the face of an angel, and I felt perfectly sure he would never come back."

Ellen was sadly correct, as it turned out. After the parade had wound down, the men of the 54th Massachusetts said their goodbyes to their friends and families, boarded a transport ship in Boston Harbor, and sailed off for South Carolina. On June 3, 1863, their ship arrived at the port on Hilton Head Island and Shaw reported for duty to General David "Black Dave" Hunter, commander of the X Corps of the U.S. Army's Department of the South, who ordered the Massachusetts Regiment to the nearby Low Country city of Beaufort, South Carolina. Beaufort had been a bastion of the Union's presence in the Confederate heartland since November 1861, when the Union navy decimated the Confederate defenders on Hilton Head and Saint Phillips Island at the mouth of the Broad River, allowing the occupation of Beaufort and nearby Port Royal for the remainder of the war. Beaufort's position as a deep-water coastal port between the major mercantile cities of Savannah, Georgia, and Charleston, South Carolina, allowed it to become a key strategic asset from which naval blockades could be deployed to sever the Confederacy's access to ocean-going trade with their key European partners and supporters.

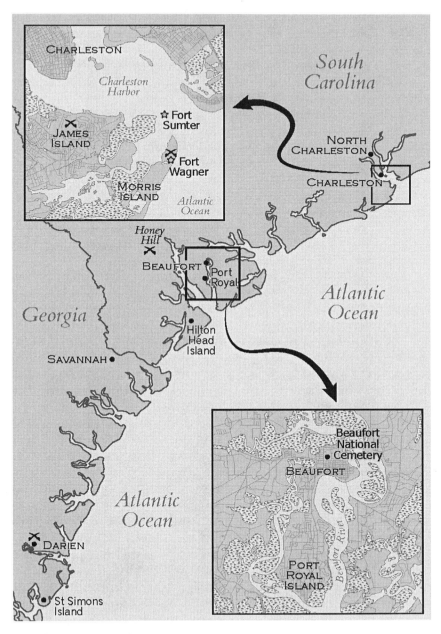

Map of the 54th Massachusetts Infantry Regiment's major landmarks in the Georgia and South Carolina Low Country (Liz Cruz).

The 54th Massachusetts's arrival in South Carolina was not without its difficulties, as the men, who had been promised upon conscription the normal wage of $13 per month plus subsistence paid to White soldiers, were informed that the Department of the South would pay them only $10 per month, with $3 of that amount being withheld from their wages as a uniform fee; White soldiers were not required to pay for their uniforms. Colonel Shaw, to his credit, fought for his men to receive their fair due, leading a regiment-wide boycott against accepting pay stubs through the remaining time that he commanded the unit. Claiming their refusal of reduced pay as a badge of honor, the men of the 54th were known to shout "Massachusetts and Seven Dollars a Month" as a motivational marching cadence. Their case was not resolved until September 28, 1864, long after many members of the 54th Massachusetts were dead; the survivors received their full wages for the roughly 18 months of service during which they had refused to accept the unjust compensation offered to them.

After a brief stay in Beaufort, the 54th Massachusetts Infantry Regiment was sent to Saint Simons Island in Georgia, and on June 11, 1863, they were deployed with the Second South Carolina Volunteers (another African American unit) to conduct a raid on the town of Darien, Georgia. The (White) commander of the Second South Carolina, Colonel James Montgomery, was given overall command of the combined force, and upon arriving and securing Darien against little resistance, Montgomery set his troops to looting the town, clearing it of livestock and other commodities, after which he burned it to the ground, to the great hardship of the civilians then resident there. Shaw was appalled by Montgomery's actions, writing to the X Corps' assistant adjutant general after the campaign to seek clarity on whether such actions were expected or required of him and his men. "I am perfectly willing to burn any place which resists, or gives such reason for such a proceeding," his letter noted. "But it seems to be barbarous to turn women and children adrift in that way; and if I am only assisting Colonel Montgomery in a private enterprise of his own, it is very distasteful to me."

It didn't take long for Shaw and the men of the 54th Massachusetts to encounter "any place which resists," as the unit was finally sent into combat on July 16, 1863, engaging in the Battle of Grimball's Landing on James Island, just south of Charleston, South Carolina. The attack on James Island was designed to draw Confederate resources away from Fort Wagner in Charleston Harbor, in advance of a planned Union attack on that key coastal asset. The men of the 54th Massachusetts

28

repulsed a Confederate advance at Grimball's Landing, suffering 45 casualties in the engagement, before making a strategic retreat back toward their camp, firing all the way, and still attempting to spread and harry the Confederate defenses and resources. The 54th was formally praised for their "steadiness and soldierly conduct" in the post-battle report by Brigadier General Alfred Terry, who had commanded their division in the engagement.

That "steadiness and soldierly conduct" was to meet its most fierce test two days later, when the Union army attacked Fort Wagner, which held a key position above the shipping approach to Charleston Harbor. The men of the 54th Massachusetts spent most of the two days between Grimball's Landing and Fort Wagner on the move from James Island without adequate rations, arriving at the staging ground for the frontal assault severely fatigued and hungry. Fort Wagner was a massive earth-work, some 600 feet wide, situated on the low-lying Morris Island, and surrounded by 30-foot-tall earthworks built from sand. The only viable land approach to Fort Wagner was across a narrow stretch of exposed beach between the Atlantic Ocean and the treacherous muck-rich marshes that define the topography and geography of South Carolina's Low Country. In preparation for the assault, Union artillery bombarded Fort Wagner throughout the day on July 18, but were unable to cause any significant damage to the fortifications.

As the sun began to set over the marshland to the west, Union troops were sent forward to take the fort. The 54th Massachusetts Infantry Regiment was chosen to lead the attack at 7:45 p.m., forced to march about a third of a mile down the exposed beachfront toward and then beyond the fort's outer bastions, then turning back across a water-filled moat to access the fort itself. The men were completely exposed to Confederate fire throughout their approach, and the rebel riflemen opened and maintained fire as the Union forces scrambled forward, inflicting grievous casualties. Against formidable odds, Shaw's unit and other Union regiments did actually penetrate the fortifications around Fort Wagner at two points, though they did not have sufficient resources to take and hold the fort itself. By 9:00 p.m., the battle was over, and the Union troops were withdrawn.

Of the 600 men who marched on Fort Wagner that night, 270 were killed, wounded, or captured during that terrible 75-minute span. Colonel Robert Gould Shaw was among the fatalities: eyewitnesses reported that he was killed early in the battle, hit by as many as seven bullets as he mounted a parapet to urge his men forward. Total Union casualties (killed, wounded, or captured) among all units assaulting Fort Wagner that night numbered over 1,500. The Confederates lost just over 200 soldiers. From a strictly situational military standpoint, the engagement changed nothing, with depleted forces ending the day exactly where they had begun it. But from a strategic and historic standpoint, as word of the 54th Massachusetts Infantry Regiment's valor spread via military and civilian media networks throughout the Union, the battle served to dramatically increase enlistment and mobilization of additional African American troops and units (over 180,000 African Americans eventually enlisted in the Union armed services before the end of the Civil War), a fact that President Lincoln later noted was absolutely crucial to the final victory against the Confederacy. There's little doubt after the fact, when looking at the narrative and the battlefield maps of the Fort Wagner engagement, that the men of the 54th Massachusetts and the other units sent behind them were, in the worst senses of the phrase, pushed into harm's way as cannon fodder in a quixotic campaign of questionable value. But there's also little doubt after the fact that they went forward willingly, fighting for a just cause, and that they purported themselves as well as anyone ever could under such heinously fraught battlefield conditions.

If the actions of the men of the 54th Massachusetts Infantry Regiment on July 18, 1863, mark a heroic high-water mark in terms of battlefield conduct and valor during the Civil War, the actions of the Confederate troops and their commanders at Fort Wagner offer an opposing example of the ways in which the copious horrors of war can be made even more horrible in the aftermath of battle.

For all of the grim changes that came to war-making during the Civil War as a result of new killing technologies being deployed on battlefields, while scorched-earth policies prevailed in the spaces and places between the battles, there generally remained some modicum of chivalry and respect shown and held between the Confederate and Union military leadership, many of whom had served together before the war. An example: Colonel Haldimand Putnam of the Seventh New Hampshire Infantry was also killed in the assault on Fort Wagner. Contemporaneous reports note that he "received all the honors of sepulture which the circumstances of his death permitted, from the fraternal hands of his West Point classmate, General Robert H. Anderson, of the Confederate Army." Most other dead Union officers were also returned to their lines for burial by their fellows, as was then customary.

But when Union Brigadier General Quincy Granville asked the

Chapter One. Robert Gould Shaw and Soldiers

Confederate commander of Fort Wagner, General Johnson Hagood, about the disposition of Colonel Shaw's body, he was informed that Shaw had been "buried with his [racial epithet]" in an unmarked trench along the coast of tiny Morris Island, an open act of contempt for the White officer who would dare to lead Black soldiers into battle. The location of the burial trench was made even more loathsome when the geography of the fort and its environs were considered: low-lying Morris Island was and remains subject to extensive land shifts and erosion by storms, tides, and currents. As it turns out, much of Fort Wagner's original location has long been eroded away in the years since the battle was fought there, including the site of the mass grave where the fallen of the 54th Massachusetts had been unceremoniously dumped.

Although General Hagood's actions in dishonoring the Union dead at Fort Wagner were most certainly intended as a deliberate slur, they actually quickly served in the North to flame abolitionist sentiment and to lay the groundwork for Colonel Shaw's status as a principled martyr for the cause of Black emancipation. Military, political, and media figures quickly began to call for Union forces in South Carolina to exert every effort to exhume Shaw's body and return his remains for reinterment as a hero in his hometown of Boston. But Shaw's parents and widow wanted no part of that, correctly noting that there was, in fact, no dishonor in the colonel being buried with his men. Francis Shaw was explicit in his public feelings about his son's resting place, explaining, "We would not have his body removed from where it lies surrounded by his brave and devoted soldiers. We can imagine no holier place than that in which he lies, among his brave and devoted followers, nor wish for him better company—what a body-guard he has!"

As fate would have it, though, the Shaw family's wishes were simply not viable, in some large part because General Hagood was so fixated on spitefully being dishonorable that he didn't consider the largely predictable aftereffects associated with his cavalier approach to burying the fallen soldiers in a completely inappropriate site. By September 1863, the bodies in the trench had begun to decompose in the fetid South Carolina heat and humidity, soon contaminating Fort Wagner's sole fresh water supply, which ultimately forced the Confederates to abandon the fort. Hagood's malfeasance didn't hurt him in his home state, for what that's worth: he went on to become governor of South Carolina and was widely hailed for reopening The Citadel (the state's private military academy) in 1880. The school's football stadium bears his name to this day.

Union troops secured and held Fort Wagner after the Confederates abandoned it, but in the immediate aftermath of the Civil War, the ramparts and earthworks (and even the island itself) surrounding the fort quickly began to deteriorate. The army elected to disinter all of the remains found there, presumably including Colonel Robert Gould Shaw, though no positive identifications could be made at the time. All of the bodies were then reinterred at the then-newly commissioned Beaufort National Cemetery in Beaufort, South Carolina, where they lie as a group in perpetual proximity, each one under a headstone marked "Unknown," their equality in memoriam finally affirmed, even if their ranks in life and their renown in death were perceived differently.

And what of the men of the 54th Massachusetts Infantry Regiment who survived Fort Wagner? Colonel Edward Hallowell was named as Colonel Shaw's replacement as the unit's commander, and under his leadership, they participated in the Battle of Olustee (the most significant engagement of the Civil War to be contested in Florida) in February 1864 in a rearguard capacity that, among other things, involved manually pulling a disabled train carrying wounded Union soldiers for over three miles to nearby Camp Finegan. Returning to South Carolina, the men of the 54th were assigned to an all-Black brigade under the command of Colonel Alfred Hartwell. Their unit was defeated with heavy casualties by an entrenched Confederate militia at the Battle of Honey Hill in November 1864, and they also fought in the Battle of Boykin's Mill in April 1865, one of the final engagements of the Civil War. The unit was officially mustered out on August 4, 1865, one of the most celebrated groups of warriors to emerge from the narrative of our nation's greatest military undertaking.

(As a historic aside and footnote, the Battle of Honey Hill was fought on one of your authors' ancestral family land, and the Confederate commander at that engagement, Colonel Charles Jones Colcock, is J. Eric Smith's direct ancestor. Colonel Colcock is buried in Smith's family cemetery at Stoney Creek in South Carolina, adjacent to an abandoned rice paddy that the family once farmed with the slave labor that the 54th Massachusetts and countless other Union forces fought to eradicate.)

Among the many men who fought and died with the 54th Massachusetts, Sergeant William Harvey Carney is arguably the best known after Colonel Shaw. In 1900, he was awarded the Medal of Honor for his bravery in saving the regimental flag during the Battle of Fort Wagner. Although he was not the first African American to receive that highest of military honors, the actions for which he received the award preceded

32

those of any other African American Medal of Honor recipient, and his medal was one of the last to be awarded for Civil War service. In the film *Glory*, Denzel Washington's fictional Private Trip is credited with the honors that properly belonged to Sergeant Carney.

Although the graves of the 54th Massachusetts's Fort Wagner fallen aren't particularly high-visibility or high-traffic destinations, one of several major markers honoring their service and sacrifice sits squarely in one of the most visible and widely visited sections of Boston. Unveiled in 1897, after the acclaimed artist Augustus Saint-Gaudens spent 14 years designing and creating it, the Robert Gould Shaw and Massachusetts 54th Regiment Memorial is a vast bas-relief of Shaw and some of his men located in Boston Common, across Beacon Street from the Massachusetts State House. It's a striking work of art and important in being the first large-scale public art work to honor Black American soldiers, but its appearance still returns us to this chapter's opening questions on why we remember Shaw as a unique individual but his men as mostly nameless and faceless masses, most suitable for fictional aggregation. Shaw's family actually objected to the original memorial design, a fairly typical "equestrian statue" of their son, preferring instead that the monument honor the unit in its entirety. But even in the adapted, final version, the famous monument depicts Shaw on horseback, above the figures of the Black enlisted men around him on foot. To Saint-Gaudens's credit, while he could not portray as many of the soldiers as he (and successive generations) might have liked, he did work to ensure the striking individuality of the faces portrayed, working with a variety of African American models of various ages and from various regions, even if each of them were chosen to represent yet another idealized and fictional Private Trip/Radio Raheem amalgamation for public consumption.

In the 1990s, after the film *Glory* brought the story of the 54th Massachusetts into wider public recognition, a level of public reassessment regarding the monument was undertaken by civic and community leaders in Boston, attempting to better frame the interpretation of the titanic work of art around the service of the Black soldiers themselves and not only their White commanding officer. Key to that effort was, finally, adding inscriptions of the known names of the members of the 54th Massachusetts Regiment to the monument, which somewhat shockingly had only presented the names of the unit's White officers until that time. That change, and public efforts to more accurately tell the story of the 54th, although appreciated by many, still didn't stop the

Augustus Saint-Gaudens' dry-plate negative of the Shaw Memorial, taken in 1897 (Library of Congress).

Saint-Gaudens bas-relief from becoming a flashpoint site in the unrest following the George Floyd killing, when the monument was defaced with anti-police slogans and expletives.

At the time of this writing, the monument is again undergoing restoration and renovation, with many prominent leaders calling for it to be removed and relocated into a museum setting and others arguing just as strongly that the work should remain but with more accurate educational support materials and signage placing it and the men it honors into their proper historical perspective. It seems fair to say, though, that while the visual telling of the story presented by the memorial may be problematic to modern sensibilities, the intentions behind it, in its time, were essentially just and sound, perhaps best evidenced by the fact that Boston's African American community was highly supportive, both emotionally and financially, when the monument was originally erected. But although the memorial can be visually appreciated as a work of art requiring contextualization, we strongly believe that the most important aspect of the modern incarnation of the monument is the listing of the names of the 54th Massachusetts's soldiers themselves, so long overdue.

The graves of the fallen at Beaufort National Cemetery bear no names because of the tragic circumstances surrounding the mass and cavalier original disposition of their bodies, so it is compelling and comforting to know that there is a place of remembrance for the 54th Massachusetts where people can go to read, learn, and *say their names*, with all of the freight and consequence that that phrase carries within today's racial discourse in America. Colonel Robert Gould Shaw is an admirable, memorable historical figure, worthy of study and acclaim, certainly, but he would not have been so without his soldiers, who in the most accurate telling of their collective story elevated their commander to glory and not the other way around.

CHAPTER TWO

Susan Bogert Warner (1819–1885) and Anna Bartlett Warner (1827–1915)

*West Point Cemetery, U.S. Military
Academy, West Point, New York*

*"Adversity has the effect of eliciting talents which in pros-
perous circumstance would have lain dormant."*
— Quintus Horatius Flaccus (Horace)

*"Let not the emphasis of hospitality lie in bed and board,
but let truth, love, honor, and courtesy flow in all thy
deeds."*
— Ralph Waldo Emerson

Your authors were classmates at the United States Naval Academy
in Annapolis, Maryland, many more years ago than either of us generally care to actively consider. We're both pleased and proud to have
completed the course of training there, and we'd both cite it as among
the most difficult personal achievements of our lives. Although the
Naval Academy rates highly for the competitiveness of its admission
process and for the quality and rigor of the education it provides as a
top-tier American university, the academic challenges posed by the cur-
riculum are compounded and magnified by the facts that navy's midshipmen also undergo strenuous military training (including summers,
when most of our friends and peers were cooling their nonmilitary jets
at home), are required to participate in organized athletics, must hew
to stringent standards of conduct and performance in myriad everyday
activities (and must suffer penalties for failures to do so), and are considered active-duty members of the United States Armed Services upon
taking the Oath of Office on Induction Day, in most cases mere weeks
after the majority of any class members graduated from high school.
Even though some midshipmen may have long-term strategic dreams of

fortune and success in the civilian world, all of them know that the first five or more years after graduation will be spent in service to the country, often in harm's way, far from family, friends, and loved ones.

It goes without saying that both of your authors would count our four years of training along (and often on) Maryland's Severn River as deeply formative in the shapes of our subsequent lives and careers, as would most of our fellow alumni at navy and the nation's three other military service academies: the U.S. Military Academy in West Point, New York, the U.S. Air Force Academy in Colorado Springs, Colorado, and the U.S. Coast Guard Academy in New London, Connecticut. (Although the United States Merchant Marine Academy in Kings Point, New York, is considered a national service academy, its students are not considered to be on active duty in the United States Armed Forces upon entering their academy, though many of them do eventually serve in the Navy Reserve or other nonmilitary uniformed services.) The bonds forged at the service academies are profound, and the personal sacrifices required to achieve them are significant.

Some years after your authors graduated, one of us was at an airport in Iowa the day before Thanksgiving, awaiting the arrival of family members from the East Coast. Another family group was there awaiting their own visitor, filling their corner of the baggage claim area with various navy-themed signs and balloons. After the flight's arrival, as the tired passengers worked their way out through the security checkpoint, a midshipman fourth-class (i.e., a freshman at a "normal" college and colloquially a "plebe" in the halls at Navy) in uniform eagerly pressed his way through the crowd to cheers from his awaiting loved ones. It was, most likely, the first time that he had left the immediate environs of the Academy since taking the oath on "I–Day" some five months earlier. He rushed straight to the arms of his mother, who hugged him closely. The first thing he said to her, with a catch in his voice, as he emotionally returned the hug was "Mom, it's *so hard!*" Your author in the airport will admit to becoming misty-eyed at the sight and sound of that reunion, reminded and remembering just what it had felt like many, many Thanksgivings before.

"Hard" was an interesting choice of a word by that young midshipman to summarize his first (and, typically, most difficult) half year at the Academy. In Navy folklore, "hard" is actually something to be proud of on some plane, per the required response that any plebe must spout on demand when queried about how long he or she has been in the navy. To wit, and from memory, decades after it was first drilled into our heads:

All me bloomin' life! Me mother was a mermaid, me father was King Neptune. I was born on the crest of a wave and rocked in the cradle of the deep. Seaweed and barnacles are me clothes. Every tooth in me head is a marlinspike; the hair on me head is hemp. Every bone in me body is a spar, and when I spits, I spits tar! I'se hard, I is, I am, I are!

"Hard" is also a standard subjective concept in the evolving histories of all of the service academies in that it is an absolute given that regardless of when any alumni of any of those fine institutions graduated, they will, without doubt, without pause, without thought tell any and all subsequent graduates that things were harder "back in the day" than they have been ever since. And, to be somewhat fair and objective, there's probably something accurate in that assessment over the long haul, just in terms of the ways in which the military and higher education have evolved since the older academies were founded in the 19th century, such changes rendering once-standard training practices obsolete, offensive, or even criminal.

The programs at the academies, then and now, were and are certainly designed to be hard (as in difficult), and they probably did and do make those who endure them hard (as in tough), and they are anchored in hard (as in strict) rules, regulations, and requirements. Which makes the occasional "soft" moments, like a mother's hug after five months of absence, or an afternoon sitting on the sofa doing nothing structured, or even the spoken admissions of feelings of doubt, or hurt, or concern all the more special when they occur. Although cadets and midshipmen at the military service academies are training to be leaders, soldiers, sailors, aviators, warriors, and more, they're also generally quite young, they're not married, and their time at their chosen academies may be their first time away from the "soft" comforts of home for any period of time. It's standard practice to put on the tough face while in training, gritting the teeth and bearing the burdens, but that doesn't mean that those talented and service-oriented young people don't miss the familial touches they've left behind.

To their credit, the academies have, over the years, recognized that there's a legitimate human need for such "soft" moments over the course of a brutal four-year training regimen, beyond the occasional trips home around the holidays, especially for midshipmen and cadets in their first years of training. One key and highly effective way in which such simple comforts are provided are through organized "sponsor" programs. In essence, families living near the various academies can sign up to serve as sponsors for one or more service academy students, and during the limited free time available to their sponsorees, they can offer home-cooked meals, casual "out-of-uniform" time, transportation, entertainment, mentoring, and the opportunity to do, see, talk about, and experience things that the rigid constraints of daily life inside the walls simply do not allow.

Sponsors essentially serve as surrogate local family members, and the emotional support benefits they provide can be profound, often leading to lifelong relationships that are just as important as those forged within the academies themselves. The Naval Academy launched its formal program in August 1956 under the direction of Superintendent W.R. Smedberg III, and focused on providing mentoring and personal support specifically for fourth-class "plebe" midshipmen. Rose Clark, the current sponsor director, noted that the initial cohort of sponsors certainly made an impact on their charges, as the son of original sponsor Barbara White (whose husband was an Academy professor) had contacted her office in 2015 to mark his mother's 100th birthday, hoping to reconnect her with the plebes she had first welcomed into her home some six decades earlier. The Air Force, Army, and Coast Guard academies also offer similar programs, again with a focus on establishing relationships between their students and sponsors during their freshmen years but recognizing that such relationships may provide succor and nourishment through the grueling four-year training program and then beyond.

A pair of unique graves in a cemetery high on the western bluffs above the Hudson River pay tribute and testament to ways in which local residents have long enriched the lives of the cadets and midshipmen who attend the nation's service academies, as formal sponsors or simply as concerned and connected neighbors and citizens. Sisters Susan Bogert Warner (July 11, 1819–March 17, 1885) and Anna Bartlett Warner (August 31, 1827–January 22, 1915) lie side by side at the West Point Cemetery, the only civilian women interred in that deeply historical memorial site. The funerary respect and honor shown to the sisters by the U.S. Military Academy was based largely on the hospitality, courtesy, and moral instruction that Anna and Susan had provided to generations of cadets, including some who emerged as the greatest military leaders of the late 19th and early 20th centuries. But even absent their de facto "sponsor" work, the Warner sisters' remarkable lives were worthy of acclaim and recognition well beyond the confines of the historical river community and nearby military campus where they spent their adult lives, as the pair were also among the most accomplished authors of their era, even if their works have been largely forgotten in 21st-century America, with one very notable exception.

The U.S. Military Academy is the oldest of the nation's service academies, founded in 1802 atop West Point, a strategic river overlook that has been continually operating as an army post since 1778, when the great Polish military engineer Tadeusz Kościuszko oversaw the building of garrison defenses to protect a tight S-shaped curve in the mighty Hudson River. During the Revolutionary War, the "Great Chain" was engineered, constructed, and laid across the Hudson to preclude British warships from advancing up the strategic river waterway. The Great Chain was 600 yards long, forged with massive links supported by logs, and running from the shore near West Point to Constitution Island on the eastern side of the river; that island was separated from the actual eastern shore by a largely impassible marshland. The Great Chain successfully stopped British ships from harrying Upstate New York, and it remained in use until 1782.

Constitution Island (known to earlier Dutch settlers as Martelaer's Rock) had been part of a large 17th-century land grant from the British Crown to the Philipse family, an immensely prominent Dutch clan who controlled a vast swath of modern Westchester County, then known as Philipsburg Manor. The family were fiercely loyal to the British Crown and therefore had most of their holdings seized in the early days of the Revolutionary War. General George Washington selected Martelaer's Rock as a key naval defensive position, with construction of Fort Constitution commencing in 1775, making it the earliest American fortification in the Hudson Valley. The British briefly captured and occupied the island in the immediate aftermath of the Battle of Saratoga in October 1777, but abandoned it a mere three weeks later. After retaking the island, a series of redoubt fortifications were built to provide clear cannon shots at passing shipping traffic until the Great Chain put an end to waterway passage past West Point.

Half a century later, Constitution Island's fortifications and barracks lay abandoned and derelict, while the U.S. Military Academy was thriving on the west side of the river. Thomas Warner, of a prominent New York and New England family that could trace its ancestry back to the early Puritan settlers, was serving as the chaplain to the army units training and stationed at West Point in the 1830s. His brother, Henry, was a successful and wealthy lawyer living in New York City's fashionable Hudson Square. Henry's wife, Anna Bartlett (from an equally old and prosperous New England family), died young, leaving Henry to raise their daughters, Anna and Susan, with assistance from his sister, Fanny, who came to live with the family. In 1836, Henry visited Thomas at West Point and had his first glimpse of Constitution Island. Smitten by its location and views, Henry acquired the property, intending to build a fine mansion to serve as a summer retreat for his family.

Unfortunately for the Warner family, Henry's fortunes took a severe turn for the worse during the panic of 1837, a financial crisis that led to a recession lasting approximately seven years, the collapse of countless banks and business, and widespread unemployment. A series of poor investment decisions quickly rendered Henry Warner insolvent, and so with Anna (then 13 years old), Susan (18), and his sister Fanny in tow, Henry vacated the family's New York City mansion and moved to an empty Revolutionary War–era barracks-cum-farmhouse on Constitution Island, after adding an eight-room Victorian-style

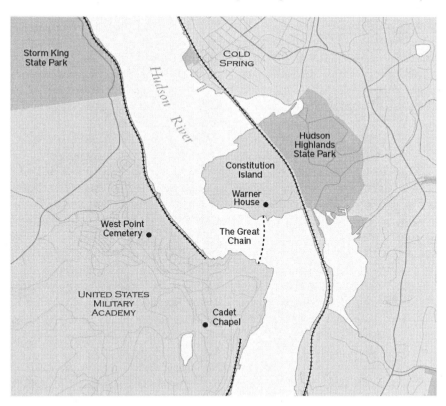

Map of Constitution Island and its environs (Liz Cruz).

wing to the stone-walled original structure. The teenaged sisters, who had once amused themselves by riding a matching pair of black ponies around their fine urban property, found themselves thrust suddenly into an extremely rough-hewn and rural environment, where the family's abilities to work the land for sustenance and shelter became of paramount importance. The sisters bravely determined that they would live self-sufficiently like pioneer women on the island, a resolution that lasted through the remainder of their lives, which they spent together, never marrying or moving away from their Hudson River home.

Both Anna and Susan had become devout Christians around this time, after youthful but profound religious experiences in the latter days of the Second Great Awakening, a period in which Protestant revivals fueled rapid growth among various evangelical (in the historical religious use of that word, not the modern political one) sects; the sisters had aligned themselves with the Mercer Street Presbyterian Church community in New York before their forced emigration from the city. The Presbyterian Church in America was, at the time, highly engaged in the creation of "moral reform organizations," including Sunday schools, temperance associations, Bible tract publishers, and orphanages, among other activities. Those movements were encouraged by the emergence of post-millennialism as a theological doctrine, which posited that the second coming of Christ would occur only at the end of an era of peace and prosperity that was to be fostered by human service and charity.

The Warner family spent much of the 1840s struggling to make ends meet on Constitution Island. When not engaged in the domestic and gardening work necessary to survival on their isolated island, the sisters spent much of their time through that decade reading voraciously and living vicariously through their stereopticon, an image viewer that allowed users to experience "3-D" views of the world's great scenes. Although the deleterious effects of the panic of 1837 lingered, Henry Warner exacerbated his dire fiscal situation by engaging in various ill-conceived legal conflicts, most especially with his neighbors across the marsh on the eastern banks of the Hudson. Henry ultimately lost that property case, and his island was temporarily placed in the hands of a receiver, reducing the family to destitution and possible eviction from their home.

Although they may have been oblivious to their dire circumstances in their early days on the island, after ten years of struggle, it had become increasingly clear to Anna and Susan that their father's fortunes were not likely to rebound in any meaningful fashion. In considering how they might best help their family and enhance their own long-term security after their father was gone (Henry actually lived to the ripe old age of 88, dying in 1875), Anna and Susan decided to become writers, supplementing their religious interests and inclinations with what they had learned as beneficiaries of that era's typical schooling for affluent young women: music, art, history, religion, and languages.

Susan was the first of the sisters to succeed in placing her written work in the public domain, and she did so with aplomb. Published in 1850 under the pseudonym Elizabeth Wetherell, *The Wide, Wide World* simply exploded on the American literary world before being widely translated and republished around the globe. Although it is impossible to ascertain accurate sales figures over its long run (in large part due to rampant literary piracy, poor enforcement of copyright protections, and chauvinistic practices in paying women authors their due), it is credibly believed that Susan Warner's debut novel is rivaled only by Harriet Beecher Stowe's *Uncle Tom's Cabin* as the best-selling novel in 19th-century America. (Louisa May Alcott's willfully creative writer Jo March reads *The Wide, Wide World* in a scene in *Little Women*, published in 1868–1869, as but one note on its lasting influence.) The book is unapologetically anchored in Susan's faith and is explicitly intended to teach Christian lessons, most especially that faith in one's God may allow the true Christian to triumph over the hardships of life on this mortal coil. (The novel's protagonist, Ellen Montgomery, certainly endures more than her fair share of travails throughout *The Wide, Wide World*, including the loss of her mother at a young age, mirroring Susan's own experiences.)

Anna Warner's first book, *Dollars and Cents*, was published in 1853 (she took the pseudonym Amy Lothrop); it was a lightly fictionalized account of the family's financial hardships. The sisters went on to write singly and collaboratively for the next three decades, creating an immense body of work, with well over 100 novels and shorter works (including nonfiction religious treatises, hymns, and children's stories) between them, earning favorable and fond comparisons to England's own sisterly literary marvels, the Brontë family. The pair even developed an educational game called Robinson Crusoe's Farmyard, which for many years was sold by Susan's publisher, George P. Putnam. (In an example of the injustices that women creators experienced in that time, searches for the game and its accompanying text now cite Putnam as the work's author and creator.) Anna's nonfiction 1872 work (published under her own name) *Gardening by Myself*, also proved to be hugely influential, as the proud island pioneer explicitly detailed how and why she gardened for pleasure. Prior to the success of that work, gardening was largely seen as a menial chore for farmers and domestic staff, not a pleasurable pastime suitable for ladies or gentlemen of substance or accomplishment.

The Warner sisters' most widely known legacy in modern times sprang from a collaboration between the pair. In 1860, while Susan was working on the novel *Say and Seal*, a scene required a song for a teacher to sing to inspire a dying child. She asked Anna to create a suitable text, and this is what the younger Warner wrote:

> *Jesus loves me—this I know,*
> *For the Bible tells me so;*
> *Little ones to Him belong—*
> *They are weak, but He is strong.*

Composer William Batchelder Bradley found this literary snippet in 1862, and inspired by its sentiments, he penned the now-familiar melody, adding the *"Yes, Jesus loves me ..."* refrain. Although she did not achieve quite the same level of lasting ubiquity as Anna did, Susan also wrote her own instructional hymns, and her "Jesus Bids Us Shine" remains a common musical component of many contemporary worship experiences.

As Susan and Anna Warner's works and successes spread over the years, the army's cadets across the river at West Point (or their instructors and officers) must have become increasingly aware of their isolated neighbors' fame. At some point after the Civil War, a delegation was dispatched to inquire whether the sisters would be willing to teach a Sunday school class to interested cadets. Susan accepted the invitation and for some years boated across the Hudson to teach a weekly class at the Academy's chapel. But as Susan grew older and frailer, the cadets began to reverse the commute, traveling to Constitution Island in warmer months for classes held on the sisters' property.

For the remainder of their lives, those Sunday school classes were the anchors of Susan and Anna Warner's social interactions. Although the gatherings were ostensibly to teach "hard" lessons about education and spirituality, there was no denying the "soft" appeal that the classes offered to the cadets, providing lemonade and gingerbread cookie–fueled respites from the rigors of their military and academic training, with fresh berries and whipped cream added to the board when they were in season. Anna regularly wrote new hymns to teach to their young guests, and "Jesus Loves Me" quickly became a popular, wistful marching refrain that the cadets carried back across the river to their duty station at West Point and thence around the world as they served, suffered, lived, and often died abroad.

Writer and philanthropist Olivia Egleston Phelps Stokes published a collection called *Letters and Memories of Susan and Anna Bartlett Warner* in 1925, in which one of "Miss Warner's Boys" (referring to Susan, in this case) remembered a typical visit to Constitution Island thusly:

> Miss [Susan] Warner awaited her guests in the orchard. She always sat in the same big chair, supported by many cushions. She was a frail little woman with a long face deeply lined with thought and care, lighted with large, dark, very brilliant eyes. As she sat in her chair with the boys in a semi-circle around her on the grass, she looked like a print from Godey's Lady's Book [a once-popular magazine] of half a century before. After each of the boys had read a Bible verse, Miss Warner, choosing her subject from some New Testament text, talked to them for perhaps half an hour until her enthusiasm and interest had obviously almost exhausted her small strength. She always gave to the boys the brightest and most optimistic side of the faith she loved so well. When she had finished and lay back pale and weary against her cushions, her sister, Miss Anna, came down from the house with the rarest treat of the whole week, tea and homemade gingerbread.

Susan Bogert Warner died in 1885 at the age of 65 and was buried at the West Point Cemetery, an extraordinary honor and an affirmation of the affection in which the corps of cadets had come to hold her. You can just see Constitution Island from Susan's grave, at least when the glorious old trees along the bluff below the cemetery are not in full bloom. After Susan's passing, the Sunday school classes became Anna's driving passion, and she continued her service to and hospitality for "her boys" until her own death in 1915 at the age of 87. General (and later President) Dwight D. Eisenhower was one of her final beloved pupils, forging a personal, temporal bond between her island's Revolutionary War history and the great conflict that roiled the world in the middle years of the 20th century. Anna is buried next to Susan, close by countless military heroes and warriors, many of whom they nurtured and tutored, providing simple pleasures like gingerbread and cold drinks to those in need of such "soft" reminders of home, family, faith, and love.

Before her passing, Anna Bartlett Warner provided the U.S. Military Academy with one final selfless gift that has endured just as profoundly as "Jesus Loves Me" does. Having been pressured for years by developers wanting to acquire Constitution Island (biographers routinely note that the Warner sisters could have become millionaires had they been willing to part with their beloved home), Anna elected to sell the property for a modest payment in 1908 to philanthropist Margaret Sage, who was the widow of prominent railroad magnate, financial mogul, and New York Whig politician Russell Sage. Margaret had inherited Russell's fortune upon his passing in 1906, and dedicated her own final decade to distributing it to worthy causes, establishing the Russell Sage Foundation in 1907 and founding the Russell Sage College for Women in 1916.

Margaret Sage and Anna Warner then jointly granted Constitution Island to the U.S. Military Academy by way of a letter to President Theodore Roosevelt in which they noted two stipulations on their gift in perpetuity. First, the donors noted that "the Island be for the use forever of the United States Military Academy at West Point, and that no part of it shall ever be used as a public picnic, excursion, or amusement ground, operated by private enterprise, individual or corporate, for profit." And

second, that "Anna Warner be allowed to live out her days there, in full possession of her house and the gardens appurtenant, to use the springs for water, pastures for her cows and horses, and to take such firewood as will be necessary." President Roosevelt accepted the terms and the gift, writing back to Margaret Sage, "I wish to thank you for your very generous gift to the Nation, and I have written Miss Warner thanking her. Permit me now, on behalf of the Nation, to thank you most heartily again for a really patriotic act."

The next year's graduating class at West Point, which included one George

Anna B. Warner, half-length portrait, circa 1913 (Library of Congress).

S. Patton, dedicated their edition of the school's annual yearbook, *The Howitzer*, to Anna Bartlett Warner. When she died six years later, she was granted full military honors at her burial with the entire corps of cadets (Eisenhower and General Omar Bradley would have been there) serving as her honorary final escort. The Warner sisters' home on their island remains much as it was when Anna left it, cared for since 1916 by the Constitution Island Association, a not-for-profit historical society. The gardens and arbors surrounding the house have also been restored with guidance gleaned from Anna's detailed descriptions of her beloved plots in *Gardening by Myself.*

Just as the modern service academies provide small doses of "soft" familial support to today's midshipmen and cadets, the leadership at West Point during the Warner sisters' time as Sunday school teachers must be commended, a century on, for supporting and sustaining the relationships between Susan and Anna and their "boys," who rowed across the river to share small tastes of joy and pleasure in their company, even while being expected to learn something. And also, unquestionably, for providing joy and pleasure back to the sisters, who so deserved it, for all they did, under such circumstances, and for so long. Good relationships, like good contracts, are those that benefit both parties. Clearly, the relationship between the U.S. Military Academy and Anna and Susan Warner was one of the very best of its kind, then, now, and forever more.

CHAPTER THREE

The Virginia Military Institute Cadets and the Battle of New Market (c. 1830s–1864)

New Market Memorial, Virginia Military Institute, Lexington, Virginia

"Experience: that chill touchstone whose sad proof reduces all things from their false hue."
—George Gordon Byron,
6th Baron Byron (Lord Byron)

"Tragedy has the great moral defect of giving too much importance to life and death."
—Nicolas Chamfort

The humid air is as heavy with expectation as it is with moisture in the Shenandoah Valley village of New Market, as the threat of imminent battle rises with the sun. Men mingle, mumble, sweat, curse, and pray; horses prance nervously beneath their mounts or in harness required to move massive artillery pieces; ordnance, ammunition, dining tins, bayonets, and uniform buttons glitter and flash as the sun creeps upward through breaking clouds and the day warms. The Civil War has been raging for three years at this point, and Union forces have been working steadily to break the will of the Confederate armies and civilians through aggressive regional campaigns designed to press the secessionists and their supporters into submission. The Valley Campaign is the latest Union initiative on this front, designed to devastate crops, communities, infrastructure, and emotions along the agriculturally and commercially important Shenandoah River. Even though the local Virginians have the advantages, mental and physical, associated with defending their own home territory, the Union forces generally outnumber the Confederate ones, have superior military matériel, and better logistics and supply chains.

In a concerted "all hands" effort to thwart the Union advance into the Shenandoah Valley, the student cadets at the Virginia Military Institute (VMI), located south down the Shenandoah Valley in Lexington, Virginia, have been ordered into action as part of the Confederate forces. After an 85-mile march over four days, VMI's 257 soldiers in training join the Department of East Tennessee and West Virginia Army forces near Staunton, Virginia. Rather than awaiting a Union push southward through the valley, Confederate leaders make the decision to march northward to meet their foes near New Market in an effort to mitigate and minimize the damage the invading troops might do, engaging in various provocative skirmishes designed to draw the Union forces into actively deploying their calvary and artillery pieces. When the Union forces refuse to budge from their seemingly strategically superior position at the northern outskirts of New Market, the Confederates have no choice but to force an aggressive attack.

The Union response is strong, and the Confederate troops are briefly thrown into disarray, the center of their line devastated by withering artillery and rifle fire. Facing a potential rout and with few other options available, the Confederate battlefield leadership reluctantly calls on the VMI cadets to fill a gap in the line of combat and press the charge against the Union positions. As the unit crosses a field near a local orchard, many of the VMI cadets lose their shoes in the mud remaining from recent steady rainfalls; yet onward they press. Following their slog through what has come to be called the Field of Lost Shoes, the military school students (the youngest of them 15 years old, the oldest 25) perform heroically and play a key role in turning the tide of battle, with Union forces suddenly and unexpectedly finding themselves on the opposite side of an emerging rout. As the sun sets on the day, New Market emerges as one of the increasingly rare significant Confederate military victories of the Civil War, ending only when the Union forces beat a hasty retreat across Mill Creek and burn its bridge behind them to keep the Confederates from further pursuit.

The date: May 18, 2019.

The event: The most recent reenactment of the Battle of New Market, with more than 1,500 volunteers from across the country assembled in accurate uniforms, carrying accurate arms (sans accurate ammunition), massing in accurate positions, all to re-create the look and feel of the Battle of New Market, fought in earnest on May 15, 1864, between ~6,300

Side by Side in Eternity

Union troops under Major General Franz Sigel and ~4,200 Confederates under Major General John C. Breckenridge, once an accomplished U.S. senator and representative from Kentucky and, on the eve of hostilities, the vice president of the United States in James Buchanan's disastrous administration. (The scheduled 2020 and 2021 New Market reenactment events were canceled due to COVID-19 concerns.) The reenactors don't revisit New Market's history as a private undertaking but rather, stage and rewage the day's carnage before even larger armies of paying spectators gathered to watch the event, the crowd also drawn from the farthest points of the modern nation rebuilt over decades from the gutted and broken remnants of the Confederacy and the homelands of the victorious Union, which were largely spared from firsthand battle damage, at the cost of the lives and health of a full generation of young men.

New Market is the oldest American Civil War reenactment still held on the original battlefield site, having been staged since 1914, currently under the auspices of the Virginia Museum of the Civil War. Its popularity as a cultural and historical happening has remained strong throughout its history. In 1923, for example, legendary Marine Corps brigadier general Smedley D. Butler and a detachment of marines stationed at nearby Quantico, Virginia, reenacted the battle before a crowd estimated at over 150,000 people. Guests can supplement the actual battle re-creation with guided tours, visits to the associated museum, lectures, small-scale demonstrations, and plentiful souvenir shopping. "Heritage tourism" is estimated to provide an annual economic impact of more than $200 million in the Shenandoah Valley's National Historic District.

The Civil War holds a special place in the United States' collective psyche, and myriad modern political tussles are clearly and demonstrably anchored in many of the same cross-regional concerns that shaped the more problematic components of the American Constitution that culminated in the nation's great schism, that manifested themselves into and through the heyday of the civil rights movement, and that remain germane in a time when "red states and blues states" have replaced the old "blue and gray" reckoning of North versus South, with residents of different regions of the country seemingly living in different worlds, experiencing different realities. The modern interest in "battlefield tourism" is also anchored in the historical Civil War realities; in the early days of the great conflict, affluent Washingtonians (including various members of Congress) traveled with picnic baskets and opera glasses to the bucolic countryside outside Manassas, Virginia, to watch one of the first major battles of the conflict, now known as the First Battle of Bull Run. The day's planned and expected excitements were brought relatively quickly to a horrifying finish, as the Confederates defeated the Union forces in a shockingly bloody battle that forced many of the formerly jolly picnickers to flee for their lives, suddenly, vividly, and viscerally aware that war is actually a terrible spectator sport when it is being waged in earnest.

And yet, hundreds of thousands of people visit scores of Civil War battlefield reenactments every year and tens of thousands of volunteers regularly dress their parts and play their roles in such events (or at least they did pre–COVID-19 and will presumably continue to do so in its aftermath), while many of the greatest works of 20th-century American film and literature are expressly designed to give readers and moviegoers a sense of what wars and battles looked and felt like for those who fought them and those whose land such battles were fought across and upon. Books, movies, and reenactments may certainly give eager audiences some increased and perhaps valuable perspective on the experience of battle, e.g., in the case of the American Revolutionary and Civil Wars' surviving battlefields, one of the more acute realizations for many modern visitors comes from gaining a personal sense of what close quarters and across what small fields the combatants shot at, stabbed at, and wrestled hand to hand with their rivals. But when no actual limbs are severed, no viscera are spilled, no one is blinded or deafened or maimed or burned, no survivors are subjected to long-term traumatic psychological duress in the aftermath of combat, and no one dies on the field, page, or screen, the experience is, thankfully, destined to be an incomplete one for most who encounter it.

But that doesn't diminish or demean the experience for those who re-create it. "In this thing that we call the 're-enacting hobby' there's a lot of nuances," said New Market reenactor Franklin Van Valkenburg (a member of VMI's Class of 2013) in an interview with the authors.

> You have a reenactment, yes, very traditional and straightforward, you're re-creating the event, you're re-creating the maneuvers and what happened there on that day. But then on the other side of it you have living history, so that might be a little bit more generic. It's not necessarily tailored to a specific event and re-creating it. It's more of a static setup or something that has a little more maneuvering but it's not necessarily re-creating a very specific battle. And it's done that way to afford spectators or visitors the opportunity to more closely engage with the reenactors and to ask them the questions about what they're wearing and what they're doing and what

they're eating, all that kind of thing. So what we do is to convey a sense of what happened. We obviously cannot get to the exact numbers, we can't get to the exact details, and I don't think you'd want to, given the very horrific carnage of a war, of a battle. So there is, obviously, a certain threshold that

Franklin Van Valkenburg (VMI '13) interpreting a captain in the Army of Northern Virginia at Gettysburg in July 2021 (Franklin Van Valkenburg Personal Collection).

you just aren't able to cross, and you wouldn't want to cross. But, at least in the sense of seeing several hundred or several thousand men on a field in formation, maneuvering, and shooting in volleys, or hearing cannon and seeing horses and wagons, well, those are all things that make history jump off the page of the history books. And that's really what a reenactment is all about.

"I've always been a bit of a material-culture-focused individual," Van Valkenburg continued.

I like learning about not just the people and the places and what happened, but what were they wearing, and what were they eating. What were they experiencing in the small ways that you can't really describe in a book. And so I've been to events where, for example, we re-created, to the man, about 250-odd men, the 13th Virginia Infantry as they appeared just before they stepped off into the overland campaign in 1864, and we, per what they did back then, were woken up and put on a forced march in the middle of the night, and marched in darkness. We didn't have any light pollution from a nearby city. We were in a very remote part of central Virginia area, and so as we marched along this dirt road, I could hear men stubbing their toes and cussing, and wondering where we were, and asking if the officers knew what they were doing, and it dawned on me that these men had to have experienced the same thing in 1864. And that's probably why I do it. Because you get these little vignettes, these little moments where something jumps out at you like that and you realize, well, these guys are all laying on their sides next to their arms in a field and just waiting to start up another march, and they're writing in their journals, and they're playing a fiddle or talking amongst themselves about where they're going, and they did the same thing back then. And so I do appreciate that ability to put myself in their shoes, if you will, for just a moment and get a glimpse of that experience. Short of, obviously, the horror and the sadness and then all that other stuff.

Of horror and sadness, there were no shortages in the historic Battle of New Market. Of the roughly 10,500 combatants in the day's brutal melee, Union casualties totaled 841 (96 killed, 520 wounded, and 225 captured or missing), while the Confederates experienced 43 killed, 474 wounded, and 3 missing for a total casualty count of 524. Both sides' casualty rates worked out to about 13 percent of the day's combatants. Tragically, or heroically (depending on your perspective), the VMI cadets carried the day but at an even greater cost: of the 257 students conscripted into live combat service at New Market, 10 were killed on the battlefield or died of their wounds soon after, and 45 were injured in the battle, for an effective casualty rate of nearly 22 percent. The American Battlefield Trust recognizes the Battle of New Market as the only time in U.S. history when the student body of a college fought (and suffered) in direct infantry combat as its own independent unit.

"Several military schools were called into active service during the Civil War, to include The Citadel, North Georgia College, Georgia Military Institute, and others," explained Colonel Keith Gibson, executive director of the VMI Museum System, in a recent interview with the authors.

> But the VMI situation has the distinction that the cadets were not brigaded with any other veteran unit. They went into battle as their own independent cadet command structure, with their own commander, rather than being attached to some preexisting regiment that may have been a little more seasoned, a little more understanding of the nature of a battlefield, and so on. The cadets were recognized as their own regiment, and they stood right beside the 62nd Regiment and the 51st Regiment, as their own unit, with their own VMI commander [Lieutenant Colonel Scott Shipp], who was the cadet commandant at the time. Virtually all of the cadets then at VMI, to a man, they went. Now, there were some that were very young, some that were ill, and some whose parents had specifically said "I do not want my son participating in this," you know. And those cadets were assigned to guard the institute, and left here during the time that the corps was away on the campaign.

Although New Market marked the sole point when VMI's students were put in harm's way under combat conditions, it was not the first time that the academic and training regimen at the institute was strained by the nation's greatest military conflict, with many of the most grievous battles of the war unfolding within a few days' march or ride from the campus in Lexington. Founded in 1839 as America's first state military college just over two decades later, VMI cadets were deployed to Charles Town, Virginia, in the aftermath of John Brown's raid on Harper's Ferry; a detachment of VMI cadets actually stood guard at Brown's execution on December 2, 1859. In April 1861, just after the Battle of Fort Sumter marked the opening of the Civil War, the corps of cadets was dispatched to Richmond, Virginia, to drill Confederate army recruits under the command of Major Thomas "Stonewall" Jackson, then a professor at the institute. VMI reopened its Lexington campus in January 1862, and in May 1862, they were ordered to aid now-general Jackson by marching in pursuit of federal troops, though they did not engage in combat. Jackson was killed in May 1863, and his remains were returned to Lexington for burial. The corps of cadets were called into action again in the latter part of 1863 to defend their home region against Union raids by General William Averell, but, once again, they were not pressed into active combat situations.

Wood engraving of VMI from the 1863 *Register of the Officers and Cadets of the Virginia Military Institute* **(Virginia Military Institute).**

But then came May 1864, when the VMI cadets' fortunate run of close calls came to an end. Colonel Gibson picks up the story:

So, the battle evolves in that Franz Sigel, a German immigrant of high training and political position, was given a command and sent into the Shenandoah Valley to basically take its resources away from the Confederacy, and to occupy any Confederate forces that might attempt to try to join Robert E. Lee on the eastern side of the Blue Ridge Mountains, where he was getting ready to get engaged in the Battle of the Wilderness and Spotsylvania and that whole series of battles that's going to take place in the spring and summer of 1864. So Franz Sigel is headed "up the valley," that is, down south; as you move south in the Shenandoah Valley, you're gaining altitude. When the Confederate forces assigned to the valley discover this, the Confederate general John C. Breckinridge is *way* down in southwestern Virginia, and he immediately begins a forced march to try to engage the Union army as far northward as he possibly can.

"Breckinridge is picking up any kind of home guard, any units that he can possibly find, on his way north," Gibson continues.

And of course, as he comes through Lexington, the cadets were a target of opportunity. So, for the next four days, they march from VMI to the little town of New Market, Virginia, 80 miles north of Lexington. Breckinridge had no intention of putting the cadets in the battle at all. They were to be held exclusively in reserve, but if everything went horribly wrong, they knew that they might be pressed into service. In fact, Breckinridge told the

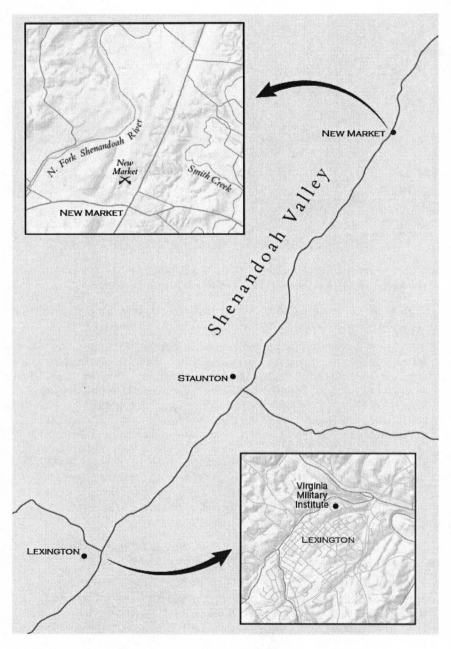

Map of Lexington and New Market, Virginia (Liz Cruz).

cadets as much that morning. He came by and said, "It is not my intention to use you today, but I know if I have to, you will perform your duty as Virginians." And, of course, the cadets cheered and yelled and all of that, as you would imagine.

The Union troops had taken up a very defendable position on the northern ridgeline of a piece of land owned by Jacob Bushong, and the line was roughly three-quarters of a mile wide. Franz Sigel had about 20 pieces of artillery lined up hub to hub. He was ready for the Confederates to arrive. So Breckinridge begins his movement to engage the Union infantry, and all this time the cadets remain in a reserve position. Breckinridge is on the front line; he takes a position on the Bushong farm along a split-rail fence, and that fence separated an orchard from a wheat field, and the wheat field was literally like a little pond at the moment, because it had been raining for a week, and it was in a depressed area and it was just saturated.

The Confederates pause at that fence, and they come under the collective fire of all of the Union infantry, plus artillery fire, and the center of the Confederate line just melted away, totally destroyed. Sigel sees that, and he tries to send three regiments forward to rush through that gap and start presenting insulating fire to the left and right to destroy the rest of the Confederate line. Breckinridge is told what the situation is and that he has to send in his reserves. At first, he says, "I'm not going to do that. I'm not going to commit the cadets." But he was reminded that he either had to commit the cadets or withdraw from the field, because there were only a few seconds before the Union forces arrived at the line. So Breckinridge gave the order to send the cadets in. Now, it is circumstance, it's fate, that he had positioned the cadets right behind the section of the Confederate line that had been destroyed. Men of the 30th Virginia, the 62nd Virginia, and the 51st Virginia. They just disappeared. Where those regiments came in contact with each other, the very center of the line, well, the cadets were literally right there, just a few yards away. So the cadets get there in time and reestablish the Confederate line, and at that moment, the entire Confederate line now moves forward into the wheat field.

The Confederates repulse the oncoming three regiments of Union soldiers, and then are approaching the Union position along with the artillery. By this time, Sigel realizes that his window of opportunity has closed. His infantry assault was not successful, and he orders a withdrawal from the field. So the Union forces are trying to get off the field as quickly as they can, pulling their artillery through the mud. It's chaotic. And the cadets are able to come upon and capture a Union artillery piece, which, you know, again to them was just beyond belief. This is just a great excitement. Shortly later, it becomes a rout. Breckinridge just misses totally destroying the Union army, but they manage to get back to the other side of the river, destroy the bridge, and save themselves.

"Then Breckinridge comes by the position where the cadets were located, he takes them out of the assault and tells them, 'Well done, men of the institute! Well done, Virginians!' And that was the day for the cadets," summarizes Gibson.

> Breckinridge credited them personally with turning the tide of battle. They performed in a way that no one would have necessarily expected a bunch of schoolboys, even VMI cadet schoolboys, fresh out of their classroom. These days, when I have VMI freshmen, we call them "rats" here, with me on the battlefield, I often tell them the story of John Howard, who survived the battle. He later wrote about his experience and said that when the cadets crossed the split-rail fence between the orchard and the wheat field, he felt every Union musket was pointed right at him. But then he looked to his left and right as the corps crossed over that rail fence, and here I quote him, "All concerns of individuality left me. It was the Corps forward." In other words, brother rats working together to do something that as individuals they could never accomplish.

When word of the Union defeat at New Market reached Commanding General of the U.S. Army Ulysses S. Grant, he was quick and decisive in removing Sigel from his command, replacing him with Major General David Hunter. The Confederate victory allowed local crops to be harvested to support General Lee's Army of Northern Virginia, while also preserving Lee's communications lines to and from western

Contemporary photograph of the Field of Lost Shoes with the "Rats" of VMI's Class of 2023 preparing to reenact the charge of their forebears (Virginia Military Institute).

Virginia. Lee suggested that Breckinridge pursue the Union army northward and invade Maryland, but the overextended logistics supply lines
and springtime high-water marks of the Shenandoah River and its trib-
utaries made such an assault impractical. Although New Market was a
tactical and emotional victory for the Confederates, its beneficial out-
comes were short lived: Hunter and his forces returned "up the valley"
mere weeks later, occupying Staunton, Virginia, on June 5, and Lexington, Virginia, on June 11. The corps of cadets did not reengage the Union
troops, instead retreating to camp in the nearby Blue Ridge Mountains.
A day later, Hunter's troops burned VMI. The corps were posted to various positions around Virginia for the remainder of the war, then were
formally disbanded in April 1865, with the cadets left to their own individual devices to find their ways home or wherever else they could find
shelter through the closing months of the Civil War, their side defeated,
their home state largely destroyed, and countless thousands of their fellow Confederates dead, maimed, or imprisoned.

Somewhat surprisingly through the long lens of history, it was a
mere six months later when VMI reopened and resumed the pursuit of
its academic and military missions in its home city of Lexington, Virginia. And just six more months after that, the long celebration of the
Battle of New Market as a defining element of VMI's culture and history began to take shape, as the remains of fallen cadets Henry Jen-
ner Jones, William Hugh McDowell, Thomas Garland Jefferson (a
great-grand-nephew of President Thomas Jefferson), Joseph Christopher Wheelwright, and Samuel Francis Atwill were brought to VMI for
reburial. Atwill had been a sophomore member of the Class of 1866; the
other four were all freshmen members of the Class of 1867. On May 15,
1866, the second anniversary of the Battle of New Market, the five bodies were escorted in an honorary memorial procession of the corps of
cadets for interment in a vault in the Old Porter's Lodge in Lexington.
In 1878, the remains of the five cadets were moved again, this time to a
newly created but short-lived Cadet Cemetery. They remained there for
just over three decades, before being moved once again in 1912 to their
current resting place in a copper box set into the foundation under *Virginia Mourning Her Dead*, a statue dedicated in 1903. A sixth New Market cadet casualty, Charles Gay Crockett (freshman '67), was reinterred
with his fellows in 1960. The other four (William Henry Cabell, junior
'65; Alva Curtis Hartfield, sophomore '66; Luther Cary Haynes, freshman '67; and Jaqueline Beverly Stanard, freshman '67) are buried in private or family plots elsewhere in Virginia.

Side by Side in Eternity

Virginia Mourning Her Dead was a labor of love for its sculptor, Moses Jacob Ezekiel (1844–1917), who was a member of VMI's Class of 1866 (the first Jewish cadet in the institute's history), who served as corporal of the guard over "Stonewall" Jackson's body the night before the general's burial and who fought and was wounded at the Battle of New Market; he was a close friend to Cadet Jefferson, now buried beneath the monument. After the Civil War, Ezekiel lived, worked, and studied in Cincinnati for several years before settling in Rome, Italy, in 1874, where he completed most of his significant sculptures and paintings. Although his fame has faded over the past century, in his time he was highly regarded and well known, ultimately being knighted three times for his accomplishments by the grand duke of Saxe-Meiningen, the emperor of Germany, and the king of Italy. He was a longtime friend of Robert E. Lee after the Civil War, and he remained a die-hard supporter of the Confederate cause until his death. Notably, given his level of attainment in his time, he refused payment for his work on the memorial statue to honor his peers at his beloved alma mater.

Since the initial interment of the five fallen cadets in Lexington on the second anniversary of the Battle of New Market, VMI has faithfully

Contemporary photograph of *Virginia Mourning Her Dead* at VMI (Virginia Military Institute).

60

observed the anniversary of the battle, instituting a formal ceremony in 1878, when the five cadets were moved to the (no longer extant) Cadet Cemetery. In the 1880s, the institute implemented a roll call of the dead as part of the ceremony, with the names of each of the ten fallen cadets of New Market being called by the commander of the company in which each served. In response to each name being called, another member of the company offers the reply, "Died on the field of honor." The ceremony was moved to the site of *Virginia Mourning Her Dead* in 1912, and (again, COVID-19 years exempted) a memorial service has taken place on May 15 annually since that time. The Battle of New Market is also a key framing element of the training experience at VMI, as the "rats" take their oath of office only after a grueling orientation program capped by running a symbolic charge across the "Field of Lost Shoes" (the muddy wheat field below the Bushong farm), at which point they receive their uniform shoulder boards from VMI seniors, who have ceremonially marched them to New Market from Lexington in remembrance of the corps' long slog into their memorable moment of active combat.

These are all grand, earnest, and meaningful traditions for those who have partaken of them over the decades, and there is no questioning the bravery and commitment to their cause demonstrated by the VMI cadets who were mostly mere boys turned into cannon fodder on a battlefield that had little long-term impact on the war surrounding it or the nation that was rebuilt in its aftermath. But there's an uncomfortable truth that must be addressed as a counterbalance to their valor and sacrifice, and that's the fact that they died defending an insurrectionist regime dedicated to the preservation of human chattel slavery and the economic system built on that great affront to basic human rights and dignity, within a nation ostensibly founded to allow its citizens to pursue those same basic rights to the best of their abilities and will.

At the time of this writing, we can count as fresh and recent memories the violent "Unite the Right" rally in Charlottesville, Virginia (farther "up the valley" from New Market and Lexington), the murder of George Floyd, and the stunning day when modern-day insurrectionists, many of them carrying or wearing Confederate flags or symbols, attempted to thwart Congress's recognition and ratification of the 2020 Electoral College results. The nation's views of and growing discomfort with such Confederate and Confederate-adjacent stories, memories, monuments, and memorials has come into ever sharper focus in the aftermath of those and other recent events, with many such monuments being removed quietly by local, state, and federal governments and agencies or being torn down by citizens when official channels are not flowing quickly enough to stanch the swelling fires of outrage.

Moses Ezekiel was an early and vociferous proponent of what's come to be known as the "Lost Cause" movement, which casts the Confederacy as a noble and honorable proponent of states' rights and economic freedom, rather than as a treasonous rebellion to preserve the institution of slavery to the interest and benefit of the Southern planter class. (As disclosed earlier, one of your authors is descended from an old South Carolina family who were slave-owning rice farmers, prominent legislators, and soldiers and officers in the Confederate army; it remains dismaying, frankly, to visit the family cemetery and see the Confederate battle flag monuments placed there regularly atop Confederate States of America veteran's graves by friends and followers of the United Daughters of the Confederacy.) Ezekiel's works have not been on the front line of the Confederate monument removal movement in large part because he eschewed straight portraiture of prominent soldiers, politicians, and

Moses Jacob Ezekiel's *New South Monument* at Arlington National Cemetery, shortly after its unveiling in 1914, photo by Harris & Ewing Photographers (Library of Congress).

generals, instead creating symbolic representations of the Confederacy's noble (to Ezekiel) attributes. That said, his allegorical and massive *New South* monument at Arlington National Cemetery, created on commission from the United Daughters of the Confederacy and unveiled and dedicated by fellow Virginian and then–American president Woodrow Wilson (whose stock has fallen with historians over the past century in large part due to his blatant racism) has been a regular source of political churn in recent years; in 2017, 20 of Ezekiel's descendants wrote an open letter to the *Washington Post* calling for its removal.

To their credit, the administration at VMI recognized some of the problematic aspects associated with the veneration of the New Market soldiers and have taken steps in recent years to adapt the services and celebrations surrounding it. "We began to get ahead of the power curve several years ago when we began to think in terms of this grander role that *Virginia Mourning Her Dead* plays," explains Colonel Gibson.

> We have made a rather long inventory to determine how to best handle things that have a Confederate connection or iconography, and *Virginia Mourning Her Dead* is on that list. However, after much discussion and deliberation, the feeling, as it relates to that statue, is that it really is not a Confederate piece of Confederate iconography. It's the Commonwealth of Virginia that's actually represented in that statue. And the fact that it was inspired by the friends that Moses Ezekiel lost in that battle is how the statue comes into existence. Ever since that statue has been created, we've continued to add to that list of those that are mourned. And that is the prevailing sentiment and the compelling argument for the statue staying where it is and continuing to tell its story.

"Now, there may be some adjustment to the plaques that are found on the base of the statue that list all of the names of the cadets who were in the corps in the year 1864," he continues.

> There was no distinction made of whether or not they actually were in the battle or whether they were some of those cadets that stayed at VMI, or they were on furlough. If their name was on the roster, their name ended up getting put on those tablets. So in some ways, it really doesn't even actually connect one to one with the Battle of New Market. But we may wish to update those tablets, with this broader thought of Virginia mourning all of her dead, whether they fell in a rice paddy in Vietnam, or a trench in Verdun, or a mountainside in Afghanistan. Virginia mourns *all* of her dead. So we have wanted to expand the concept so that when we have that commemoration on May the 15th, we're really remembering the 600 VMI alumni who have died in times of a national call to duty, killed on battlefields around the planet. We began to make the transition and introduce that concept at least six or seven years ago. And for the past couple of years,

the program that's printed for that ceremony—and it's now called the VMI Memorial Day parade—lists the names of all of those 600, which includes the cadets from New Market and the three that we know of that died wearing Union blue uniforms during the Civil War.

The reenactment community at New Market also recognizes that changing times, values, and perspectives merit consideration in the ways in which they present "living history" for a paying audience. "We live in a time now where there's a lot of stuff being called back up into question, and folks are asking themselves whether it's appropriate to engage in this hobby," noted Franklin Van Valkenburg to the authors.

> How do we commemorate or remember our past? Is it appropriate to commemorate the past versus just knowing that it happened, and leaving it at that? I look at it this way: history is good, bad, and ugly. There are all kinds of places where you can see yourself as the hero, while someone else can see you as the villain. But then there are other places that are a lot murkier. For example, there were many soldiers that took up arms not by their own choice but through conscription and being drafted into service, in both the North and the South. There's a lot of gray area in war and in what is understood to be the causation, or what is the personal motivation of the soldiers who find themselves on battlefields. I certainly think that we need to have a discussion about that, and I'm not the one to say to you that this side was right or that side was wrong. What I am going to say is that we need to put ourselves in a position where those conversations can be had, maturely, and with tact and with an open mind.

"I do think that the reenacting hobby has obviously looked over its shoulder in recent years and asked, 'Hey, are we going to be around in the next few years, or is the country going to shift in a direction where it's just no more,'" Van Valkenburg continued. "Personally, I would say that, very much, now more than ever, this is needed, and this is something that I thankfully, optimistically see a lot of people taking a lot of interest in reenacting. Not just the people who are getting into it as a hobby but the spectators who come up to us and talk and say, 'Thank you for doing this.'"

Outside of New Market hobbyists, even VMI's current commandant, Colonel Adrian T. Bogart III (a member of VMI's Class of 1981), concurs with and supports the changing role of New Market in the institute's modern remembrances.

> The annual New Market ceremony has improved, and the way it has improved is that we are now celebrating all VMI graduates who have paid the ultimate price and made the ultimate sacrifice for their country. We're remembering and celebrating all of them, and that's appropriate, so I think

that's how we advance VMI. You know, we wear these great overcoats that keep you very warm in the winter, and the underside of our capes are red, to symbolize the blood that VMI has spilt in the service of this nation. That's the philosophy behind it, and in the ceremony, we recount all of the great sacrifices. So I think we're taking an expanded view, recognizing that today's cadets are going into a lot of environments that are different from what other earlier cadets graduated into. So my view as commandant is that we need to embrace VMI's *entire* history and not just one series of pages in the many chapters that this great institute has.

With the Battle of New Market reenactment having been shut down for at least two years due to the coronavirus pandemic, it will remain interesting to see whether or how it is further adapted, when and if it does eventually return. The emotional weight of the Civil War, and the depths of its causes and its impacts, all lend themselves to active and thoughtful conversation and interpretation all these years on. Ignoring and hiding such elements of our history is just as fraught with peril as is blind adherence to a narrative penned when one human being could own another, solely by virtue of their relative skin color. VMI is taking steps to engage such a dialogue, to their credit. Of course, not every recipient of an adapted or evolved message wants to hear it, especially in today's often toxic, social media–fueled political environment. When the Virginia Museum of the Civil War announced that they were canceling the 2021 reenactment, no doubt after careful and cautious review, comments on their social media pages included "New communist in charge compliments of [Virginia governor Ralph] Northam" and "Covid or Woke Virginia?" and "Pitiful." If a potentially lethal virus is not sufficient grounds for giving a conscientious nonprofit organization a break in its cultural programming, it's hard to imagine that a more open and telling interpretation of the events of May 15, 1864, is likely to find a warm response from those prone to see malfeasance in any changes to the ways things have "always" been done.

But that doesn't mitigate the need for such changes, nor does it diminish the admirable, yet difficult, work being undertaken by those tasked with helping Americans of the 21st century better understand those who came before us, warts and all.

Douglas Albert Munro (1919–1942) and Edith Fairey Munro (1895–1983)

Laurel Hill Memorial Park, Cle Elum, Washington

"True bravery is shown by performing without witnesses what one might be capable of doing before all of the world."
—François de La Rochefoucauld

"Our virtues are dearer to us the more we have had to suffer for them. It is the same with our children. All profound affection admits a sacrifice."
—Luc de Clapiers, Marquis de Vauvenargues

As gentlemen of a certain age (ahem), your authors were within the core target audience of military-recruiting advertisements in the late 1970s and early 1980s, as an all-volunteer armed services began to take shape in America in the years following the Vietnam War. Per the recommendations made in February 1970 by the Gates Commission (headed by Thomas S. Gates, Jr., a former secretary of defense in the Eisenhower administration), President Richard Nixon and the Joint Chiefs of Staff accepted the not-astonishing reality that adequate military strength could be achieved and maintained without involuntary conscription. The last draft call of the modern conscription era was held on December 7, 1972, and the authority to induct conscripts expired in June 1973, after which registration with the Selective Service System (SSS) was suspended in April 1975, and registrant processing was suspended in January 1976. (In 1980, President Jimmy Carter reinstated the requirement that all young men register with the SSS within a month of their 18th birthdays, a policy that remains in force to this day, despite various occasional legislative and legal challenges to the SSS's charter and authority.)

Chapter Four. Douglas Munro and Edith Munro

Of course, in the age of an all-volunteer military, the role of professional military recruiters changed dramatically, moving from a facilitation role in processing often unwilling conscripts to a role highly dependent on convincing young people, who may or may not have other, better employment options, that a stint in the armed forces would be a worthwhile life step, the benefits of which (education and training, job security, healthcare and retirement, sense of purpose and patriotism, etc.) ostensibly outweighing the challenges (spartan lifestyles, long deployments, high mortality risks, etc.). Since the emergence of broadcast and (later) cable or streaming television services in the post–World War II years, punchy and pithy 30- to 60-second broadcast commercials have often served as the armed forces' most effective instruments of persuasion, planting seeds through repetition, repetition, repetition of basic, simple, aspirational message, designed to produce crops of recruits as their messages take root and blossom alongside their young target audience's own advancing maturity.

Spend an afternoon watching pretty much any major sporting event after reading this chapter, decades on from the end of the draft, and you're likely to be bombarded (no pun intended) with military recruitment commercials that are often visually and thematically indistinguishable from the equally ubiquitous "first-person shooter" military console game advertisements. Things weren't quite as high budget and sophisticated around the time that your authors were in high school, though. Back then, one of the most ubiquitous marketing campaigns of the era was built around a cheesy low-budget multiservice recruiting commercial with an earworm tune so damnably memorable that Bill Murray even sang it for comedic effect in his 1981 comedy *Stripes*. We don't have to look it up online, all these years on, to remember the words, and we apologize in advance for replanting them in your brain if you'd successfully managed to extract them at some point over the past half century:

> *Army! Navy! Air Force! Marines!*
> *We don't ask for experience, we give it.*
> *You won't read it in a book, you'll live it.*
> *Pick a service, pick a challenge, set yourselves a course.*
> *Army! Navy! Air Force! Marines!*
> *What a great place, it's a great place to start.*

At the commercial's end, a garish yellow tagline noted, "See your local recruiter. Paid for by the U.S. Armed Forces." (It apparently worked for the two of us, as we joined the navy soon thereafter, though to be fair, we were both conditioned to do so, having been raised by Marine Corps fathers.) Although the exhortation to see a recruiter was probably heartfelt and accurate from the perspective of those who produced the commercial (military recruiters have quotas to meet, after all, just like most of their civilian colleagues do in their own worlds), we suspect that the tagline "Paid for by the U.S. Armed Forces" was not quite 100 percent accurate since had that been the case, the fifth component of the armed forces, the U.S. Coast Guard, would likely have negotiated itself into the jingle, rather than being left out of any potential recruiting bonanza that the advertising campaign might have produced. It could have been more accurate for the text to have read "Paid for by the U.S. Department of Defense (DoD)," since the army, navy, air force, and marines were and remain components of that federal civilian-headed department, while the Coast Guard at the time was a component of the Department of Transportation; it has since been reassigned to the Department of Homeland Security (DHS) as of 2003, and had been part of the Department of the Treasury prior to 1967.

Still and all, we feel fairly confident that if you were to survey a random sampling of folks near our age, even including other veterans, about the components of the U.S. Armed Forces, a majority of them would likely reply, "Army, Navy, Air Force, Marines," in that order, entirely missing the Coast Guard and the newly established U.S. Space Force, which was peeled off from its historic placement in the Air Force Space Command in late 2019 and established as its own military branch under the Department of the Air Force, much as the U.S. Marines are an independent branch of the military under the Department of the Navy. If specifically reminded of the Coast Guard, we suspect that many thoughtful respondents might presume that it is one of the nonmilitary uniformed services, a cohort that includes the U.S. Public Health Service Commissioned Corps and the National Oceanic and Atmospheric Administration Commissioned Officer Corps, but that would also be wrong. As would a guess that the Coast Guard was analogous to the U.S. Merchant Marine, which is neither a military branch nor a nonmilitary uniformed service branch, even though it maintains its own Federal Service Academy, as does the Coast Guard, but which the Marine Corps lacks.

The nuances between those various organizations may be subtle, but let there be no debate on one point: the U.S. Coast Guard is, in fact, a component in equal standing within the U.S. military organizational structure, even if its senior officers report to the Executive Branch of the federal government via DHS instead of the DoD. In a just and fair world, we old folk would have a jingle stuck in our heads that included that coequal branch, and general popular understanding of the nation's military forces would hold the Coast Guard to the same level of acclaim and import that the better-known (or at least better-marketed) branches of the armed forces command.

As with the army, navy, and Marine Corps, the Coast Guard's history can be traced directly back to the Revolutionary War era. (The air and space forces are, for obvious reasons, constructs of the post-flight 20th and 21st centuries.) At the direct request of Alexander Hamilton, Congress created the U.S. Revenue-Marine (later known as the U.S. Revenue Cutter Service) in August 1790, making it the oldest continuous seagoing service of the United States. The primary purpose of the original revenue-marine was to collect customs duties and tariffs at U.S. seaports, one of the most important sources of revenue for the newly independent nation. As the original Continental navy (along with the Continental marines and army) was demobilized between 1785 and 1797, the revenue-marine maintained and operated the nation's sole seagoing force for over a decade. In 1848, an independent federal agency known as the U.S. Life-Saving Service was established to protect, and often save, the lives and property of shipwrecked mariners, their passengers, and their cargoes. The modern Coast Guard was organized in 1915 when the Revenue Cutter Service (the former revenue-marine) and the Life-Saving Service were merged into a single entity under the auspices of the U.S. Department of the Treasury; the Coast Guard later assimilated the U.S. Lighthouse Service and the Bureau of Marine Inspection as part of its core organization as well.

In keeping with the roles of its historical predecessors, the modern Coast Guard's mission focuses on maritime security, search and rescue functions, and law enforcement, the last role making it unique among the nation's uniformed services. At the time of this writing, the Coast Guard employs approximately 40,000 active-duty personnel, 7,000 reserve personnel, 9,000 civilian employees, and 30,000 members of the Coast Guard Auxiliary, a civilian volunteer component founded in 1939 with a primary focus on recreational boating safety and education and to serve as a crucial force multiplier for Coast Guard missions that do not involve direct law enforcement or military engagement. The Coast Guard's charter allows it to be transferred, in part or in whole, under the control of the U.S. Navy during times of war. Selected subunits of the Coast Guard have been transferred to the navy at various crucial times in the nation's history, beginning with the quasi-war with France in the 1790s and continuing to this day as part of the Global War on Terrorism. The U.S. Congress authorized the first wholesale transfer of the entire Coast Guard to navy control in 1917, and then in 1941, President Franklin D. Roosevelt again authorized the entire Coast Guard to operate under Department of the Navy oversight during the various seagoing and amphibious campaigns of World War II.

The nature of the Coast Guard's mission means that its service members and auxiliaries are engaged on a nearly constant basis in a variety of crucial, though perhaps lower visibility from a general public perspective, missions on or near the nation's ports, waterways, and coastal regions, lending credence to their motto, *Semper Paratus* (Always Ready). The routine risks, dangers, and challenges associated with pursuing their missions are also embodied in the oft-cited Coast Guard quote, "Regulations say we have to go out. They say nothing about coming back." Another common summary of the essence of the Coast Guard's mission is evident in the equally common (but equally unattributable) maxim, "We do this job because every once in a while, someone is out there without hope, desperately praying for their life, and we get to be the answer." The selfless calling embodied by those rubrics was certainly true and centrally defining in the short but heroic life of Signalman First Class Douglas Albert Munro, the only service member from the U.S. Coast Guard ever to be awarded the Medal of Honor, the nation's highest military encomium, out of the ~3,600 cumulative recipients in the history of the American armed forces.

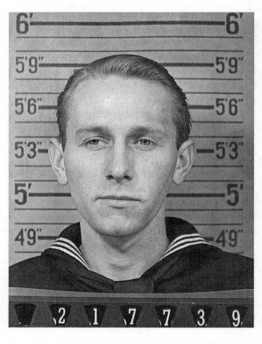

Douglas Munro's service record photograph (U.S. Coast Guard).

Douglas Munro was born in Vancouver, British

70

Columbia, in the autumn of 1919. His father, James, was an American citizen born in Sacramento, California, who had moved to Canada as a child when his mother married a Canadian citizen. Douglas's mother, Edith Thrower Fairey, was born in Merseyside, Liverpool, England, and also immigrated to Canada as a teenager with her family. James and Edith married in 1914 in Vancouver, which, under the immigration laws of the time, bestowed American citizenship on Edith and her children. The Munro family returned to the United States in 1922, with James taking a job as the manager of a Milwaukee Railroad electrical substation in South Cle Elum, a town of some 2,500 souls in scenic central Washington State. The senior Munro also attained a commission in the Coast Guard Reserve and was an active member of the local American Legion post.

The Munro family weathered the Great Depression relatively comfortably, as James was able to work regularly throughout that most challenging decade. Young Douglas was an excellent student and athlete, and his sound character was made manifestly obvious within his home community as he regularly gathered, cut, and split wood for neighboring families who could not afford to heat their homes with coal. Doug also evidenced exceptional musical talent, playing in school bands and orchestras throughout his high school years, then joining the Sons of the American Legion Drum and Bugle Corps (which was managed by his father), eventually assuming the roles of music director and march leader for the corps. After graduating from high school in 1938, Doug enrolled at Central Washington College of Education, a relatively short drive from Cle Elum, allowing him to pursue his studies while continuing to serve in and support the legion's drum and bugle corps.

After a year of college studies, Doug began to seriously consider whether his talents could be better deployed beyond the confines of central Washington, as the threat of war increasingly moved from the realm of the possible to the realm of the probable. After considering his various options for meaningful public service, he elected to join the Coast Guard, telling his sister Patricia (two years his elder) that he was moved by the guard's fundamental commitment to saving lives. After gorging himself with rich foods in an effort to fatten up his slender frame to meet minimum weight requirements for his height, Douglas Munro traveled to the U.S. Coast Guard Recruiting Center in Seattle, passed his physical, and enlisted as a seaman apprentice. On that same day, Raymond J. Evans, Jr., of Seattle, also visited the Coast Guard Recruiting Center and swore his own oath of office alongside Doug Munro. The two quickly struck up a deep friendship, and Munro spent the vast majority of his Coast Guard time serving with Evans, the pair earning the affectionate nickname "the Gold Dust Twins" from their crewmates in the years that followed.

Evans and Munro were initially sent to the Coast Guard Air Station at Port Angeles, Washington, where they spent their time mowing lawns, performing routine service jobs on aircraft, and conducting maintenance tasks around the base. Within a week, however, the pair had jumped at the opportunity to fill crew vacancies on the U.S. Coast Guard Cutter (USCGC) *Spencer* as the ship was transferring its permanent home port from Valdez, Alaska, to Staten Island, New York. The Gold Dust Twins served together on the *Spencer* until early 1941, earning their signalman third class ratings along the way. Late in 1941, with the war now "hot" in both the European and Pacific theaters after the Japanese bombing of Pearl Harbor, the Coast Guard was tasked with manning three transport ships that were being converted for naval purposes at industrial shipyards near the Staten Island Coast Guard Station. After days of pleading with the *Spencer*'s executive officer, Signalmen Munro and Evans managed to talk themselves into assignments on the USS *Hunter Liggett* (APA-14), a "Design 1029" merchant ship originally commissioned in 1921 as the *Palmetto State*, for operation by the United States Shipping Board, then the Munson Steamship Line, then the U.S. Army; the "1029" ships were built with the understanding that they could and would be converted for military applications should national interests so dictate.

Whereas the *Liggett* and its two adopted sister ships, USS *American Legion* and USS *Joseph T. Dickman*, were to be almost entirely crewed by Coast Guard personnel, the senior command were naval officers, in keeping with President Roosevelt's dictum that the Coast Guard be managed by the Department of the Navy for the duration of the war. The ships were assigned to Transport Division 7, under the command of Commodore G.B. Ashe; the senior Coast Guard officer in the Gold Dust Twins' chain of command was Commander Dwight Dexter. The *Liggett* carried nearly 700 crew members, 35 "Higgins Boats" (personnel and vehicle landing craft, also known as LCVPs), and 2 landing craft tanks (LCTs), all of whom and which were ordered to the Pacific theater in April 1942. Following port calls in the Panama Canal Zone and the island of Tongatapu (now the capital of the Kingdom of Tonga), the *Liggett* arrived in Wellington, New Zealand, on May 28, 1942. Two months later, she and her crew sailed for the Solomon Islands to take part in the first major American offensive operation in the Pacific, the occupation of Guadalcanal. Commander Dexter, USCG, was selected to command the naval operating base on Guadalcanal, and Signalmen Munro and Evans volunteered to be part of the initial waves of invaders, ideally with the goal of building and manning beach signal stations. Their plans to undertake such endeavors together, however, were foiled when Munro was transferred to the USS *McCawley* (APA-10) in July 1942, with Evans remaining aboard the *Liggett*.

From the *Liggett*, Evans landed on Guadalcanal on August 7, 1942, with the marine invasion force, their team surprised to find that their landing was relatively peaceful as the Japanese soldiers occupying Guadalcanal initially withdrew back into the highlands of the island's center, only later returning to the beach area to spark an increasingly fierce engagement. From the *McCawley*, Munro's unit was not so fortunate when they landed on Tulagi Island some 20 miles away from Guadalcanal, with the Japanese forces unleashing ferocious fire that killed or wounded some 80 percent of the marines' first wave. Munro spent the night on the beach with the marines, using blinker lights and semaphore flags to communicate message between the marines and the ships beyond the breakers. The next morning, Munro evacuated marine casualties back to the *McCawley*, after which he learned that he was being transferred to "Cactus" (the code name for the emergent naval operating base at Lunga Point on Guadalcanal); he was soon delighted to discover that Evans had also been transferred to "Cactus" from the *Liggett*.

The reunited Gold Dust Twins spent most of August and September leading rescues, ferrying casualties to ships, and moving supplies. Munro did undertake another twin-free mission on September 20, volunteering to lead a rescue team after a navy bomber had been forced to ditch off the coast of nearby Savo Island. Munro selected a small crew of sailors and set out in a powerboat to rescue the downed pilot and gunner. Unfortunately for Munro, the aviators were quickly rescued by another flying boat, though radio silence protocols prevented such information from being relayed to Munro and his team, who plowed forward with their mission, not knowing that it had already been completed by others. Their boat got within 1,000 feet of the beach on Savo before they were driven back by steady machine gun fire, effectively maneuvering their small craft under Munro's command to minimize damage and injury before eventually returning safely to their base at Guadalcanal.

While Evans and Munro were so engaged, the U.S. Marines at

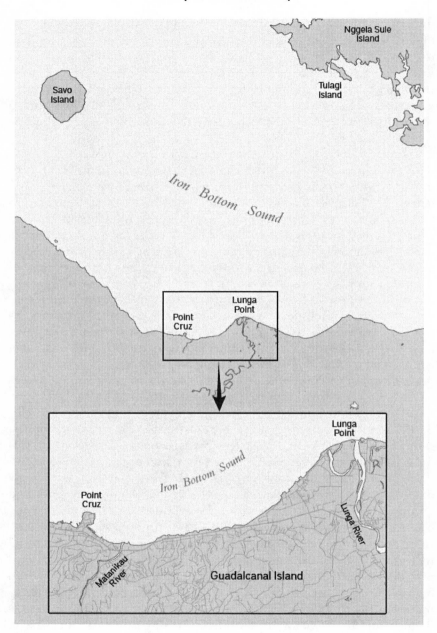

Map of Guadalcanal's North Central Shore, where Douglas Munro served (Liz Cruz).

Chapter Four. Douglas Munro and Edith Munro

Guadalcanal continued to struggle with expanding and securing the American perimeter throughout the remainder of August and September. With the arrival of reinforcements late in September, the Marine Corps command elected to make a firm push beyond their established defensive perimeter, planning to cross the Matanikau River from its east to west banks in an effort to prevent dispersed Japanese units from combining their forces and making more effective strikes on the American positions. Their efforts to cross the river from the east were met with fierce resistance, so on September 27, legendary marine Lieutenant Colonel Lewis B. "Chesty" Puller elected to transport three companies of his marines by sea to the west side of the Matanikau River, disperse the Japanese forces entrenched there, and establish a small base to facilitate the larger marine force's crossing of the river. Douglas Munro was given command of eight Higgins Boats and two LCTs, and tasked with transporting "Chesty" Puller's marines from Lunga Point to a small cove west of the river along Point Cruz.

Decades after Signalman Munro left Lunga Point with his small flotilla, the U.S. Coast Guard Historian's Office conducted an oral history interview with Raymond Evans, by then a retired Coast Guard commander, to preserve the story of what had happened that day. We could summarize the tactical details, but such a telling could never do justice to the story in the ways that hearing it in the words of Munro's own greatest friend could. We therefore respectfully quote a portion of Commander Evans's testimony below:

> The boats loaded, Munro and [I] were in separate LCVP's, each with an air-cooled Lewis .30 caliber machine gun and ammunition. The flotilla proceeded to a point about one mile offshore of Point Cruz and rendezvoused with the destroyer USS Ballard, which laid down a covering barrage and then gave us the go ahead to land. The landing was marred by shallow water preventing the landing from occurring where planned. The Battalion Major was informed that as soon as they landed, he should direct his troops to the left to compensate for the landing site, but as it turned out he was killed instantly by a Japanese mortar round and did not so direct his troops. They charged through the narrow fringe of trees and jungle at the beach and emerged into a field rising steeply up to a ridge. They started up only to find the Japanese in single man pits with camouflaged lids behind them. They had charged right up the hill past these defensive positions and were then placed under a murderous field of fire and were forced into fighting their way back to the beach losing about twenty-five casualties in the process.
>
> Meanwhile the Battalion Major had requested that when the boats returned to base, one LCVP remained offshore for a short time to receive

immediate wounded. I volunteered to do this while Munro led the other boats back to base. The coxswain, whom I believe was named [Samuel] Roberts, from Portland, Oregon, and I lay-to off the beach waiting. Due to our inexperience, we did not anticipate fire from the beach and allowed our boat to lay too close in. A sudden burst from a Japanese machine gun hit the coxswain and I slammed the combined shift and throttle lever into full ahead and raced the four miles back to the Lunga Point Base. Roberts was placed on an air-evac[uation] plane to Espiritu Santos, New Hebrides, but I understand he died while en route. I should add that the Japanese gunner had punctured all three hydraulic control lines on the LCVP so that arriving at the base at full throttle, probably about 20 mph, I could not get the engine out of gear and ran full throttle up on the gently sloping sand beach. Scratch one LCVP.

As soon as I arrived back at the base, Munro and I were told that the Marines were in trouble and had to be evacuated from the same beach we had landed them on. So, with approximately the same LCVPs and three or four LCTs we headed back to get them off. On arrival Munro and I elected to stay in an empty LCVP with our two Lewis machine guns and furnish some sort of covering fire for the Marines on the beach as they boarded. As the LCVP we were in would be filled we transferred to a waiting empty boat, until at last, all the Marines had been loaded, including about twenty-five walking wounded, and the last boat, an LCT and our LCVP turned and headed to sea. As we passed the end of the point, we saw another LCT loaded with Marines stranded on the beach and unable to back off. Munro directed the LCT with us to go in, pass a tow line and get them off, which it did. During this procedure, which took about twenty minutes, there was no gunfire from the Japanese on the beach nor did we see any movement on the beach. When both LCTs were headed out to sea we fell in after them and were at full power when I saw a line of waterspouts coming across the water from where the LCT had been grounded and realized it was machine gun fire. I don't think Munro saw the line of bullets since he was facing forward and did not at first react to my yelling over the engine noise. When he did, he turned far enough to receive a round through the neck at the base of the skull. He was dead on arrival back at the Naval Operating Base.

Signalman First Class Douglas Albert Munro was buried on Guadalcanal on September 28, 1942, under a wooden cross made by Evans. Two weeks after his death, a larger force of U.S. Marines successfully crossed the Matanikau River, inflicting heavy casualties on the Japanese infantry regiment entrenched there, forcing them to retreat and hindering their preparations for an assault on Lunga Point in what came to be known as the Battle for Henderson Field, which turned into a decisive defeat for the Japanese. Although word of Douglas Munro's heroic actions filtered into the American media by mid–October, after

Painting of Douglas Munro providing covering fire for the marines at Guadalcanal, by artist Bernard D'Andrea (1923–2016) (U.S. Coast Guard).

the marines had secured the west bank of the Matanikau, Doug's parents were not informed of his death until about October 19, 1942. A memorial service was held soon thereafter at the Holy Nativity Episcopal Church in South Cle Elum, with the town's American Legion post, which had meant so much to Doug and his father both, providing sentries and a cordon of honor.

Colonel Puller clearly understood the role that the Coast Guard crews had played in saving his marines to fight, and win, another day, with Munro obviously offering the ultimate sacrifice, but not before he had cleared the last marines from the beach where they had been pinned down. Puller himself nominated Munro for the Medal of Honor, and his nomination was endorsed by Admiral William Halsey, Jr., before being approved by President Roosevelt in May 1943. Doug's posthumous medal was awarded to his parents on May 24, 1943, in a ceremony at the White House, the only time in the nation's history when a member of the Coast Guard received such an honor. Commander Dwight Dexter, the senior Coast Guard officer who had been with the Gold Dust

Side by Side in Eternity

Twins since they had arrived on the USS *Liggett* in 1941, provided Munro's parents with some additional insight into his final moments via a letter containing the following narrative:

> On Sunday the 27th of September an expedition was sent into an area where trouble was to be expected. Douglas was in charge of the ten boats which took the men down. In the latter part of the afternoon, the situation had not developed as had been anticipated and in order to save the expedition it became necessary to send the boats back to evacuate the expedition. Volunteers were called for and true to the highest traditions of the Coast Guard and also to the traditions with which you imbued your son, he was among the first to volunteer and was put in charge of the detail. The evacuation was as successful as could be hoped for under fire. But as always happens, the last men to leave the beach are the hardest pressed because they had been acting as the covering agents for the withdrawal of the other men, and your son, knowing this is so, placed himself and his boat so that he could act as the covering agent for the last men, and by his action and successful maneuvers brought back a far greater number of men than had been even hoped for. He received his wound just as the last men were getting in the boats and clearing the beach. Upon regaining consciousness, his only question was "Did they get off" and so he died with a smile on his face with the full

Douglas Munro's "Glimmer Twin" comrade Raymond Evans receives the Navy Cross (U.S. Coast Guard).

knowledge that he had successfully accomplished a dangerous mission. In the year and half that I have known Douglas, I have grown to admire him and through him, you. He was the true type of American manhood that is going to win this war and I hereby promise that I will make all efforts to call on you whenever it is my privilege to be near Cle Elum and pay homage to you as the parents of Douglas.

While experiencing the unknowable grief associated with losing a child in battle overseas, most parents would take at least small measure of comfort in receiving a letter like that sent by Commander Dexter, demonstrating a personal knowledge of and understanding of their beloved deceased, and crediting them for their role as parents in raising and educating such an exemplar of human strength and heroism. But in one of the more extraordinary codas to any Medal of Honor story, Edith Munro was not to be satisfied with the knowledge that she had mothered a Coast Guard hero, feeling that in order to pay proper tribute to her son, she herself needed to make a service commitment mirroring the one that he had made. So on November 23, 1942, just shy of two months after Douglas's death, Edith became one of the first women who volunteered to serve their country in the newly established Women's Reserve of the Coast Guard, known as the "SPARs" after the guard's slogan in both Latin and English: "Semper Paratus—Always Ready." Edith completed her training at the Coast Guard Academy in New London, Connecticut, on May 27, 1943, three days after she received Doug's Medal of Honor from President Roosevelt, and she was commissioned as a lieutenant (junior grade) in the United States Coast Guard at the age of 48. (Doug's sister, Patricia, also attempted to join the guard, but she apparently did not follow her brother's lead in bulking up before her physical and was rejected for being underweight. Her son, Douglas Sheehan, however, did join the Coast Guard, just like his namesake uncle, eventually retiring with the rank of commander.)

The SPARs were authorized to accept women into the reserve as commissioned officers and enlisted personnel for the duration of World War II plus six months, ostensibly to release male officers and sailors for sea duty, replacing them with women at shore duty stations. Following her commissioning, Edith was initially assigned to the 13th Coast Guard District, where she commanded the SPARs barracks in Seattle, then later served in the Women's Reserve's personnel office with duties and assignments that took her across the full reach of the continental United States. She retired as a lieutenant in November

1945, 18 months before the SPARs were dissolved as an organization following the cessation of wartime hostilities.

Around the same time as the SPARs' dissolution, Edith's son's remains were recovered from Guadalcanal and returned to the United States for his final interment. Edith and James declined the opportunity to have Douglas buried at Arlington National Cemetery simply because they would have been unable to regularly tend his grave from their home in the Pacific Northwest. Doug was laid to rest instead with full military honors at Laurel Hill Memorial Gardens in Cle Elum. His grave site has become a significant and resonant monument for the Coast

Lieutenant Edith Thrower Munro's official Coast Guard portrait (U.S. Coast Guard).

Guard, which flies its flag, along with the American and POW/MIA flags, daily above his marker, adjacent to a monument honoring his life, a large ceremonial anchor chain taken from a Coast Guard cutter, and (as of 1999) a memorial wall listing the names of over 700 local veterans, living and dead. James Munro passed away in 1962, followed by Edith in 1983; they have joined their son at Laurel Hill in perpetual proximity.

The Coast Guard and the navy have also granted Munro perhaps the finest homage possible beyond his Medal of Honor, commissioning not one, not two, but three ships in his honor: the Destroyer Escort USS *Douglas A. Munro* (DE-422) and the Coast Guard Cutters USCGC *Douglas Munro* (WHEC-724) and USCGC *Munro* (WMSL-755). Lieutenant Edith Munro, USCGR, served as the ship's sponsor for the first two vessels commissioned in her son's name, and Patricia's granddaughter, Julie Sheehan, served as sponsor for the latest addition in her great-uncle's name, which was commissioned in 2017 and remains a powerful component of the modern Coast Guard fleet. There is also a

Munro Hall at the U.S. Coast Guard Academy and a Munro Barracks at the U.S. Coast Guard Training Center at Cape May (the service's "boot camp"), while the Coast Guard's headquarters in Washington, D.C., is known as the Douglas A. Munro Building. Finally, following "Chesty" Puller's lead in nominating a non–marine for the Medal of Honor, in 2006, Douglas Munro's name was added to the Wall of Heroes at the National Museum of the Marine Corps in Quantico, Virginia, the only non–marine to be so honored.

Although the organizational and historical vagaries associated with the placement and structure of the various branches of the U.S. Armed Services may lead the general public to consider the Coast Guard as *something different* from those elements highlighted in the "Army! Navy! Air Force! Marines!" refrain from that vintage recruiting commercial, the stories of Douglas and Edith Munro demonstrate, each in their own distinct fashions, the ways in which that vital component of our nation's defensive portfolio has long cultivated its own heroes and heroines, who serve admirably and impressively, perhaps recognizing that the heart of their mission and their duty is ultimately in quiet, steady service to others, and not in managing gaudy advertising campaigns.

CHAPTER FIVE

Leavenworth's German Prisoners of War (1910s/1920s–1945)

Fort Leavenworth Military Prison Cemetery, Fort Leavenworth, Kansas

"The only way to make the mass of mankind see the beauty of justice, is by showing them, in pretty plain terms, the consequences of injustice."
—Sydney Smith

"The public have more interest in the punishment of an injury than he who receives it."
—Marcus Porcius Cato (Cato the Elder)

Physical places and spaces often come to exist as easily synopsized snapshots and snippets within America's collective public consciousness. A mention of "Las Vegas," for example, immediately conjures up images and narratives of "Sin City" and "What happens in Vegas stays in Vegas." A mention of "Chicago" evokes wind, fire, and noxious political machines. "Paris" calls to mind springtime, romance, and artistic aspiration, while "Ibiza" summons images of parties raving on through the night with beautiful people behaving beautifully badly. "Gettysburg," "Bunker Hill," and "Little Big Horn" are all integrally associated with transformative military engagements, while "Wall Street," "K Street," "Bourbon Street," "Broadway," "Route 66," and "Beale Street" all demonstrate that even roads and highways can have overarching narratives that succinctly evoke and summarize a variety of historical, political, and cultural tropes and memes.

Tucked away on the bluffs along the Missouri River in northeastern Kansas, the otherwise mostly innocuous small city called Leavenworth has also come to claim a large bit of infamous mental geography for the average American, evoking "prison" perhaps as strongly as any spots in the country beyond the confines of Alcatraz's, San Quentin's, and Ossining's ("Sing Sing") barbed-wired boundaries. The association is a fair one, borne out by facts, as the city, the adjacent army base at Fort Leavenworth, and the nearby city of Lansing, Kansas, are currently home to five major detention centers: the U.S. federal penitentiary (the most famous of the group and the one that most people would envision when presented with the word "Leavenworth"), the United States Disciplinary Barracks (USDB), the Joint Regional Correctional Facility (JRCF), the CoreCivic detention center, and the Lansing Correctional Facility.

Although the United States has seen a somewhat troubling and problematic emergence over the past quarter century of pop-up prisons-for-profit that may fuel questionable convictions for corporate bottom-line reasons, Leavenworth's history as a destination for detainees runs far deeper than modern prison paradigms: the U.S. Penitentiary (a civilian facility) opened in 1903, and the original USDB traces its roots all the way back to 1874. (Its current physical facility was opened in 2002; visitors to Fort Leavenworth can now order paninis, wraps, soups, and salads at the 12th Brick Grill located in a restored portion of the original prison facility.) Although the federal penitentiary at Leavenworth enjoys more fame via its popular depictions in various seminal films and books over the past century, its status as a medium-security facility with a nearby associated minimum-security satellite farm camp

The original U.S. Disciplinary Building at Fort Leavenworth (U.S. Department of Defense).

actually makes it pale a bit correctionally when compared to the USDB, which is the nation's only maximum-security prison for male military personnel. (Female military prisoners are generally incarcerated at the Naval Consolidated Brig in Miramar, California.)

The USDB now houses all four of the U.S. military's current death row inmates, the most recent addition to that terrible roster being army major Nidal Hasan, who killed 12 soldiers and wounded more than 30 others in the tragic Fort Hood shooting in 2009. Barring some significant changes in the implementation of punishments under the Uniform Code of Military Justice, Hasan and his three current death row colleagues will likely die behind bars, as the last actual execution to occur at the USDB was in April 1961, when army private first class John A. Bennett was hung for the rape and attempted murder of an 11-year-old Austrian girl.

The armed forces had not been so sparing when it came to capital punishment during World War II itself, though, with 141 U.S. service members having been executed between 1942 and 1945, with an additional six executions conducted in the immediate aftermath of the war, for crimes committed during the period of active conflict. All of the American soldiers and sailors executed during World War II had been convicted of murder and/or rape, with one exception: army private Eddie Slovik was executed by firing squad in Sainte-Marie-aux-Mines, France, for desertion, becoming the first (and last) person to be killed for that crime since the Civil War.

Leavenworth's USDB played a small role in the final dissemination of extreme military justice during World War II, with Private Levi Brandon (rape) and Private Edward Reichl (murder) having been hung in 1943 and 1945, respectively, but the vast majority of military executions during World War II were conducted in the campaign theaters where the capital crimes occurred. Over two-thirds of those executions took place in the European theater of operations, with 98 convicted servicemen being (mostly) hung or (occasionally) killed via firing squad, their remains then interred near the sites of their executions. In the late 1940s, after the end of the war, the armed forces worked to recover as many remains as possible from across the European continent, offering their fallen soldiers' survivors the option to either have the remains brought back to the United States or to be reinterred in formal U.S. military cemeteries established in Europe, much as the U.S. government managed reburials after the Civil War by opening national cemeteries throughout the former Confederate states.

The families of the 98 servicemen who were executed in the European theater did not receive such options to bring their deceased home, however, nor have them buried with honor among their fallen colleagues and comrades. In 1949, the Army Quartermaster Corps' Graves Registration Service established Plot E at the Oise-Aisne American Cemetery in France, relocating the remains of the executed service members to a private section there, reserved for "the dishonorable dead." Plot E is deliberately hidden from public view by thick hedges and is accessible only through a secured entryway in the cemetery superintendent's office. No American flags may fly over the section, the grave markers are nondescript index card–sized stone placards with only sequential grave numbers engraved on their surfaces, and the bodies in Plot E are laid down with their backs turned to the "honorable" cemetery across the road. (Private Eddie Slovik's remains were originally interred in Plot E, though President Ronald Reagan authorized his remains to be exhumed and returned to the United States for reinterment in 1987. Private Alex Miranda's remains were also returned to the United States in 1990, after his conviction for murder was posthumously reduced to manslaughter due to his being deeply intoxicated at the time when he shot Sergeant Thomas Evison in the head with a carbine.)

Fort Leavenworth is home to one of the nation's major national cemeteries, known to locals as "the Old Soldiers' Home," with nearly 31,000 interments since its consecration in 1886, including six Medal of Honor recipients. But there's no analogue to Plot E for the "dishonorable dead" at Leavenworth National Cemetery, even though the presence of the USDB on Fort Leavenworth has long meant that service members have died there at the army base (naturally or with government assistance) and require a resting place for their mortal remains. Rather than comingling their deceased with fellow soldiers who died as free men, the USDB established its own cemetery early in its history, located in the less-trafficked northern portions of Fort Leavenworth, with a first recorded burial on March 10, 1884. This old half-acre military prison cemetery contains the remains of about 250 men who died or were executed while incarcerated at the USBD and whose families did not or could not claim their remains for burial elsewhere. The latest interments there were made in 1957, though it technically remains available for additional burials should current prisoners' remains be unclaimed after their deaths, an increasingly uncommon phenomenon. (There are about 60 available burial plots remaining on the site.)

Entrance to the prison cemetery at Fort Leavenworth (Office of Army National Cemeteries).

Unlike Oise-Aisne's Plot E, at the USDB cemetery, the decedents' crimes in life have not been used as justification to debase or deny their humanity in death, as the graves are all formally and respectfully marked, the stones and grounds are well maintained, and guests, though not common, may in fact walk among the graves, leaving flowers or other mementos of their visits behind. The care that the cemetery's staff demonstrate for their charges recently resulted in the cemetery being accorded National Shrine status by the Office of Army Cemeteries, joining the military cemetery at Fort Knox, Kentucky, as the only two army cemeteries to be accorded such recognition. If you didn't know its backstory, you'd simply presume you were in a proper military cemetery, not visibly different from any of its sibling sites around the country and abroad.

But the differences are there, nonetheless. A well-maintained sign at the USDB cemetery provides the following introduction to the site for visitors, briefly summarizing one of the more remarkable, yet largely unknown, stories associated with wartime justice in mid–20th century America:

MILITARY PRISON CEMETERY: This half acre cemetery was established in 1884 for inmates who died or were executed. They had no next of kin, or the next of kin refused the remains. On the back row are the graves of 14 German prisoners of war who were hanged in 1945 for crimes committed while POW's. No family members are buried here.

The graves of the 14 executed German POWs are (slightly) physically removed from those of their American neighbors, with an empty row between the tightly massed stones in the front part of the cemetery and their 14 burial sites along the back fence line of the plot. The German POWs ranged from 21 to 32 years of age at the times of their executions, which were conducted in three waves on July 10, July 14, and August 25, 1945. Their stories are illustrative of a rarely discussed but major facet of the United States' engagements in Europe and Asia during World War II—namely, the ways and places in which enemy prisoners of war were held and treated following their surrender or capture.

The singular phrase "Geneva Convention" has entered popular public parlance as the governing body of international law documenting humanitarian treatment of combatants and civilians. The more technically correct term would be the plural "Geneva Conventions," which comprise four treaties and three supplemental protocols and which were most recently and significantly updated in 1949, in the aftermath of the horrors of World War II, most especially the war crimes brought to light by the Nuremberg trials. The Geneva Conventions trace their roots to 1864, when the Swiss government invited various European and American delegations to negotiate and enact the First Geneva Convention "for the amelioration of the condition of the wounded in armies in the field." By the time that hostilities erupted in the early days of World War II, the conventions had been adapted and expanded to include elements negotiated in The Hague Conventions of 1899 and 1907, as well as additional protections that emerged in the aftermath of World War I, where technological innovations had made possible new heights of carnage and suffering within the act of making war.

Most germane to the lives and deaths of Leavenworth's German POWs was "The Convention Relative to the Treatment of Prisoners of War," enacted on July 27, 1929, and entered into force on June 19, 1931. Key elements of that 1929 convention included:

- Clearly defining that POWs are prisoners of the government which holds them, and not the property of the specific unit which receives their surrender or captures them;
- Protocols surrounding the capture of enemy soldiers, who may not be coerced into giving any information beyond their true

name and rank, and whose personal possessions, other than
arms or transport, may not be taken from them;

- Policies for evacuating POWs from combat zones within the
shortest possible time, and for notifying enemy forces of said
captures;
- Standards for Prisoner of War Camps, which must be constructed
to be materially similar to conditions experienced by the
captured soldiers in their own base camps; related articles also
codify expectations for food, medical treatment, religious needs,
compensation, transfers between locations, work expectations in
the camps, and relations between guards and captives;
- Protocols for termination of captivity, either through
repatriation (especially for sick and seriously wounded
prisoners), through the cessation of hostilities (release of
prisoners should ideally form part of any negotiated armistice,
which caused problems at the end of World War II as the Axis
powers' surrender was unconditional, meaning that there was
no formal armistice agreement), or through death in captivity
(prisoners should be honorably buried, and their graves
respectfully marked and maintained).

Most modern American readers, when asked to consider POW
camps, likely envision places abroad where U.S. soldiers were captured
and then held by forces mostly native to the combat zones, relatively
near to the places of their captures. We will address one most notable
example of Vietnam-era POW experiences in the final chapter of this
book, and popular military histories are rife with depictions of American soldiers being held by German or Japanese forces in Europe or Asia.
But how was the 1929 Geneva Convention regarding the treatment of
POWs to be implemented when American captors took prisoners in or
near their own countries but thousands of miles away from the American homeland? As U.S. soldiers made their way across the battlefields of
Europe toward the German homeland, most of their infrastructure was
ephemeral, sufficient only to meet basic military requirements, and certainly not suitable for the humane incarceration of captured prisoners
for however long the war was then yet to grind on.

The scale of the prisoner problem was further exacerbated after
1941, when the government of the United Kingdom requested American support for the housing of 175,000 German POWs due to a shortage
of viable facilities in England. The United States had only had limited

experience in processing and housing prisoners in World War I, when approximately 2,000 German prisoners were held, briefly, at Fort Douglas in Utah, and Fort McPherson and Fort Oglethorpe, both in Georgia. Despite a lack of preparation and resources, the United States agreed to support the United Kingdom with its own prisoner of war camps, rapidly building watchtowers and fencing various federal and state properties, generally well removed from urban or industrial areas, in regions with moderate climates that allowed for easier construction, and for the deployment of prisoners to nearby farms, which were expected to experience labor shortages as nearly 16 million young soldiers and sailors were enlisted or commissioned to pursue the war's course to its bloody, bitter end.

When all was said and done, the Americans addressed the formidable human and logistical problems associated with the large-scale housing of captured enemy combatants through a massive and under-documented relocation program that brought over 425,000 German soldiers captured in Europe between 1941 and 1945 to the U.S. mainland, where they were held in over 700 camps, located in all of the then-48 states except for Montana, North Dakota, Nevada, and Vermont. Had the Germans been housed in a single location, their camp's population would have roughly equaled that of Newark, New Jersey, then the 18th largest city in the country. American military and combat-related civilian deaths in World War II are estimated at about 419,000 souls lost, just slightly fewer than the total number of German prisoners of war brought to the United States during the war.

It was a mammoth undertaking, at bottom line, and on some plane was a noble one, too, underscoring the United States' commitment to the law of armed conflict and the conventions that governed war-making and its aftermath. The prisoners were typically brought to the United States on "Liberty ships" (large cargo vessels that had been mass produced to support the war effort) that otherwise would have returned home empty. German prisoners were then generally transported to their camps via commercial trains that had been repurposed to support the massive relocation effort; many German soldiers expressed amazement at the comfort of their transport ships and Pullman cars, at the quality and quantity of the food they were provided, at the vast scale of the American continent, and at its undamaged nature, compared and contrasted to the utter devastation that was then wracking the European continent. The camps themselves were supervised by the army's Office of the Provost Marshal General, which generally worked to honor basic tenets of the 1929 Geneva Convention, with enlisted prisoners being accorded the same 40 square feet of personal space that their American counterparts were allocated in their own camps, and German officers being provided with 120 square feet, again per the standards of camp housing design for American officers. Since many of the camps were being constructed as their prisoners were arriving from abroad, German POWs often had to sleep in tents while permanent structures were being completed, and in such cases, it was expected that their guards would also be housed in tents.

None of this, of course, is intended to sugar-coat or undermine the psychological and emotional damage experienced by the German prisoners as they were being incarcerated thousands of miles from their homes and families. Nor is it intended to infer that there were not abuses within the camps themselves, no matter how diligently the army's leadership might have worked to hew to the spirit and the letter of the governing conventions. But in relative terms, many German soldiers did express gratitude that they had been captured by English or American forces, rather than by Soviet forces on the European theater's eastern fronts, as the Soviet prisoner of war camps often made little to no effort to comply with international humanitarian standards, and the suffering and mortality rates within their camps were far higher than those in the United Kingdom and the United States.

None of the 14 German soldiers who currently lie along the fence at the USDB cemetery in Fort Leavenworth began their American incarcerations there. Five of them (Walter Beyer, Hans Demme, Hans Schomer, Willi Scholz, and Berthold Seidel, all once members of General Field Marshal Erwin Rommel's elite Afrika Korps) were originally housed at Camp Tonkawa in Oklahoma. In early November 1943, a fellow POW named Johannes Kunze was revealed to be collaborating with his American captors by spying on his countrymen and providing written reports incriminating other prisoners to the camp's leaders via secret notes passed to an American doctor during sick calls. A faction of the prison population held a kangaroo court on November 4, 1943, and Kunze was beaten to death by Beyer, Demme, Schomer, Scholz, and Seidel. The federal case against the five killers was prosecuted by army lieutenant colonel Leon Jaworski, better known for his later role as the special prosecutor in the Watergate scandal. The five were found guilty, sentenced to death, and sent to the maximum-security USDB in Leavenworth.

Chapter Five. Leavenworth's German Prisoners of War

The murder of Johannes Kunze highlights two of the problematic aspects associated with the sheer number of German troops imprisoned in the United States at the time. First off, most American soldiers with German linguistic talents had been deployed, leaving the camps to often be managed by soldiers who had little to no ability to communicate with the detainees under their control and command. This led to many camps often essentially relying on the Germans to self-police and self-discipline throughout their captivities, which allowed for some of the most committed members of the Nazi Party, especially officers, to wield undue and unjust influence within the camps. Especially problematic were the Afrika Korps soldiers who had been captured early in the war, when Germany was ascendent, and before their home continent had disintegrated into a war-torn hellscape; their collective vision of Germany's likely ultimate vision was not clouded by the visions of despair and destruction that most POWs captured later on the European continent experienced, and so they were often the instigators of work stoppages, prisoner intimidation, and the sorts of kangaroo courts that found Johannes Kunze guilty of collaboration and ordered his killing.

The second problematic issue associated with maintaining order and enforcing criminal sentencing among the German prisoners was the fact that American leadership was leery of having word of prisoner deaths (much less executions) reach Germany, lest American prisoners of war there be subjected to retaliatory treatment, up to and including their own executions. (It's worth noting that this concern was proven highly valid in the aftermath of the war, when the freeing of both prisoner of war and concentration camps and the subsequent Nuremberg trials revealed the true inhumanity of what had been happening at those same camps, though that was not common knowledge in 1943.) Although Kunze's murderers were duly shipped off to death row at the Leavenworth USDB, their actual execution was stayed after their arrival for an unspecified and unknowable period of time. Their fate was ultimately to be determined by individuals working well above the pay grades of any of the soldiers overseeing their final confinement.

A similar scene to Kunze's murder unfolded at Camp Aiken in South Carolina in April 1944, when prisoner Horst Günther was suspected of collaborating with his American captors and was strangled to death by fellow prisoners Erich Gauss and Rudolf Staub; the murderers then hung Günther's body from a tree in hopes that his death would be seen and reported as a suicide. It wasn't, and Gauss and Staub were also tried, found guilty of murder, sentenced to death, and sent to the Leavenworth USDB to await their execution, or (optimistically) the commutation of their sentences and their repatriation to their homeland. Staub stated that he and Gauss had killed Günther "as German soldiers under orders" and that if they had not followed said orders, presumably given by German loyalist senior enlisted or officer personnel at Camp Aiken, then they would have been punished when they were returned to Germany. Perhaps Staub considered his murder conviction to be his "get out of jail" pass if the pair ever made it back to Germany. It was to be proven a moot point in the end.

The third German cohort buried at the USDB cemetery came from Camp Papago Park, Arizona. There were seven men in this group: Helmut Fischer, Fritz Franke, Günter Külsen, Heinrich Ludwig, Bernhard Reyak, Otto Stengel, and Rolf Wizny, all of them former submarine sailors. This septet was convicted en masse for the murder of Werner Dreschler, who had been a crewman on a German submarine that was sunk by the Allies in 1943. After his rescue from the torrid seas surrounding the Azores, Dreschler avidly and enthusiastically cooperated with his captors to the point where American intelligence officers actively recruited and trained him to serve as a spy at a POW camp in Fort Meade, Maryland, where he worked to tease out information about German submarine operating tactics and technology, sharing it with his intelligence handlers. Unfortunately, said intelligence handlers were caught by surprise when Dreschler was transferred to Camp Papago Park, where numerous other submariners, including some who had served directly with Dreschler, recognized him and quickly divined that he was engaged in undercover espionage within the camp community. Once again, a kangaroo court was convened by loyalist German prisoners, and Dreschler was beaten and hanged that night in its aftermath. His seven countrymen were convicted to death before a general court-martial and, like the murderers of Günther and Kunze, were sent to Fort Leavenworth to await their fate in maximum-security settings.

The 14 German men who lie at the USDB cemetery actually had a 15th companion for much of their time on death row: Edgar Menschner had beaten fellow prisoner Hans Geller (another suspected collaborator) to death on March 23, 1944, at Camp Chaffee, Arkansas. Menschner was tried for the murder, sentenced to death, and sent to Leavenworth, just as his colleagues had been.

As the German prisoners awaited their fates at Leavenworth, the U.S. Army informed their German counterparts that the soldiers were to be executed for their crimes. The Third Reich quickly responded by identifying 15 American prisoners being held in Germany for a similar fate, leading President Franklin D. Roosevelt and his military advisors to delay the executions based on a reassessment of their crimes and cases. A military board of review soon recommended that the German POWs' sentences be commuted to life in prison, but before their recommendation could be implemented, President Roosevelt died on April 12, 1945, and weeks afterward, on May 8, Germany unconditionally surrendered, ending the "hot" phase of the war in Europe.

That news bode most ill for the death row inmates at Fort Leavenworth, and not just because of any emotions associated with reevaluating their futile service to an utterly defeated and globally humiliated former great power. On July 3, 1945, military judge advocate general Myron C. Cramer wrote a memorandum to President Harry S. Truman that stated, in part, "the threat to execute American prisoners of war has been removed by reason of the Allied military victory over Germany; I recommend that the sentence of each accused be confirmed and ordered executed." Truman accepted the memorandum's recommendation later that same day, though he then commuted Menschner's sentence from death to 20 years of hard labor on July 6, 1945.

That commutation likely gave the other 14 some sense of hope, but it was to be short lived. On July 10, 1945, the five Afrika Korps soldiers who had killed Johannes Kunze were hung from makeshift gallows erected in an elevator shaft in a warehouse adjacent to the USDB's main prison building. Four days later, Horst Günther's two killers met a similar fate. And on August 25, 1945, the seven submariners who had killed Werner Dreschler were led to the gallows and hung until dead. The local base's print news outlet of record, *The Fort Leavenworth News*, dispassionately reported on the mass execution, noting, "The trap was sprung on the first man at 12:10, and the last man went to his death at 2:48 a.m. A new system for mass hangings has been devised at the institution which saved more than an hour in the procedure."

Although various online resources inaccurately report that the Germans were buried face down or that their headstones faced away from the other graves in the USDB cemetery, the facts of the matter are that the Germans were laid to rest with more decorum than their American counterparts interred in France's Plot E, with comparable grave markers to the other American prisoners buried around them, in a site that has received appropriate perpetual care in the ensuing decades. It seemed the prison keepers at Leavenworth, perhaps simply because that city is so dependent on its local correctional facilities as core parts of the regional economy, were less inclined to display spite over the mortal remains of men who already suffered the ultimate indignity of having their lives cut short in a mass act of institutional killing. There have also been calls over the years to return the 14 Leavenworth POWs' remains to Germany, but neither our government nor theirs has seen it as a priority meriting action, so the odds are that the 14 will indeed remain in perpetual proximity for as long as that USDB cemetery is maintained.

There are also a variety of online interviews and research resources readily found and cited that embrace a narrative that the 14 Leavenworth German POWs were just doing their jobs and being good soldiers by killing their countrymen whom they had judged guilty of collaboration without any legitimate legal proceedings. Many of the online pundits making such arguments also express the view that if American soldiers had killed their countrymen who were collaborating in prison camps abroad, the killers would have been welcomed home as heroes at war's end. That's a sticky argument to make, though, when it comes to loyalist Nazi soldiers, just as it's a sticky argument to make with regard to the bravery exhibited by soldiers fighting for the American Confederacy in the Civil War. Is being an obedient soldier, killing your comrades who oppose or undermine unjust regimes that sent their soldiers into harm's way to defend their ability to enslave or commit genocide against another group of people, truly a noble narrative? And if not, does it then become a more noble narrative when said soldiers are members of our own armed forces? We'd argue against such a view, simply because the act of taking justice into one's own hands, even in a prison camp, defies the spirit and intent of the international laws and conventions designed to protect all soldiers and sailors from harm while in custody. Few people would applaud a civilian prisoner killing a fellow in one of America's modern megaplex correctional facilities, so cheering a narrative of similar murders in military prisons seems incongruous with the nature of managing captives in ways that don't demean the overarching moral essence of the governments holding such captives.

We find the perspective of Colonel Karlheinz Ammann, a German federal armed forces liaison assigned at Fort Leavenworth in the late 1990s, to ring the truest of all the sources we've considered. In an interview with the *Los Angeles Times* in 1998, Colonel Ammann offered the following thoughts: "It was a bad time in 1945. The Allies had found the concentration camps, and there was no desire to show mercy for the Nazis at that time. And that is understandable. These POWs were educated in the Third Reich. They were convinced the guys they killed were traitors. They had no chance to learn differently. And this is not a bad place to stay, this little cemetery. Nazis remain outcasts in Germany, the party officially banned. But a right-wing minority still supports Nazi concepts, and any effort to repatriate Nazi POWs buried in the United States could make the situation worse. There are German graves all over Europe and no place to bring them back. So why would you bring these remains to Germany?"

Perhaps the most surprising epilogue to Leavenworth's German POW story has been the fact that the hanging of the seven submariners was to become the last mass execution in American history. Was that because the story was widely disseminated, resulting in political or social outcry and reaction and resultant prison and capital punishment reforms? No, not in the least. In fact, many of the documents concerning the facts of the Leavenworth POWs' lives and deaths were not declassified and released to the public until the early 1970s, so the story has been an obscure one, by and large. As noted earlier, the Geneva Conventions were updated in 1949, incorporating lessons learned and experiences documented in World War II, just as the 1929 conventions were similarly responding to World War I's atrocities. But the death penalty was not then and is still not now banned under the terms of the Geneva Conventions, except that it "shall not be pronounced on persons who were under the age of eighteen years at the time of the offence and shall not be carried out on pregnant women or mothers of young children."

As a general matter, the death penalty is also not forbidden under international law if the governing laws of a given nation allow capital punishment for its most serious criminals, so long as such sentences are pronounced "only as the result of a final judgment, rendered by a competent court established by law and in conformity with due process rules and norms." At the time of this writing, only 54 nations still pronounce and practice death penalties for a variety of offenses, but with the United States, China, India, Pakistan, Indonesia, Nigeria, and Bangladesh (all among the top ten largest nations in the world by population) counted in that cohort, some 60 percent of the world's people are still legally subject to the ultimate punishment, and in some parts of the world, public mass executions remain a regular part of various countries' collective consciousness.

It would probably feel morally satisfying, on some planes, if we could conclude that we have not experienced a government-sanctioned mass execution in the United States since 1945 because we collectively decided as a nation that it was ethically wrong to conduct such spectacles, even in the privacy of a prison warehouse's elevator shaft, and so we took action to stop them from happening again. But we think the truth of the situation is less idealistic, believing instead that the nature of American law and litigation has evolved since the end of World War II in ways that make such mass executions improbable and impractical, for both military and civilian matters, given the ever higher burden of proof required to secure a capital sentence and the lengthy appeals processes that are allowed to play out before an execution actually takes place. Even in cases where a group of individuals committed a capital crime together at the same time and the same place, their trials would likely run on different schedules, their defenses would take different tacks (often turning one perpetrator against the other), their judges and juries could reach different results based on the nature of rules regarding admissibility of evidence, their appeals could have different timelines and results, and the likelihood of all of those factors aligning in a way that seven co-convicted criminals could be marched to the gallows, electric chair, rifle range, or gas chamber together at the same time is small accordingly.

Which is ultimately not a bad result, even if it's not for a good reason.

CHAPTER SIX

Quentin Roosevelt (1897–1918) and Theodore Roosevelt, Jr. (1887–1944)

Normandy American Cemetery and Memorial, Colleville-sur-Mer, France

"We never seem to know what anything means until we have lost it. The full significance of those words—property, ease, health—the wealth of meaning that lies in the fond epithets—parent, child, friend—we never know 'til they are taken away, 'til in place of the bright, visible being, comes the awful and desolate shadow where nothing is, where we stretch out our hands in vain, and strain our eyes upon dark and dismal vacuity."

—Orville Dewey

"We do not choose our own parts in life, and have nothing to do with selecting those parts. Our duty is simply confined to playing them well."

—Epictetus

In our nation's quarter-millennium history, there are a relatively small number of political figures who have become so iconic (though often also inaccurately represented) that their persons and their essences can be invoked and evoked with the smallest of cultural cues. Think George Washington's wooden teeth and "I cannot tell a lie" cherry tree–chopping backstory, or Abraham Lincoln's stovepipe hat and "Four score and seven years ago" narrative at Gettysburg. Think disheveled genius Benjamin Franklin flying a kite in a thunderstorm, or Franklin Delano Roosevelt and his jaunty cigarette holder and fireside chats (all conveniently staged to hide his disability), or Richard Nixon declaring "I am not a crook," and throwing hunch-shouldered victory signs as he retreated into ignominious political exile. Although history and political science may be arcane academic pursuits for many Americans, these icons are readily recognized almost instinctually, even by those carrying but the faintest knowledge of the nation's history, as universally branded in their own ways as a Coca-Cola, Nike, Amazon, or Facebook logo.

Theodore Roosevelt must certainly be counted among that list of the most recognizable personages in American political history, just over a century on from his passing. A sketch of a small, myopic, roundish man wearing a distinctive eyeglasses-and-mustache combination will be recognizable to most as "Teddy" or "T.R.," and if there's any confusion remaining, offering a verbal prompt of "Bully!" or "Speak softly and carry a big stick" will generally nail down the subject in question. The fact that Roosevelt is memorialized on the Mount Rushmore statue, alongside Presidents Washington, Jefferson, and Lincoln only serves to affirm both the visual image of T.R. and his perceived standing among the list of America's greatest presidents. Although that was not necessarily Mount Rushmore sculptor's Gutzon Borglum's intention (he choose the four to represent the nation's birth, growth, development, and preservation, with Roosevelt embodying that fourth value), modern historians and scholars do indeed tend to rank the first President Roosevelt among the top tier of its executive leaders, and the fact that Borglum began the work on Mount Rushmore in 1927, a mere eight years after Roosevelt died, clearly indicates that his stature was already well recognized and appreciated relatively soon after his vibrant walk on this mortal coil had ended.

Theodore Roosevelt's life and accomplishments are so iconic that they often frankly beggar belief. If your authors were to propose a novel to any contemporary publisher based on the facts of his life, we'd likely be faced with rejection after rejection for pitching a personal story that was too fantastic to be embodied by a single believable human being. Born in Manhattan in 1858 to businessman/philanthropist Theodore Roosevelt, Sr. (one of the founders of the city's Natural History Museum), and socialite "Millie" Bulloch, his childhood was defined by physical frailty and poor health, both overcome in his telling by his active embrace of a rigorous, strenuous, adventurous lifestyle. The young Roosevelt was homeschooled by his parents and a series of tutors in large part because his health issues rendered classroom attendance impractical. His studies were supplemented by experiential activities, including a trip with his family down the Nile River in 1872, after which he prepared a strikingly sophisticated, nuanced, and mature essay titled "Ornithology of Egypt between Cairo and Assuan."

Roosevelt developed into a precocious intellectual titan with sweeping interests in a variety of historical and then-current topics, earning admission to Harvard College in 1876. He experienced the first of many devastating personal losses midway through his time at Harvard when his father died suddenly, but he stoically subsumed his grief and went on to become a successful member of the school's rowing and boxing teams, while excelling in his studies, although in later years he was often dismissive of Harvard's pedagogical approach. Roosevelt then moved on to Columbia Law School, where he spent much of his time researching, writing, and publishing a well-received and still well-regarded and widely studied book titled *The Naval War of 1812*. Roosevelt's political career began in 1882, when he was elected to the New York State Assembly. In 1884, Roosevelt experienced further personal tragedy, as his beloved mother, Millie, and his first wife, Alice Hathaway Lee, died within 12 hours of each other, in Alice's case soon after she had given birth to their daughter, Alice Lee Roosevelt.

In 1883, Roosevelt had visited the Dakota Territory for the first time, fully embracing the cowboy lifestyle with his usual vigor and enthusiasm, investing a sizable portion of the inheritance he had received from his father in a ranch he dubbed Elkhorn. After an unusually severe winter in 1886–1887 decimated his cattle herd, he returned to New York and married his childhood friend Edith Kermit Carow. After an unsuccessful campaign for election as New York's mayor, Roosevelt wrote *The Winning of the West*, another publishing success about the westward migrations and aspirations of Americans of European descent.

President Benjamin Harrison appointed T.R. to serve on the United States Civil Service Commission in 1888, and in 1894 he became president of the New York City Police Commissioners. In both cases, he was a zealous reformer, attacking the long-established "spoils system" that dominated the era's politics, professionalizing policing in New York, and actively working to alleviate the suffering of New York's millions of disenfranchised immigrants. His established expertise in naval history led President William McKinley to appoint Roosevelt as assistant secretary of the navy in 1897; he resigned from that post in 1898 with the outbreak of hostilities in the Spanish-American War, electing to form, with his friend Colonel Leonard Wood, the First U.S. Volunteer Cavalry Regiment, known to history as "the Rough Riders." Under Roosevelt's leadership, the Rough Riders became one of the more famous units in military history in large part for their heroic charge up Cuba's Kettle Hill (part of the San Juan Heights and often referred to as "San Juan Hill" accordingly); Roosevelt later declared that assault as "the great day of my life," and for the remainder of his days, he was regularly portrayed in popular media wearing his Rough Riders' uniform.

Later in 1898, bolstered by the celebrity that his wartime exploits bestowed on him, Roosevelt was narrowly elected as governor of New York, a post he held for two years until he was tapped to serve as McKinley's vice president in the election of 1900, following the death of incumbent vice president Garret Hobart. McKinley and Roosevelt decisively defeated William Jennings Bryant and (the first) Adlai Stevenson in the election, and Roosevelt served (somewhat unhappily) in the nation's second-in-command position until McKinley was assassinated in 1901, elevating Roosevelt to the presidency. He was, remarkably, given his eventful life, but 42 years old at the time of his inauguration, and he remains the youngest person to ever hold the nation's senior executive position to this day.

When Teddy and Edith Roosevelt moved into the White House in 1901, they brought six children with them. Alice (daughter of T.R.'s deceased first wife) was 17 years old and quickly emerged as a celebrity and fashionista, scandalizing "proper" social circles with her outspoken ways, for riding in cars with men and smoking in public, for placing bets with bookies, and for keeping a pet snake named Emily Spinach. "I can either run the country or I can attend to Alice, but I cannot possibly do both," T.R. once confessed to his friend, author Owen Wister. Alice's younger half siblings included Theodore Jr. (14 years old and officially named Theodore III, though with his father having eschewed his own "Jr." suffix, it was and remains customary to refer to the two Teds in the White House as Sr. and Jr.), Kermit (12 years old), Ethel (10), Archibald (7), and Quentin, a mere four years old when he became an occupant of one of the nation's most famous homes.

Although it is considered gauche by most these days to identify a "favorite child," there's little debate that Quentin held that special place in President Roosevelt's heart. Edith dubbed her youngest son "a fine bad little boy" and his antics in the White House remain somewhat unparalleled in American history. T.R. dubbed Quentin and his friends (including Charlie Taft, the son of then–secretary of war William Howard Taft) "the White House Gang," and among many other adventures, the group were (in)famous for defacing official presidential portraits, throwing snowballs at Secret Service agents, destroying the White House lawn to make a baseball diamond, and riding on top of the elevator to the family's quarters in the White House, surprising and/ or scaring the occupants below them. (Quentin also brought his pet pony up the family elevator once to cheer up his sick brother Archie.) The media of the day loved Quentin and his antics, and he demonstrated child-star quality skills in dealing with them, once answering a reporter's probing questions about his father by declaring "I see him occasionally, but I know nothing of his family life."

With Alice scandalizing the capital city's social circles and Quentin emerging as a prototype "Little Rascal," the other four Roosevelt children hewed to somewhat more conventional roles during their time in the White

Alice Roosevelt, circa 1903, photo by Frances Benjamin Johnston (Library of Congress).

House. Ted Jr., as the eldest son, was held to a higher standard and burdened with greater expectations by his father than his younger siblings; he allegedly suffered near-nervous breakdowns in his adolescence from the responsibilities associated with living up to the examples set by his once-in-a-generation, broke-the-mold father. Kermit took after his father in a different way, spending much of his childhood being desperately ill and spending his time in bed reading and writing avidly; he also suffered deeply from depression for most of his life. Ethel served as a demure, low-profile counter to her flamboyant sister, Alice, often taking on adult "hostess" responsibilities with the White House staff and among her siblings, with Edith otherwise engaged in her First Lady responsibilities. Archibald ("Arch" or "Archie" to family members) was particularly close to Quentin but was often the target for terrible bullying by his older brothers.

Quentin Roosevelt, 1902, photo by Frances Benjamin Johnston (Library of Congress).

The rambunctious Roosevelt brood spent nearly eight years in the White House, with their father being elected president in his own right in 1904; he had pledged that he would not seek another term in 1908, believing that a limited number of presidential terms was an important check against the threat of dictatorship. (For the record, President Roosevelt had added to his long list of unbelievable accolades when he was awarded the Nobel Peace Prize in 1906 for his efforts in negotiating a settlement to the Russo-Japanese War.) Roosevelt put his considerable cultural clout behind the campaign of his secretary of war William Howard Taft in the election of 1908, which Taft handily won, defeating William Jennings Bryan in the latter's third futile attempt to secure the presidency. T.R. then headed off (with Kermit in tow) for a long-term safari in East and Central Africa, hunting specimens for the Smithsonian Institution and the American Museum of Natural History. All four of the Roosevelt boys continued their private school educations after leaving the White House, and all four of them eventually earned admission into their father's alma mater, Harvard College. Alice continued on as a source of scandalous and salacious material for the nation's yellow press, marrying Congressman Nicholas Longworth III, while maintaining a long romantic affair with Senator William Borah, who fathered her only daughter, Paulina. Ethel, who had made her society debut at the age of 17, "coming out" as a debutante just before the family left the White House, remained true to type, keeping a lower profile in her personal and professional life, measured and responsible in her family and community connections.

When T.R. had stepped down from the presidency, he had expected Taft to serve essentially as a Roosevelt clone, but by the time the ex-president returned to the United States in 1910, it had become increasingly clear that Taft intended to serve as his own man, with his own team, in his own ways, with his own policies, many of which were opposed by his outspoken predecessor. By the end of 1911, Roosevelt and his followers had come to think of T.R. as the savior of a Republican Party seemingly (though not actually) adrift under Taft's executive leadership, and Roosevelt stated that he would "accept the nomination for president if it is tendered to me." The 1912 elections were the first where presidential primaries played a key role (as a result of the progressive, Roosevelt-empowered party reforms), and Taft carried the day as the Republican standard bearer at the end of that new and convoluted vetting process. Unaccustomed to not getting what he wanted through dint of his hard work and energy, Roosevelt then declared that he would "accept the progressive nomination on a progressive platform," so desperate was he to prevent a Democrat from reclaiming the White House.

Toward that end and along with an assortment of prominent political allies, Roosevelt formed the Progressive Party (better known as the "Bull Moose Party," after Roosevelt declared himself as fit as that large male mammal when questioned about his health), running as a third-party option against Taft and Democrat Woodrow Wilson. In October 1912, while campaigning in Milwaukee, Wisconsin, Roosevelt was shot point blank in the chest by a psychotic saloon keeper who believed his hand was directed by the ghost of William McKinley. The bullet was blunted as it passed through T.R.'s eyeglasses case and the folded manuscript of his planned speech, lodging in his chest muscles without penetrating the pleura and entering his lung. Roosevelt declined medical attention on the spot and went on to deliver his planned speech, bleeding from his wound, and with a new introductory statement: "Ladies and gentlemen, I don't know whether you fully understand that I have just been shot, but it takes more than that to kill a Bull Moose." The bullet remained embedded in his chest for the remainder of his life.

Wilson and Taft both suspended their campaigns for two weeks while Roosevelt recovered, but the end result of the electoral process once again disappointed T.R., who split the Republican vote with Taft, allowing Wilson to claim the White House for the Democrats. Roosevelt left the country again after the election, this time for an expedition to South America, once again collecting specimens for the American Museum of Natural History. He returned to the United States in 1914, just in time for the outbreak of the Great War in Europe. President Wilson spent the ensuing 30 months desperately attempting to keep the United States out of the emerging European conflagration, much to Roosevelt's chagrin. As American involvement became increasingly likely in the latter part of 1916 and early part of 1917, T.R. saw before him yet another opportunity for greatness and adventure, attempting to muster four divisions to fight in France, under his leadership, essentially mirroring his efforts with the Rough Riders in the Spanish-American War. Not surprisingly, President Wilson declined to send the nation's former chief executive and commander in chief into a combat situation, and to Roosevelt's credit, while railing against Wilson's policies, he did send a written missive to the men who had pledged to follow him into battle, encouraging them to seek military opportunities through other means or to serve the country in its civil life to the best of their abilities.

With the aging, ailing (he had been sickened by various tropical illnesses over the course of his many safaris and expeditions, to the long-term detriment of his health, never mind having been shot), and cantankerous Bull Moose relegated to the sidelines in the Great War, the burden of carrying the Roosevelt name and honor into combat fell on his children, who embraced it with aplomb. Early on during the conflict, before the United States' formal involvement, Ted Jr., Archie, and Quentin all attended a "businessman's" military training summer camp in Plattsburgh, New York, founded by President Roosevelt's old Rough Rider buddy, now major general Leonard Wood. When the United States formally entered the war, graduates of such private programs were offered commissions in the armed forces, a practice eventually codified in the Officers' Reserve Corps and Reserve Officers' Training Corps (ROTC). (Kermit briefly attended the camp in the summer of 1917, but had less training time there than did his three brothers.)

After the declaration of war by the Americans, Archie was commissioned as a second lieutenant in the U.S. Army and Ted as a major in the same service. Kermit elected to volunteer with the British army in Mesopotamia, in what is now Iraq, where he was in charge of transport in that theater, and became an expert English-Arabic translator; he transferred to the U.S. Army in 1918 and participated in the Meuse-Argonne offensive. Ethel also served in France as a nurse, alongside her husband, Richard Derby, who was a surgeon; she later became a prominent advocate and champion of the Red Cross. Alice somewhat scandalously remained stateside, eventually being banned from the Wilson White House for an off-color joke at the touchy president's expense.

Ted Jr. and Archie were the first of the Roosevelt boys to see hard combat, both serving honorably and admirably and both also being seriously wounded in the meat grinder of the western front; Archie's injuries were so severe that he was discharged from the army with a full medical disability. Young Quentin was still at Harvard when America entered the war, having recently become engaged to Flora Payne Whitney, an heiress of the extended and extravagant New York Vanderbilt clan. He shared his father's wrath at President Wilson's pacifism and neutrality, writing to Flora, "We are a pretty sordid lot, aren't we, to want to sit looking on while England and France fight our battles and pan gold into our pockets."

Quentin soon put his money where his pen was and followed his brothers to Europe as a member of the newly formed First Reserve Aero Squadron, where he thought his mechanical skills would be of most use to the army. While proud of all of their children's service, President and Mrs. Roosevelt obviously worried about their sons and daughter as they went off to Europe to do their parts in the war, and it was Quentin whom they worried about most of all. "It was hard when Quentin went," Edith later noted. "But you can't bring up boys to be eagles, and expect them to turn out sparrows." Quentin passed his military physical only by memorizing the eye chart (like his father, he was desperately myopic) and lying about a chronic back injury. He trained as an aviator at Hazelhurst Field on Long Island and sailed for France in July 1917, where he continued his flight training on the infamously finicky French Nieuport 28 fighter planes, and served in a supply capacity as the air service training base at Issoudon was being established.

Quentin eventually became a pilot in the 95th Aero Squadron, posted first to Touquin and then to Seine-et-Marne, France. He recorded his first and only kill of a German aircraft on July 10, 1918. Captain Eddie Rickenbacker, commander of the 94th Aero Squadron and one of the greatest combat aviators in history, met Quentin during his service in France and remembered him thusly in his memoirs:

> As President Roosevelt's son he had rather a difficult task to fit himself in with the democratic style of living which is necessary in the intimate life of an aviation camp. Everyone who met him for the first time expected him to have the airs and superciliousness of a spoiled boy. This notion was quickly lost after the first glimpse one had of Quentin. Gay, hearty and absolutely square in everything he said or did, Quentin Roosevelt was one of the most popular fellows in the group. We loved him purely for his own natural self. He was reckless to such a degree that his commanding officers had to caution him repeatedly about the senselessness of his lack of caution. His bravery was so notorious that we all knew he would either achieve some great spectacular success or be killed in the attempt. Even the pilots in his own flight would beg him to conserve himself and wait for a fair opportunity for a victory. But Quentin would merely laugh away all serious advice.

Sadly, Quentin's fate followed the second course predicted by Rickenbacker, as his Nieuport 28 was shot down a mere four days after his sole combat triumph during an intense aerial combat over Chamery. During that dogfight, Quentin was struck in the head by two machine gun bullets, his plane falling, wrecked, behind enemy lines. Upon realizing who the fallen aviator was and with a modicum of respect to the Roosevelt family, the German military buried him where he fell with full battlefield honors, creating a marker from two basswood boards bound with wire cut from his plane. Their magnanimity was limited, though, as the German military also staged and shot grisly photos of Quentin's body and plane and distributed them widely as postcards for propaganda purposes. The backlash from such crass propagandizing was swift and strong in the German homeland, where many citizens held President Roosevelt in high respect and were impressed that a former president's son would elect to serve, and die, under such circumstances. (Quentin remains the only child of a U.S. president to die in combat, and Hazelhurst Field on Long Island was renamed Roosevelt Field in his honor; a mega-shopping mall now sits on that site, still bearing his name.) The French government also honored Quentin for his bravery and sacrifice, awarding him the Croix de Guerre with Palm.

American forces captured the area surrounding Quentin's grave within a week, removing the German handmade cross and replacing it with one of their own, around which the French built a fenced enclosure. The site quickly became a shrine and a point of pilgrimage and reflection for aviators and soldiers, American, English, French, and even German alike. After the grave site had been secured, President and Mrs.

Quentin's original grave, from a Keystone View Company stereograph, 1923 (Library of Congress).

Roosevelt learned that the army intended to disinter Quentin and bring his remains back to the United States for reburial. The senior Roosevelts were not having it, with T.R. writing to U.S. Army Chief of Staff Peyton C. March that "Mrs. Roosevelt and I wish to enter a most respectful, but a most emphatic protest against the proposed course so far as our son Quentin is concerned. We have always believed, that 'where the tree falls, there let it lie.' We know that many good persons feel entirely differently, but to us it is merely painful and harrowing long after death to move the poor body from which the soul has gone. We greatly prefer that Quentin shall continue to lie on the spot where he fell in battle, and where the foemen buried him."

In keeping with his public persona, President Roosevelt put on a (mostly) brave face for the public following the loss of his beloved son, going so far as to note, "Haven't I bully boys, one dead and two in the hospital!" But Quentin's loss hurt him truly and deeply. "There is not much to say," T.R. wrote to Kermit after Quentin's death. "No man could have died in finer or more gallant fashion; and our pride equals our sorrow—each is limited only by the other." The nation, too, mourned Quentin, as he had grown up in public before America's citizenry, who were charmed by his vigorous, vibrant, and often irreverent personality and who followed his education, his engagement, his deployment, his service, and his death as a beloved surrogate member of the greater national family.

President Roosevelt's health declined precipitously in the months following Quentin's death, and he was hospitalized for seven weeks in late 1918 due to the aggregate effects of the various jungle diseases he had contracted over the years, compounded by the psychological and emotional toll associated with losing his child in a war that he had championed. On January 5, 1919, the venerable Bull Moose died in his sleep at his home, Sagamore Hill, on Long Island's North Shore, finally felled by a blood clot that had formed in a vein in his leg, broken free into his circulatory system, and lodged fatally within his lungs. He was only 60 years old. Vice President Thomas R. Marshall famously remarked that "death had to take Roosevelt sleeping, for if he had been awake, there would have been a fight."

It's not our place to attempt to retroactively psychoanalyze Theodore Roosevelt or to speculate whether his own particular form of masculinity and the expectations that his sons would follow in his own audaciously dangerous footsteps could have played a key contributory role in Quentin's death, though many writers have done so over the years. Because for all of his frenetic activities over his working life and his deeply, loudly, widely shared opinions on myriad topics, and despite his love of public attention and affection, and despite his willingness to upset whatever apple carts required tipping, at the end of the day, there's little question that T.R. truly adored his family, took great comfort in their happiness and success, and did the best that he could, in the best ways that he knew, in the times that he lived, to let them know that in his actions and his words alike.

After his election to the presidency in 1904, T.R. wrote to Kermit, then 15 years old, "No matter how things came out, the really important thing was the lovely life with Mother and you children, and that compared to this home life everything else was of very small importance from the standpoint of happiness." Later, Roosevelt wrote, "There is no form of happiness on the Earth, no form of success of any kind, that in any way approaches the happiness of the husband and the wife who are married lovers, and the father and mother of plenty of healthy children." We choose to believe that he indeed believed what he wrote.

So with the "Old Lion" (as Arch described him in a telegram to his siblings informing them of their father's death) gone, after the beloved baby of the family flew away for the last time, the surviving Roosevelt siblings were left to carry their father's legacy to the best of their own abilities, which were proven formidable indeed.

Ethel played a key role in preserving Sagamore Hill as a National Historic Site, was one of the women to serve on the board of trustees of the American Museum of National History, was a champion of the American civil rights movement, and a prominent leader in the Red Cross organization for sixty years. When she commissioned a formal portrait of herself, she did not wear the usual jewels, furs, and evening gown, electing instead to be painted for posterity in her Red Cross nurse's uniform. She died in 1977 at the age of 86, months after making her final visit to the White House to pay her respects to President and Mrs. Jimmy Carter. Alice remained a cultural institution and media favorite in the nation's capital until her death in 1980 at the age of 96; she had come to be known as "The Other Washington Monument" for her perpetual perch atop the federal district's social hierarchy and for her near century of being exactly who she wanted to be, in all the ways that she best saw fit, dissenting opinions on propriety be damned.

Kermit Roosevelt founded the Roosevelt Steamship Company and the United States Lines after World War I, and he and Ted Jr. continued to plan and execute T.R.-styled expeditions in China and central Asia throughout the 1920s, writing best-selling books about their adventures and exploits. After serving as vice president of the New York Zoological Society in the late 1930s, Kermit again negotiated to join the British armed forces (he was friends with Winston Churchill) when war with Germany erupted again; he fought with the British in North Africa and in Norway, was injured at the Battle of Narvik, and was eventually discharged for health reasons in May 1941. His lifelong struggles with depression and alcoholism roared to the fore after he returned to the United States, eventually resulting in a four-month stay at a sanitarium in Hartford, Connecticut, at his siblings' behest. Upon his release and recovery, incomplete as it perhaps was, his cousin, President Franklin Delano Roosevelt, arranged for Kermit to be commissioned as a major in the U.S. Army. He was serving as an intelligence officer in Fort Richardson, Alaska, in June 1943, when he tragically took his own life by gunshot. He was and remains interred at Fort Richardson National Cemetery.

Like Kermit, World War I veterans Archie and Ted Jr. sought to return to active duty during World War II, despite the grievous injuries they'd both experienced earlier in their lives. Archie had spent the interwar period working in the petroleum industry, and he was a bit player in the Teapot Dome scandal that doomed President Warren G. Harding's administration. He was later involved in conservative policy advocacy, then petitioned Cousin FDR for a commission in the army following the attack on Pearl Harbor. As commander of the 162nd Regimental Combat Team, he commanded combined Australian and American forces in the Salamaua campaign in northeastern New Guinea, where a key battle landmark was named Roosevelt Ridge in his honor. In August 1943, he was wounded by an enemy grenade and was once again medically discharged from the army. He worked in investment banking after the war and became active with a variety of right-wing organizations, including, controversially, the John Birch Society and the Veritas Foundation. Archie died in 1979 at the age of 85.

As accomplished as all of T.R. and Edith's children were, Ted Jr.'s career most closely mirrored the absurd levels of achievement that his father had patterned before him. After recovering from his wounds in World War I, he went on to serve as a member of the New York State Assembly (1920–1921), as the assistant secretary of the navy (1921–1924), as the governor of Puerto Rico (1929–1932), and as the governor-general of the Philippines (1932–1933). (He, too, was tarred by his peripheral involvement with the Teapot Dome scandal, though he and Archie were ultimately exonerated of any wrongdoing.) Ted returned to the United States in 1935 and served as an executive with the Doubleday publishing house and with American Express. He was touted as both a presidential and then vice presidential candidate in 1936, which would have set him on a campaign against his cousin. (The two were not close. After Democrat Franklin D. Roosevelt was first elected to the presidency in 1932, Republican Ted Roosevelt, Jr., was asked how the two were related, replying, "Fifth cousin, about to be removed.")

In 1940, as he had done in the years immediately preceding World War I, Ted participated in private military training offered to businessmen. With conflicts escalating, Ted was returned to active duty in April 1941 as a colonel in the U.S. Army. Later that year, he was promoted

Brigadier General Theodore Roosevelt, Jr. (Library of Congress).

to brigadier general. He quickly remade a name for himself, leading the 26th Infantry in its attack on Oran, Algeria, in November 1942, a key part of the Allies' invasion of North Africa. Well loved by his troops, with a reputation as a general who often visited the front lines and who preferred battle conditions to distant command posts, Brigadier General Roosevelt ran afoul of Lieutenant General George S. Patton, who disapproved of flag officers who "dressed down" and did not embrace or endorse Patton's spit-shine approach to soldiering, routinely pointing out Roosevelt's iconoclastic performances and practices up the chain of command to General Dwight D. Eisenhower. With grudging consent from General Omar Bradley, Roosevelt was eventually relieved of his command and reassigned to a variety of noncommand positions in Sicily, Sardinia, and England, where he was tasked with helping to plan and execute the Normandy invasion.

Of course, being his father's son, Ted Jr. worked to make sure that his role in D-Day was not limited to logistics support from a command center. After badgering the Fourth Infantry Division's commanding general Raymond Barton both verbally and in writing, Roosevelt was granted his wish to land by sea in Normandy with the first wave of troops. He was the only general to do so, and at age 56, he was the oldest man in the invasion, with a heart condition and arthritis that forced him to walk with a cane. Accompanying him in that first wave to the bloody beaches was his son, Captain Quentin Roosevelt II. The pair were the only father-son team to fight together among the 150,000 military service members (American, British, and Canadian) who stormed the beaches as part of the D-Day invasion. (Quentin II survived World War II, then died in a plane crash in China in 1948.)

Side by Side in Eternity

While motoring across the English Channel, Brigadier General Roosevelt's landing craft had drifted off course and landed about a mile from its intended target point on Utah Beach. Clambering ashore, armed only with a pistol and his cane, he is alleged to have announced, "Well, I guess we'll start the war from right here!" As the invading troops faced blistering fire from German pillboxes, machine-gun nests, and bunkers along the beach and as soldiers blundered catastrophically into dense minefields along the beach, Ted Jr. calmly moved among his young charges, encouraging and inspiring the successive waves of troops seeking to secure the beachhead. A sergeant from his unit later recalled encountering Roosevelt presiding over the beach "with a cane in one hand, a map in the other, walking around as if he was looking over some real estate." By day's end, the Fourth Infantry had pushed over five miles inland, the crucial first step toward the rescue and restoration of Europe from its would-be Nazi overlords. When General of the Army Omar Bradley was asked, many years later, to name the most heroic action he had witnessed in battle, he replied with little hesitation, "Ted Roosevelt on Utah Beach."

Just over a month after the landing at Utah Beach, Brigadier General Roosevelt's lingering health issues finally caught up with him, and he was stricken by a heart attack while resting in a converted sleeping truck that his unit had captured from the Germans. He had spent much of the day engaged in pleasant conversation with his son and fellow D-Day veteran Quentin II. Despite medics' best efforts over a two-hour period, Brigadier General Theodore Roosevelt, Jr., died around midnight. He was buried in the cemetery at Sainte-Mère-Église, France, and his honorary pallbearers included Generals Bradley, Patton, and Barton, along with other senior officers in the regional theater. General Barton recommended that Roosevelt be awarded the Distinguished Service Cross for his valiance at Utah Beach, but that recommendation was upgraded as it worked up the chain of command. By the time it reached President Franklin Roosevelt's desk and was signed, Ted Jr. was the posthumous recipient of the Medal of Honor, the highest recognition of valor in the armed services. Ted's medal was presented to his widow, Eleanor Butler Roosevelt, in September 1944, above the following citation:

The President of the United States of America, in the name of Congress, takes pride in presenting the Medal of Honor (Posthumously) to Brigadier General Theodore Roosevelt, Jr., United States Army for gallantry and intrepidity at the risk of his life above and beyond the call of duty on 6 June 1944, in France. After two verbal requests to accompany the leading assault elements in the Normandy invasion had been denied, Brig. Gen. Roosevelt's written request for this mission was approved and he landed with the first wave of the forces assaulting the enemy-held beaches. He repeatedly led groups from the beach, over the seawall and established them inland. His valor, courage, and presence in the very front of the attack and his complete unconcern at being under heavy fire inspired the troops to heights of enthusiasm and self-sacrifice. Although the enemy had the beach under constant direct fire, Brig. Gen. Roosevelt moved from one locality to another, rallying men around him, directed and personally led them against the enemy. Under his seasoned, precise, calm, and unfaltering leadership, assault troops reduced beach strong points and rapidly moved inland with minimum casualties. He thus contributed substantially to the successful establishment of the beachhead in France.

The U.S. Army's Quartermaster Graves Registration Company had first established a temporary cemetery near the landing beaches of Normandy in 1944, and after the war ended, a more formal cemetery was established about a mile from the original burial grounds. The Normandy American Cemetery and Memorial was officially dedicated in July 1956, and despite T.R.'s exhortation that "where the tree falls, so let it lie," Ted Jr.'s remains were relocated to that profoundly moving and powerful site, allowing him to rest in perpetuity with the soldiers he led and inspired on D-Day and beyond.

The Normandy American Cemetery was specifically created to honor and remember American troops who died in Europe

Ted Jr.'s grave at Normandy (via Wikimedia, Creative Commons License CC BY-SA 3.0).

Quentin's grave at Normandy (Martin Bugelli, via Wikimedia, Creative Commons License CC BY-SA 3.0).

during World War II, but there is one exception to be found on the site, right next to Brigadier General Roosevelt's grave. Ted's younger brother Quentin's remains were relocated to the Normandy site in 1955, making him the only World War I casualty to be buried there; Quentin's original headstone is now at the Sagamore Hill family site in New York. Yes, some rules were bent, and yes, some arms were twisted to allow the brothers to lie side by side, but really, would you expect anything less from the Roosevelts, once the family had set its sights on something they wanted and believed was right?

CHAPTER SEVEN

Hazel Ying Lee (1912–1944) and Victor Ying Lee (1914–1944)

River View Cemetery, Portland, Oregon

> *"Women should do for themselves what men have already done—occasionally what men have not done—thereby establishing themselves as persons, and perhaps encouraging other women toward greater independence of thought and action."*
>
> —Amelia Earhart

> *"The categories of caste and class that affect the residential patterns of the living also touch the homes of the dead. In the cemetery, geography meets history and sociology. The sacred and the profane converge at the grave. Burial patterns reveal religious beliefs and social distinctions; they reflect intra- and intergroup as well as interpersonal relationships and project them into eternity. Racism pervades the metropoles and the necropoles, biography and memory."*
>
> —Angelika Krüger-Kahloula

World War II has been retroactively judged in popular American culture as "the last good war" and "the war that had to be fought and won." Three-quarters of a century after the cessation of its active military engagements, the defining moments and iconic images of that global conflict still stand mighty and singular in their ability to evoke and invoke the best of what the United States of America can do, and can be, when it chooses to marshal its formidable economic, human, and natural resources toward a singular purpose and when it openly engages allies from every one of the world's inhabited continents to share its causes and concerns.

The complex political, social, and military machinations beneath and behind World War II have long provided ample fodder for formal

115

historical study, rivaled only by the Civil War in the volume of scholarship and number of print pages produced to explore specific aspects
and elements of a mind-boggling human cataclysm, rife with horror and
heroism in equal measure. World War II has also provided fuel and fodder for America's arts and cultural communities, with Hollywood regularly returning to moments and battles famous or infamous, macro or
micro, tactical or strategic, continually producing some of the entertainment industry's most-acclaimed works along the way.

As the number of veterans and citizens who actually experienced
the depredations and inspirations of that great global conflict have rapidly dwindled in recent decades, the Hollywood versions of those great
stories have come to shape the ways that modern audiences see, hear,
understand, and visualize what the war looked like, and felt like, for
those who experienced it.

As a mental exercise, who do you see in your mind's eye when presented with the following biographical summary: "Born and raised in
an industrial city of the Pacific Northwest, a strong high school student and athlete, smitten young by the wonders of flight, earned pilot's
certification as a civilian, traveled abroad as a flyer for hire, returned to
the United States after Pearl Harbor, signed up for federal service, ably
flew a variety of fighter aircraft, died of injuries sustained while deliv-
ering an airplane to the Soviet Union under the Lend-Lease program."
Or perhaps this one: "Also born and raised in an industrial city of the
Pacific Northwest, also a fine student and athlete, completed three
years of high school before leaving to work as an office clerk, enlisted in
the army soon after the attack on Pearl Harbor, was assigned to a tank
destroyer battalion, landed at Normandy's Utah Beach on D-Day, fought
across northern France before being killed by anti-tank fire, just shy of
the German border."

Odds are high that most readers' mental movie screens will queue
up a pair of chiseled young White "leading man" types when presented
with those character descriptions, fantasy images that would have
worked well as still promo shots advertising one of Hollywood's great
epics of the *From Here to Eternity*, *The Longest Day*, *The Dirty Dozen*, or
Patton variety. We applaud the few (if any) of you who envisioned a Chinese American sister and brother tandem to fill those imaginary casting
roles, as Hazel Ying Lee and Victor Ying Lee did in their very real lives
until their very real deaths.

Hazel and Victor's parents, Yuet Lee and Ssiu Lan Wong, had emi-
grated to Portland from Taishan, Guangdong, China, settling in what

was then the second largest "Chinatown" on the American West Coast. The family, which grew to include eight children, ran the Golden Pheasant Restaurant, supplemented by Yuet Lee's import-export business. Hazel and Victor were both born in Portland in August 1912 and May 1914, respectively. As children, they both worked to support the family businesses, studied at the community's Chinese school, and attended Portland public schools at a time when ill-will toward the region's Chinese community was growing (again), enabled, empowered, and encouraged on a federal basis by the Immigration Act of 1924 (which restricted immigration from Asia), among other contemporary discriminatory legislation, all of which only served to deepen the hurt and harm done by such long-standing laws as the Chinese Exclusion Act of 1882, which directly contributed to the ghettoization of Asian immigrants in "Chinatowns" across the country.

Hazel graduated from Commerce High School in 1929 and took a job as an elevator operator at Portland's H. Liebes and Company department store, one of a limited number of opportunities available for the city's Chinese American women, who were essentially banned from working in high-profile public professional positions. During her years at the department store and as Victor's own high school career wound down, the entire Lee family would have been acutely aware of news from their family's ancestral homeland, as the Japanese Empire invaded Manchuria in 1931 and established the puppet client state of Manchukuo there in 1932. A variety of Chinese American civic, social, business, and political groups emerged across the United States over those difficult years, seeking to provide material, financial, and moral support for China in the face of the atrocities perpetuated in Manchuria and beyond by the invading Japanese army.

The Chinese Flying Club of Portland (CFCP) was one of the many organizations founded in response to the events of 1931–1932 in Manchuria. As the Japanese had deployed air strikes against civilian targets as acts of terror, the CFCP aimed to train pilots for service in the nascent air force of the national government of China, ostensibly to help combat the threat from above that the superior Japanese air force presented. CFCP students formally signed pledges stating their willingness to die on behalf of China, and donations in excess of $20,000 (roughly $400,000 in 2021 dollars) were collected from a global network for the would-be aviators to learn their craft and trade under the tutelage of seasoned flight instructor Al Greenwood. In the end, 32 trained aviators were sent to China in two waves, the first deployed to Guangdong in August 1932, and the second dispatched to northern China in March 1933.

Among that second group was Hazel Ying Lee.

Hazel had taken her first airplane ride in late 1931 or early 1932; sources (and memories) vary on the timing. As do sources on the nature of that excursion, the ownership of the plane in question, and who Hazel's companion(s) might have been when she first took to the air. But wherever and whenever it truly happened, that first flight changed Hazel's life profoundly, giving her a purpose and a goal—to become a pilot herself and to make her way professionally in the world aloft—that would have seemed unimaginable to most American women of the era, never mind an American woman from an often-disenfranchised cultural community that was then being especially demonized through one of our nation's regular convulsions of targeted discrimination.

Those formidable challenges notwithstanding, Hazel's focus and determination can be clearly judged from the outcome she achieved and how quickly she reached that goal, earning her pilot's license in October 1932 under the auspices of the CFCP, less than a year in any reckoning after her first trip aloft. Hazel's time with the CFCP was also influential and important in another deeply personal fashion, as she began a relationship with fellow aspiring pilot "Clifford" Louie Yim-Qun, whose parents had, like Hazel's, immigrated from Taishan, Guangdong, China, settling in Seattle, where "Cliff" (as Hazel called him) was born in the same year as Victor Ying Lee.

Hazel and Cliff left for China in the second wave of CFCP trainees, ready to volunteer for service with the Chinese air force. Cliff's proffered service was readily accepted, and he saw significant aerial combat action in the years that followed, rising to the rank of major by 1940, when he was seriously wounded in one of the first-known engagements with the now-legendary Japanese A6M "Zero" fighters; Major Louie managed to make it back to his base, safely landing his own severely damaged plane, but his injuries required a recovery period that kept him from the skies for some time.

Hazel, while ostensibly free in China from the racial discrimination that she had bravely faced and surmounted in Portland, was not, unfortunately, free from the era's gender discrimination: the Chinese air force refused her volunteered service as a combat pilot, relegating her to desk work, which was deemed more suitable for women. Joined by her mother and sister, Hazel settled in Guangdong, where she did find work as a commercial pilot, finally able to deploy her formidable skills as a flyer, if not in the ways that she saw as most befitting her talents and the ways that she believed she could have best served Chinese interests. Hazel remained in Guangdong until 1938, when the city was bombed by the Japanese in the early months of the Second Sino-Japanese War, which raged as a major combat theater until Japan's defeat and surrender in 1945. Recognizing that she was no longer in a position to make meaningful contributions to China's defense, Hazel (with her mother and sister) left their home and possessions in Guangdong and fled by foot and rail to Hong Kong, where they lived as refugees until returning to the United States. Hazel settled in New York City, where she worked as a fundraiser, buyer, and exporter of war matériel for China.

On December 7, 1941, the Japanese Empire attacked Pearl Harbor, drawing the United States into the war in the Pacific and making Japan not only the declared enemy of the nation's allies but also a military and political threat to the American heartland and populace themselves. Organizational response on a federal basis was fast and fierce. Among many other mobilizations, the 607th Tank Destroyer Battalion was activated in California on December 15, 1941. In March 1942, its ranks were bolstered by the addition of recruits from Washington, Oregon, Montana, and Idaho, including Victor Ying Lee, who enlisted and joined the unit on March 15 at the Presidio in Monterrey, assigned to its Company C.

Victor began his army career a mere three days before one of the more shameful examples of anti–Asian prejudice and discrimination in U.S. history was unveiled with the War Relocation Authority being established on March 18, 1942, to oversee the relocation of Japanese American citizens to internment camps scattered across the American West. Less than two weeks later, the first Civilian Exclusion Orders were issued by the army, giving families of Japanese descent one week to prepare for removal from their homes. By June 2, 1942, all identified Japanese Americans in "Military Area I" (California, Oregon, Washington, and Arizona) had been removed into army custody.

Victor would have been training with his unit throughout this time, undoubtedly confronted regularly with the cruel caricatures of Asian heritage that often featured in wartime public relations materials. It is also likely that the same wrong-thinking that produced the "anyone of Japanese descent will be ethnically more loyal to the emperor of Japan than to the commander in chief of the United States" paradigm would have often transmuted into "anyone of Asian descent," placing Victor in the position of defending both his American and his Chinese heritage, both of which had been grievously assaulted by the Japanese military and political leadership. His decision to enlist and commitment to serve must be judged as particularly admirable under such circumstances, and the difficulties he would have endured through training and duty would likely have been even more strenuous than those experienced by his company mates who were not judged or questioned simply for their appearances.

While Victor was training in California (his unit was originally armed with self-propelled "gun motor carriages"—think ordnance welded to an armored truck—before being reconfigured to operate towed three-inch M5 anti-tank guns in 1943), Hazel continued her work in New York, unable to enlist and serve a cause she cared passionately about, as her brother had done, due to her own gender. But late in 1942, two dueling opportunities that fit her unique interests and skill sets emerged, as the military found itself short of trained pilots for domestic service due to all available and qualified (male) aviators deploying to support the war effort abroad.

The Women's Auxiliary Ferrying Squadron (WAFS) and the Women's Flying Training Detachment (WFTD) were both launched publicly in September 1942. The goals and objectives of the two organizations were similar: allowing female pilots to take over traditional male pilot roles in such military-adjacent activities as ferrying new-construction planes from factory to airfield, flying cargo, and conducting training activities to create a larger pool of female pilots for such work. Those similarities notwithstanding, the two organizations were founded and existed (briefly) side by side in large part due to the competing alliances of charismatic and pioneering female pilots (Jacqueline Cochran with the WFTD and Nancy Harkness Love with the WAFS) and senior officers in the Army Air Corps, the precursor to the modern United States Air Force (Colonel William H. Tunner was a primary patron for the WAFS, while General Henry "Hap" Arnold was more closely aligned with Cochran and the WFTD).

The two organizations eventually merged on August 20, 1943, under Cochran's leadership as the Women Airforce Service Pilots (WASP), its flyers wearing insignia inspired by the shield of Athena, and its flight jackets and fuselages often decorated with the "Fifinella" mascot, a female "gremlin" (mystical monsters that attacked planes) created by acclaimed children's author Roald Dahl in his 1943 book *The Gremlins*, illustrated by Walt Disney.

Hazel applied for service in the WFTD in the fall of 1942, and was accepted for the highly competitive program in its fourth group of trainees. (More than 25,000 women applied to serve in WASP and its precursor organizations; only ~1,800 were accepted for training, and of those, only ~1,075 of them actually earned their wings.) Hazel entered flight training at Avenger Field in Sweetwater, Texas, on February 21, 1943, and completed the rigorous program there on August 7 of the same year, mere weeks before the formal launching of the WASPs from the foundations of the WFTD and WAFS. Upon graduation, Hazel was assigned to the Third Ferrying Group at Romulus Army Air Base in Michigan, tasked primarily with transporting new aircraft from the factories that produced them to the military air bases where they could be turned over to male combat pilots and deployed. It took over a decade for Hazel to make the journey from her first flight as an airplane passenger to her first flight as the pilot of a U.S. military aircraft, though as was so often the case for women and minorities in wartime America, the nature of her service came with some significant structural caveats.

First and foremost, the WASPs were deemed to be a civilian organization, not a military one. Its members did not qualify for military benefits (including burial expenses for the 38 WASPs who died in service to

Hazel Ying Lee in a Link flight training simulator, with an Army Air Corps instructor (U.S. Air Force).

121

their country), and they were required to fund their own transportation costs to training sites, for their uniforms, and for their room and board. Despite various federal bills and proposals to militarize the organization, the WASPs did not achieve such stature before the end of World War II. The organization itself was dissolved soon after the cessation of hostilities due to a sad sentiment that had the female aviators been allowed to continue flying in the service of their country, they would have been "stealing" jobs from male pilots, both those returning from overseas and those coming up behind the WASPs themselves. During their service, the WASPs were also paid at about two-thirds the rate of their male counterparts flying similar ferry flights, were often assigned undesirable or poorly maintained planes, were not given practice flight time, were required to stand down at age 35 lest the "debilitating irrationality of menopause" impact their flight abilities, and were quite possibly the targets of sabotage by their male colleagues and support crews.

The WASPs were often assigned the least desirable assignments, including winter trips in open-cockpit planes. Most of the WASPs were also limited in the types of planes that they were trained and authorized to fly, though an exception was made for a select group who qualified for "pursuit" duty, flying the faster, higher-powered fighters that emerged toward the end of the war. Hazel was one of the 134 WASPs to achieve that designation, allowing her to ferry such aircraft as the P-39 Airacobra, P-63 Kingcobra, and P-51 Mustang, the last of which was Hazel's favorite aircraft. Most contemporary "best of" lists ranking the various aircraft of World War II would cite the Mustang as one of the finest and most effective aircraft to serve in that era; although not necessarily a scientifically rigorous assessment, there's no question that having qualified to pilot such a machine was a brag-worthy accomplishment, then and now.

Despite the myriad challenges facing the women pilots of WASP, the sense of comradery, support, and mutual respect within their community was profound, as evidenced by both contemporary accounts and the remembrances and recollections of those pioneering flyers in the decades since their quasi-military force was forcefully dissolved, to their collective and profound distress. Hazel Lee's colleagues often commented over the years on her sense of humor, her profound love of flying, her willingness to go the extra mile (or hundred miles, often literally), and her pride in her Chinese heritage. She would often use her lipstick to inscribe Chinese characters on the tail of her planes or those of her colleagues, leaving often humorous messages for the surprised recipients of her communiqués. Hazel also took pride in her ability to identify authentic and high-quality Chinese restaurants around the country, educating her fellow flyers on menu selections, often supervising mass orders for whichever WASPs were fortunate enough to be overnighting with her.

Although she likely experienced racial or cultural prejudice in her work, the regard that Hazel's colleagues felt for her flying skills likely took precedence in her interpersonal relationships with the other WASPs with whom she lived, flew, traveled, talked, played, and partied. She even managed to turn one potentially racially fraught incident into a great dinnertime story that numerous sources and friends recall affectionately all these years on. It seems that in one of only two emergency landings that she was ever forced to make, she ended up grounded in a wheat field in Kansas. (Or Texas, in some sources, memories being fungible.) A farmer, armed with a pitchfork, arrived and proceeded to chase Hazel around her plane as he was shouting to his neighbors that the Japanese were invading. Deftly evading his attack and pointing to her plane's U.S. Army Air Corps insignia, Lee explained to the farmer who she was, what she was doing, and demanding that he stop his assault. He capitulated only when finally convinced that she was a "China gal" and not a "Jap gal." It's a testament to her personality and character that Hazel was able, and frequently chose, to share that experience through the lens of her humor and not through one hued by hatred.

Hazel's training time in Texas and early days in Michigan also found her reunited with her old friend and flame "Clifford" Louie Yim-Qun, who had been sent to the United States to attend the army's Command and General Staff College following his in-service injuries in the Sino-Japanese theater of the war. The relationship deepened while the pair pursued their respective training courses, and the couple married on October 9, 1943, an occasion that merited an Associated Press wire story with a photo of the smiling couple above the following caption:

CHINESE BRIDE AND GROOM ARE BOTH PILOTS: Major Yin Cheung Louie [sic], 29-year old pilot in the Chinese army, who gave his address as Washington, D.C., and Hazel Ying Lee, 31-year old pilot attached to the Third Ferrying Group, Romulus Air Base, Romulus, Mich., sit in a car following their marriage at the Marble Collegiate Church in New York City on October 9. The groom was born in Canton, China. The bride was born in Portland, Oregon.

Unfortunately, Cliff's career quickly took him back out of the United States, and he and Hazel never saw each other again after the brief, bright final moments they spent together on and after their wedding date. Hazel believed for months after their wedding that Cliff had either been killed or captured in China, as she had received no communications from him.

While Hazel was working to achieve her WASP wings, beginning her career as a ferry pilot, and forging her marriage bond with Cliff, Victor continued his service with the 607th Tank Destroyer (TD) Battalion, eventually achieving the rank of technician fifth grade, a designation used by the army only through World War II, which recognized (and compensated) specialized skills but with no attendant command authority. The 607th TD Battalion was finally deployed to the United Kingdom in April 1944, posted first to Macclesfield, then to Camp Barton Stacey, where they made their final secret preparations for the D-Day invasion of Normandy. Two of the 607th TD Battalion's companies landed at Utah Beach on June 17, 1944, with two others (including

Soldiers of the 607th Tank Destroyer Battalion and their M5–3 anti-tank gun, Le Bourg St-Leonard, France, August 1944 (U.S. Army).

Victor's Company C) landing at the same beach on June 23, their arrivals delayed by rough seas. The battalion spent the next six months fighting its way across France toward the German border, earning accolades and combat credits for the Normandy, northern France, Rhineland, Ardennes-Alsace, and central European campaigns.

By mid–September, the 607th had reached the Moselle River, near the tripoint border of France, Luxembourg, and Germany. Victor's Company C, supporting the 90th Infantry Division, fired ten artillery rounds toward Perl on the eastern banks of the Moselle. These were believed to have been the first fire to fall into Germany from the Third Army, under the command of General George S. Patton. The 607th remained in the region for the remainder of September and October, providing artillery support for infantry attacks targeting occupied Metz (on the French side of the Moselle) in preparation for a major push into Germany later in the year.

As Victor's unit was mired in the meat grinder alongside the Moselle in early November, Hazel received orders to travel to Bell Aircraft's manufacturing facility in Niagara Falls, New York, to ferry a P-63 Kingcobra to Great Falls, Montana. The Kingcobra was a successor to the Bell P-39 Airacobra, which the United States had provided in bulk to the Soviet Union under the Lend-Lease policy, an extraordinary wartime program wherein the American allies in the United Kingdom, Free France, China, and the Soviet Union were provided with food, fuel, and weaponry (including warships and airplanes) to pursue the Allies' collective strategic objectives. In operation from March 1941 to August 1945, the Lend-Lease program's aid was generally provided free of cost to the recipients, though some of the larger military hardware items were returned to the United States after the war. The United States had provided the Soviet air force with P-39 Airacobras in such high volume that Soviet pilots recorded the highest number of combat kills attributed to any American fighter aircraft flown by any air force in any conflict.

The P-63 Kingcobra was designed to capitalize on the economies of scale at Bell Aircraft's manufacturing facilities, while addressing operational and performance issues associated with the Airacobra, which had limited its effectiveness at high altitudes, degrading its utility as an interceptor class over time. Although the Kingcobra was deemed superior to the Airacobra in almost every operational aspect, it was not determined to be suitable for use by the Army Air Corps and was never accepted for operational service by the American military. Instead, vast numbers of P-63s were flown to Great Falls, where male pilots accepted the planes and flew them on to Nome, Alaska. In Nome, Soviet ferry pilots (many of them also women) would take custody of the Kingcobras and transport them on to their assigned units, primarily in the Soviet Far East, where they were staged for an eventual attack on Japan. Nearly 2,400 P-63s made the journey from Niagara Falls to the Russian Far East, most of them ferried at some points in their journey by WASPs and their female Soviet counterparts.

After picking up her plane in Niagara Falls, Hazel Ying Lee worked her way westward along familiar routes, but foul weather in the Upper Midwest forced her to the ground for an unplanned weather delay in Fargo, North Dakota. On Thanksgiving morning, November 23, 1944, the sky cleared and she was cleared for the final flight into Great Falls. In a 1997 oral history interview, fellow WASP and P-63 pilot Virginia Luttrell Krahn recalled the subsequent events as follows:

> "Shortly after [the group] took off, [pilot] Jeff [Russell] moved over close to me and pointed to his earphone and raised his hand. His radio was out." [The group stopped in Bismarck, N.D., hoping to have Russell's radio fixed, but

A P-63 Kingcobra, the same type of plane Hazel Lee was ferrying on her final flight (U.S. Air Force).

126

since it was a holiday, they were out of luck; the group continued on to Montana]. "By this time there were so many planes circling at Great Falls and ready to land. The air was just filled with P-63's." [After landing her own plane safely, Krahn saw, to her horror, that at the end of the runway two planes were too close together, one above the other]. "When the tower saw what was happening, they said 'Pull up! Pull up!' And the only plane that could hear it was Hazel ... and she pulled up right into Jeff, who heard nothing."

Russell's fuel tank ruptured from the impact and both aircraft burst into flames before falling to the runway. Russell escaped from his plane on the ground and survived with minor injuries. Hazel Ying Lee was knocked unconscious, trapped in her plane, and suffered severe burns before being extracted from the wreckage of her final flight. She died two days later, on November 25, 1944, at the age of 32. In that same 1997 oral interview, Virginia Lutrell Krahn recalled that "[Hazel] was conscious [that] entire time. She never complained. The doctors said they had never seen anyone so brave."

As Hazel ferried, waited for weather, made her final flight, crashed, burned, suffered, and died, Victor Ying Lee's 607th TD Battalion continued its inexorable slog toward Germany. On November 28, 1944, three days after Hazel's passing, four tank destroyers from Victor's Company C, Third Platoon, were dispatched to assist the 95th Infantry Division in an attack on the small commune of Merten, France, in the Moselle department, east of the tripoint border with Luxembourg. The infantry and artillery units were to meet at a roadblock at the western edge of the town. On their way to the designated meeting point, the infantry units met more resistance than intelligence had expected and were unable to reach the roadblock or to clear any of the German anti-tank guns positioned in and near Merten. As the American towed tank destroyer guns approached the town, the Germans opened fire with their own anti-tank caliber weaponry, hitting and destroying two of the four artillery pieces being hauled by the members of Company C, Third Platoon. Several soldiers were killed in the attack. Thirty-year-old Victor Ying Lee was one of them.

Within those terrible 72 hours, the family of Yuet Lee and Ssiu Lan Wong of Portland, Oregon, lost two of their eight beloved children, a continent and an ocean's width away from each other and the home in which they'd been raised. As a WASP, Hazel was not entitled to receive military burial honors (or financial support for an interment), though as a member of the United States Army, Victor was so entitled, though he was initially buried near where he fell in France, as was customary.

But the Lee family ultimately wanted their children buried together
and near their home, so they selected River View Cemetery on the west
banks of the Willamette River as their loved ones' final resting place,
some five miles from the heart of Portland's Chinatown.

**Victor's original burial report, from his first interment in France (National
Personnel Records Center).**

River View was a fine choice, a deeply resonant and significant part of Portland's history. Prominent city fathers Henry W. Corbett, William S. Ladd, and Henry Failing had purchased 350 acres of land along the west bank of the Willamette River in 1879, and in 1882, they opened the first nonprofit cemetery in Portland, intending for River View to be mutually owned by those who choose the site as the perpetual resting place for loved ones and expecting River View to serve as the primary cemetery for their growing riverfront city. Although it was not a military or veterans' cemetery, it was certainly a fine final resting place for Hazel and Victor, where their family could gather to celebrate their lives and the cost of their amazing service and sacrifice on behalf of their country.

Victor and Hazel's story takes an interesting twist here, in the ways that it has been told since their passing. Countless public sources, websites, videos, and books generally provide some version of this narrative: "The Lee family chose a burial site in a Portland, Oregon, cemetery but were refused permission to bury Hazel in the chosen place because cemetery policy did not allow Asians to be buried there. The Lee family wrote to President Roosevelt, successfully challenged the policy, and Hazel Ying Lee was laid to rest in a nonmilitary funeral, and buried alongside her younger brother Victor, who had also been killed in action." (Some versions of the story available online state that Hazel's remains were kept at Romulus Army Air Base for a year or more.) It was that summary telling of the story that actually led your authors to feature Victor and Hazel in this book, but our in-depth research into key primary source documents actually calls many elements of that popular public narrative into question.

First off, the timeline of key events for Hazel's interment, per primary source documents of the era, is as follows:

23 November 1944: Hazel critically injured in a flight accident at Great Falls, Montana.
25 November 1944: Hazel dies of her injuries in Great Falls.
29 November 1944: Military message from Commanding Officer L. Ponton de Arce of Third Ferrying Group, Romulus, Michigan, sent to Commanding General Army Air Forces reading:

This HQ advised by telephone that funeral F Hazel Ying Lee WASP will be at 1130 PWT Friday 1 December 1944 in Portland, Oregon. Undertaker Holman and Lutz. Portland AAB to provide V// full military funeral.

30 November 1944: *The Oregonian* newspaper runs the following announcement:

LOUIE—Nov. 23, Mrs. Y.C. (Hazel Lee), formerly of Portland; wife of Major Yin Cheung Louie of Chinese air corps; sister of Harry, Victor, Howard, David, Ben, Mrs. Bowen Hann and Mrs. Walter Chung, Mrs. Herbert Tong, Miss Ngan Lee. Friends invited to attend funeral services Friday, 11:30 A.M., in the Drawing Room Chapel of Holman & Lutz Colonial Mortuary, NE 14th and Sandy. Vault Interment Riverview.

1 December 1944: River View's interment entry from their daybook reads as follows:

12/1: Holman & Lutz, Lot 56, Sec 120–4, Friday, 11:30, Hazel Lee Louie, Goodman Vault (pd #19657)

5 September 1945: Hazel's interment card reads:

(Marker) Ledger: Delivered 9/5/1945

The timeline for Hazel's interment was actually quite brisk, certainly not beyond the normal bounds of funerary protocol, and the evidence suggests that the federal government did at least intend to provide moral and conceptual military support for her burial, despite that not being the case for the WASPs in general. It is worth noting that River View's property cards cite the purchaser for each plot in the cemetery, not the decedents buried within. There is no property card on file for Hazel's grave, and the plot map, which also generally lists buyers, not decedents, shows her plot under her married name of "Louie."

Hazel's interment entry in our Day Book

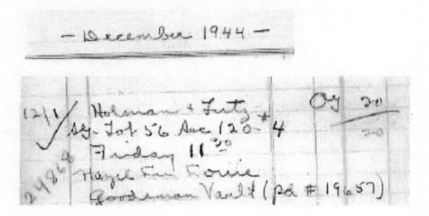

River View Cemetery's interment log entry for Hazel Ying Lee (River View Cemetery Archives).

So was Hazel's plot actually purchased? Or could it have been simply provided by River View in response to the direction that the Portland AAB would coordinate a military burial for Hazel in a civilian cemetery, despite the fact that WASPs were normally not accorded such government support for the disposition of their mortal remains? The lack of a property card and any related procurement records is a curious anomaly, and if we presume that Hazel had not purchased her plot in advance, the presence of her name on the site map, in lieu of any other purchaser, is equally mysterious.

Victor's documentation with River View Cemetery, on the other hand, clearly shows that his final resting place was purchased by his sister, Florence Chung. But the popular narrative about Victor and Hazel being buried together is also not borne out by the timeline associated with his eventual interment at River View, per the following officially documented dates:

28 November 1944: Victor is killed in combat near Merten, France, though he was originally declared missing in action (MIA).

15 December 1944: The War Department updates Victor's MIA status to killed in action status after "evidence considered sufficient to establish the fact of death was received by the Secretary of War from a commander in the European Area." Victor's remains were identified via his military paybook, the name "V. Lee" on a wallet, the initials "V.Y.L." on a watch chain, a letter addressed to Victor, and a towel marked with his name and service member number.

4 October 1945: Florence Chung purchases a plot for Victor; the property card filed for his eventual grave reads:

Sec 120, Lot 58 Grave #4, Owner CHUNG Florence L, Date Oct. 4 1945, No Monument, Name Victor Ying Lee

4 September 1946: Major General T.B. Larkin, the U.S. Army's quartermaster general, notifies Victor and Hazel's brother Harry Lee via letter that Victor's remains have been interred at U.S. Military Cemetery Limey, "eighteen miles northwest of Nancy, France … under the constant care and supervision of United States military personnel." Further, Major General Larkin noted:

The War Department has now been authorized to comply, at Government expense, with the feasible wishes of the next of kin regarding final interment, here or abroad, of the remains of your loved one.

28 April 1947: Brigadier General G.A. Horkan, chief of the Army

Quartermaster Corps' Memorial Division, provides Harry Lee with a photo of Victor's resting place at the Military Cemetery at Limey, noting:

It is my sincere hope that you may gain some solace from this view of the surrounding in which your loved one rests. As you can see, this is a place of simple dignity, neat and well cared for. Here, assured of continuous care, now rest the remains of a few of those heroic dead who fell together in the service of our country. This cemetery will be maintained as a temporary resting place until, in accordance with the wishes of the next of kin, all remains are either placed in permanent American cemeteries overseas or returned to the Homeland for final burial.

22 July 1947: Major General Larkin again writes to Harry Lee, providing two pamphlets explaining "Disposition of World War II Armed Forces Dead" and "American Cemeteries"; Harry is given a form called "Request for Disposition of Remains" and asked to reply with his wishes within 30 days. Harry requests that Victor's remains be returned to Portland for final interment.

15 February 1948: Victor's remains are disinterred from Limey cemetery; the disinterment directive notes that he was buried in military clothing, that his body was intact, with large amounts of decomposed flesh and a crushed skull and mandible. Victor's remains slowly made their way back to Portland via Antwerp, Belgium, followed by an Atlantic crossing (with numerous other fallen American soldiers) on the U.S. Army Transport Ship *Lawrence Victory* to Brooklyn, New York, then a train journey to Utah General Distribution Depot, Ogden, Utah, and again by train to the Holman & Lutz Funeral Home in Portland, after Harry Lee reaffirmed the family's intentions via telegram on August 16, 1948.

23 September 1948: River View's interment entry from their daybook reads as follows:

9/23: Holman & Lutz, Lot 58, Sec 120 #4, Thursday, 1 PM, Victor Ying Lee, Cement Box

17 March 1949: Victor's interment card reads:

(Soldier Marker) Delivered March 17, 1949

So Victor's remains did not arrive at River View until nearly four years after his death and Hazel's interment. Carol Tyler at the American Battle Monuments Commission noted that the Lee family's experiences were not at all unusual in this regard: "During WWII, American soldiers that lost their lives were immediately buried in a temporary

RECEIPT OF REMAINS

DISTRIBUTION CENTER UTAH GENERAL DISTRIBUTION DEPOT
OGDEN, UTAH

ROUTINE 14 SEP 19--

REMAINS CONSIGNED TO: HOLMAN & LUTZ
N E 14TH AVENUE & SANDY
PORTLAND OREGON

293

REMAINS OF THE LATE TECHNICIAN FIFTH GRADE VICTOR LEE

BEING SHIPPED TO YOU ACCOMPANIED BY MILITARY ESCORT ON TRAIN NUMBER ELEVEN

UNION PACIFIC RAILROAD   DUE TO ARRIVE

PORTLAND OREGON   STATION SIX FIFTEEN

PM EIGHTEEN SEPTEMBER   REQUEST YOU MAKE ARRANGEMENTS TO

ACCEPT REMAINS AT STATION UPON ARRIVAL AND THAT YOU IMMEDIATELY PASS THIS

INFORMATION ON TO NEXT OF KIN.

STEVEN F. CAPASSO
MAJOR, QMC
CHIEF, AGRD

FILE
RECORDS ANNOTATED
DATE 10/28/48
NAME

I, THE UNDERSIGNED, DO HEREBY ACKNOWLEDGE RECEIPT OF THE REMAINS OF THE ABOVE-NAMED DECEASED

THIS 18 DAY OF September, 19 48

WITNESS (Escort)   CONSIGNEE

Receipt for Victor's remains as they were returned to Portland (National Personnel Records Center).

location near where they fell. After the war ended, next of kin in the United States received correspondence from the government asking if they would like their loved one returned to the United States for burial or interred overseas in a permanent, American military cemetery. Less than 30% of families selected overseas burial."

As it turns out, the delay in Victor's interment meant that it was actually impossible for Victor and Hazel to literally be buried side by

Victor's interment entry in our Day Book

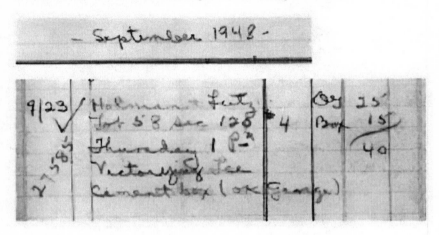

River View Cemetery's interment log entry for Victor Lee (River View Cemetery Archives).

side, though they are indeed close to each other. Between their graves, Maria F.J. Denman Rieff was buried in 1945, then joined in 1974 by her husband, John William Rieff, a professional jockey who rode the winning horses in (among many other races) the Epson Derby (twice), the French Derby, and the Kentucky Oaks; he was inducted into the National Racing Hall of Fame in 1956. Once again, the widely quoted popular narrative is close to the truth, though not quite wholly supported by the facts of the situation upon examination of primary source documents.

In laying out the facts above about Hazel and Victor's mortal remains, it is not our desire to challenge, diminish, or downplay any anguish experienced by the extended Lee family in making final arrangements for their loved ones' burials. Although an "all's well that ends well" narrative summary could be applied to the case of Victor and Hazel's funeral arrangements, it's difficult to imagine the lasting horror, indignity, and suffering that even a short delay between the request for interment and the actual burial in the desired plot would have caused, especially given the illogical and immoral reasoning behind the racial segregation of human remains or behind any institutional efforts to disallow a family from burying their loved ones as and where they desired.

Chapter Seven. Hazel Ying Lee and Victor Ying Lee

Although longtime River View employees and volunteers assert that there were never formal policies documenting "Whites Only" or "Chinese Only" sections at the cemetery, that does not mean that staff at the time could not have caused the family anguish by invoking unilateral, unofficial practices or simply pressing the Lees to have Victor and Hazel buried alongside other Chinese people in other sections of the cemetery. Searches through River View's records do indicate that there are other people of Chinese birth or descent in the same section as Hazel and Victor, and similarly there are no sections that are exclusive to Chinese interments, though there are clusters in several areas with higher densities of people of Chinese descent.

River View executive director Rachel Essig concurs with our findings and assessments, noting that "I cannot say how people spoke to the Chinese community back then. What I do know is there are a lot of Chinese buried at River View and not just one area but rather mixed in with European names. But I always say to the Chinese community and anyone else asking, that things were different back then and it could be how they were spoken to or some other racist act that caused them anguish. There are concentrations of Chinese in certain areas of the cemetery, but I've always presumed that is because of the feng shui aspect, as the highest concentration areas face east toward Mt. Hood or Mt. St. Helens and the river."

In attempting to reconcile the documented facts of Victor and Hazel's posthumous treatment with the popular stories available online, your authors also spoke at length with Marcus Lee, who has worked to document and honor Portland's Chinese community over the years through his work on the Chinese Consolidated Benevolent Association (CCBA) of Oregon, the Lee Family Association of Portland, and the Lone Fir Cemetery Foundation, among other organizations. (The remains of numerous Chinese Americans originally buried at Lone Fir were relocated to River View Cemetery in 1947, after Multnomah County paved a sizable portion of Lone Fir, later putting a building on the site.)

"Most of my Chinese American family are interred up in River View, so I'm up there quite often, caring for the headstones, taking flowers, just visiting," notes Lee. "And when you research their history, the ripples in the pond tend to spread out to encompass extended family, friends, neighbors, community, et cetera. I'm not a professional in this area, but the stories I've heard in our community about Hazel and Victor Lee pretty much align with the popular telling you have found. One of our elders, Mary Leong, recently passed away, and she was extremely knowledgeable about the history of the Chinese community here in Portland. Mary was instrumental in starting our very modest CCBA Museum, which I care for right now. One of the framed photos up in the hall there is of Hazel and it has a script of Mary's recollections, which also align with the popular public story."

"Let me tell you a personal story," Lee continues.

My grandfather, my first great-uncle, and my fourth great-uncle are all in the same section at River View. There are many other Chinese in this section, too, as well as non–Chinese, just based on the names on the headstones. This is in Section 111, which we call 'The Hole,' and our understanding is that section was where they interred the Chinese and the indigent in years gone by, so that was, in fact, kind of the Chinese section, even if that wasn't based on any documentation or direction from River View. It's kind of on a downhill slope and during the rainy months it's just waterlogged and all that kind of stuff. But in later years, they clearly did allow the burial of Chinese elsewhere within the cemetery, because my grandmother, one of my great-aunties, and some other family members, including my dad, are buried further up on the hill, in more of the "white sections."

When my Grandmother Lee passed away in 1970, the family had her interred up in that section on the hill, very beautiful place, beautiful view, mostly white people in that section. But they would not allow the family to inscribe the headstone for Grandma with any Chinese characters. In fact, if you look at the headstones of other Chinese interred in that section up there, they're all in English. But for us, traditionally, it was very important to have the Chinese characters in there, because the Chinese characters would usually tell the village that that individual came from and their true family name, not just their English "paper name." So according to my aunt, she had to threaten a discrimination lawsuit against River View before they backed down, and the family was able to have Chinese characters inscribed into the headstone along with the English. And then after 1970 you see a lot more of that up there.

"So, for the people I've known over the years up there, it can be kind of a difficult thing to share and talk about," concludes Lee. "Because we're not trying to point fingers, and we're not trying to visit the sins of the fathers upon the children, or to condemn someone. We're just saying: This is the way it was. It's a process, a process of education. In my experience, you often run into a brick wall with the elders when you bring up these things, as they just don't want to talk about some of these issues, because they're so painful. Or maybe they're humiliated by them. It's a tough line: we may not be pointing fingers or laying blame, but folks on the side of that coin perhaps see what happened from a very different perspective."

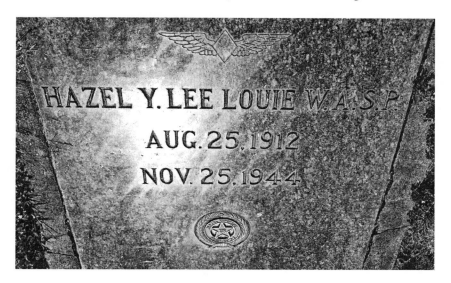

Hazel Lee's grave (J. Eric Smith).

Hazel and the other 37 fallen WASPs did not live to see it, but mere weeks after her burial, the WASP program was dissolved in December 1944. It was as if their service did not matter and was to be erased in "normal" non-wartime days, with the expectation that they would all return to the "normal" gender expectations of the times. But the trail-blazing pilots and their allies were tenacious in the years and decades that followed, seeking not only respect for their work during World War II but also recognition that they had indeed performed services that were an integral part of the nation's wartime activities and that had required them to complete and achieve levels of skill and expertise that few of their male colleagues could match or challenge.

Their efforts were belatedly rewarded in 1977, when President Jimmy Carter signed an act into law that granted the WASPs veteran status with full benefits. In 2010, around 200 of the surviving WASP pilots were further honored when President Barack Obama presented them with the Congressional Gold Medal.

Hazel's widower, "Clifford" Louie Yim-Qun, continued on as a prominent and powerful member of the Chinese air force, serving in a variety of leadership roles and eventually achieving the rank of lieutenant general. He retired from the military in 1974, and served as CEO and chairman of the board for China Airlines until 1978. He remarried, had three children, and passed away in 1999 at the age of 94.

River View Cemetery remains a beautiful, historic site, worthy of a visit should one find oneself with time and inclination in Portland; when one of your authors visited Victor's and Hazel's graves in the summer of 2021, both had coins and other objects atop them, indicating that they are remembered and that their burial places are actively being visited by others. River View's website has a historical tour page that lists prominent members of the community who have been buried at the cemetery over the years, with explanations of their accomplishments and pointers to their markers. We regret to note that Hazel Ying Lee and Victor Ying Lee are not included on the list of honorees at the time of this writing. Nor are any other Chinese Americans. Nor any other non–Caucasian deceased, for that matter.

We'll certainly presume that situation is the result of an oversight in comparing and contrasting Victor and Hazel's accomplishments to those of other River View decedents, and not an active policy decision about who may appear on the modern website. Just as we'd like to presume that the segregation of the dead (either via explicit policy or via harder-to-track unofficial practices) for racial reasons is a thing of a distant and ill-informed past in our nation. But a mere 30-seconds' worth of online searching reveals this story, with a dateline of January 2021:

> A southwest Louisiana cemetery refused to accept the remains of a recently deceased Black man, citing Jim Crow–era bylaws that permitted such exclusions. Allen Parish Sheriff's Deputy Darrell Semien, 55, died this week after a brief battle with bladder cancer, and he had hoped to be buried close to his

Victor Lee's grave (J. Eric Smith).

home in Oberlin, about halfway between New Orleans and Houston. When loved ones of Semien, who was Black, approached Oaklin Springs Baptist Cemetery, they were rebuffed by a representative who said the graveyard was for whites only.

That particular cemetery's board of directors have since amended their bylaws (written in 1955) to remove the offending and offensive policy. But, still again, imagine the shock and pain that Deputy Semien's family experienced in being told their recently deceased loved one's remains were not worthy of being buried next to the remains of other people's loved ones, just because they looked differently in life. This, sadly, has not been, is not, and will not likely be an isolated story or situation in our country since the time that Hazel and Victor Ying Lee's family suffered some form of discrimination and anguish while trying to honor their fallen heroes' memories.

We've certainly come a long way in pursuit of social justice and equity as a nation since Victor and Hazel died for our causes in November 1944. But our collective journey along that path is not yet over, not by a long shot.

CHAPTER EIGHT

James Clifton "Mandy" Colbert (1928–1951), Roosevelt Colbert (1898–1944), and Gilford Weems (Unknown–1939)

Annapolis National Cemetery, Annapolis, Maryland

"History has its foreground and its background, and it is principally in the management of its perspective that one artist differs from another. Some events must be represented on a large scale, others diminished; the great majority will be lost in the dimness of the horizon, and a general idea of their joint effects will be given by a few slight touches."
—Thomas Babington Macaulay

"We read history through our prejudices."
—Wendell Phillips

On a macro basis, the professional study of history hinges on the documentation and interpretation of events in the past, ostensibly with an eye toward predictive analysis of the ways in which events gone by can and will influence events happening now and events yet to come. Professional historians routinely apply a variety of tools to shape their written output, ideally including real-time, firsthand, primary documentation (when such is available), along with contemporaneous and after-the-fact reporting by journalists and other historians, a wide variety of public and private documentation that may or may not have ever been lifted into the realm of public discourse, and (in cases where the events being documented are recent enough to allow it) oral histories of and personal interviews with witnesses to the events being documented for posterity. Rigorous research and documentation are key tenets hewed to with fervor by any historian worth his or her salt, and the closer their sources are to the events they document, the better they are as meaningful, objective touch points for the historical extrapolations they might inspire.

It should come as no surprise if you've made it this far in this book that your authors are personal devotees of the role that cemeteries and the documentation associated with interments can play in understanding history and gleaning meaning from the burial sites and circumstances associated with the lives of our forebears. In the chapters before this one and those yet to come, we have worked as diligently as we might to begin with facts related to adjacent burials and then to follow high-level primary documentation (both written and spoken) toward deeper truths about and explorations into why certain persons lie in perpetual proximity. We see cemeteries as markers, or mileposts, or landmarks, planted at specific times, yet charting courses of longer-term narratives that both predate and survive the ostensible subjects of our work here. If history is ultimately about the act of remembering, then cemeteries stand high on the list of places where such historical reflection can occur, ideally inspiring forays into the bigger and broader questions that any grave, or any pairs or groups of graves, can inspire on their own.

When we first became aware of the stories of this chapter's subjects (three generations of African American men buried in "perpetual proximity" at the national cemetery in Annapolis, Maryland) in the early stages of our research for this book, we saw an opportunity to explore history as remembrance, celebrating their multigenerational achievements, which we presumed would be clearly documented and therefore readily available for analysis and interpretation. But as we dug deeper, we discovered that the stories of Gilford Weems, Roosevelt Colbert, and James Colbert seemed to be more about the ways in which the historical record can often overlook, or even forget, social, cultural, and political elements that, in their time, were of sizable or significant import. In assessing the stories of the Weems-Colbert family, it became increasingly apparent to us that many facets of their combined narratives were deeply anchored in the ways in which their lives, their deaths, and their final resting places occurred at the margins of popularly written and remembered history. As a result of that realization, this chapter will spin in a slightly different direction than those preceding and following it, exploring gaps, omissions, adjacencies, and other aspects and elements that shaped their lives, rather than providing a deep dig into their specific experiences and stories, admirable though they were and remain.

We begin by considering the city in which the three men are buried: Annapolis, Maryland. The modern capital of the Old Line State began its European-governed existence when the settlement of Providence was established on the north shore of the Severn River by Puritan exiles from the Dominion of Virginia. Struggling to tame and live within the local geography, the original settlers later moved to a better-protected harbor on the Severn's south shore, cycling through a series of names for their nascent community including Town at Proctor's, Town at the Severn, and Anne Arundel's Towne. The community was riven over the ensuing decades as its mother country, England, struggled through its own Civil War; the Battle of the Severn, fought between Puritan settlers and monarchists loyal to Lord Baltimore in 1655, was the first colonial naval battle to be waged in North America. Following the restoration of Charles II as king in England, Maryland's Catholic government was overthrown, and royal governor Francis Nicholson moved the colony's capital to Anne Arundel's Towne, renaming it Annapolis, after Princess Anne of Denmark and Norway, soon to become Queen Anne of Great Britain. Annapolis was incorporated as a city in 1708, and grew rapidly through the remainder of the 18th century, eventually becoming a prominent political and administrative center, a major port of entry for marine traffic and commerce, and a crucial hub for the Atlantic slave trade.

Annapolis's long history (by the relative standards of European settlement in the Americas) makes it a choice modern destination for those interested in exploring America's past through "cemetery tourism." St. Anne's Cemetery is the oldest extant graveyard in Maryland's capital city, having been established in 1692, and having long served as the sole burial site in the colonial city; one of the most aged tombs on the site hosts the mortal remains of Amos Garrett, the first mayor of Annapolis, who died on March 8, 1727. The host church of the cemetery, St. Anne's Episcopal, is an iconic part of downtown Annapolis's streetscape and skyline, though in the list of "forgotten things," the current incarnation of St. Anne's is the third church to make its home in that city's "Church Circle," two earlier versions of the sacred space having been destroyed by fire. Although burials at the main St. Anne's site ended in 1800, more than 6,500 people were laid to rest beneath its now pleasant, if busy, sward. Other notable interments at St. Anne's include:

- Brothers John and William Kielty, whose monuments are the only ones at St. Anne's to note the American Revolutionary War;
- Captain James Iredell Wadell, once captain of the Confederate States Ship (CSS) *Shenandoah*, the only CSS vessel to circumnavigate the globe; and
- Richard Randall, a free Black resident of Annapolis who served as an Army physician in the early 1800s, and was appointed in 1828 as governor of Liberia, the African nation established for former American slaves seeking to return to their home continent after achieving their freedom, often under extreme duress and after enduring extreme hardship; life in Liberia at the time remained challenging for its settlers, and Randall died there in 1829, his monument at St. Anne's serving as a cenotaph for all of his home state's freed slaves.

The unquestioned highlight in Annapolis for those interested in cemetery tourism and the stories to be gleaned from such visits is the United States Naval Academy, the federal service academy established along the banks of the Severn River in 1845. (It has long been a running joke among students, faculty, and alumni of the Academy that its official acronym, "USNA," actually stands for "University of Severn, Near Annapolis.") The most spectacular and prominent grave on the Naval Academy's grounds is the tomb of John Paul Jones, arguably the seminal commander of the nascent Continental navy in the American Revolution. Jones was essentially a Scottish maritime mercenary who fled to Virginia after killing a mutinous crew member, becoming one of the earliest ship's captains (most notably on the famed *Bonhomme Richard*) serving the emergent independent American government for which he engaged in a variety of daring and successful (and a smaller number of stupid and unsuccessful) exploits in the Atlantic Ocean. One of the very first things that incoming Naval Academy midshipmen learn is the quote attributed to Jones during the Battle of Flamborough Head off Yorkshire, England, when the *Bonhomme Richard* engaged the HMS *Serapis*, took heavy damage, and was invited to surrender by British captain Richard Pearson. "I have not yet begun to fight," replied Jones, who went on to win the battle.

After the Revolutionary War, John Paul Jones found himself without a command in the American navy, so mercenary that he was, he joined the imperial Russian navy and eventually attained the rank of rear admiral. He relocated to Paris in 1790, dying there two years later of interstitial nephritis; his remains were preserved in alcohol, interred in a lead coffin, and buried in Saint Louis Cemetery for Alien Protestants. Jones was embalmed by his admirers with the understanding that the United States might someday wish to reclaim his remains, which was the case, though it took over a century for them to be properly identified and carried to Annapolis for reinterment beneath the Naval Academy Chapel in 1906. His sarcophagus is truly opulent and spectacular, noting beneath his birth and death dates, "He Gave Our Navy Its Earliest Traditions of Heroism and Victory."

As fine as John Paul Jones's final resting place is, there are countless other impressively historic graves at the nearby Naval Academy Cemetery, including Admiral William J. Crowe and Vice Admiral James Stockdale (and their wives), whose "perpetual proximity" story is recounted in a subsequent chapter of this book. Senator John McCain also lies in the Naval Academy Cemetery next to his lifelong friend, Admiral Charles R. Larson; as recounted by Rear Admiral McNeal in this book's preface, it was their "perpetual proximity" story that originally inspired your authors to undertake this project. Less famously,

The crypt of John Paul Jones, beneath the U.S. Naval Academy Chapel (U.S. Navy).

Midshipman Fourth Class Kristen Dickmann is buried there at the Academy cemetery, too; she died tragically during her "plebe" (freshman) year and was honored most memorably by her classmates during their annual Herndon Monument Ceremony, a story first fully told in Rear Admiral McNeal's earlier book with Scott Tomasheski, *The Herndon Climb: A History of the United States Naval Academy's Greatest Tradition* (U.S. Naval Institute Press, 2020). And Fleet Admiral Ernest J. King also lies nearby; he was chief of naval operations during World War II, is one of only four people to hold the rank of fleet admiral, and is the namesake for King Hall, the massive Naval Academy dining facility where the entire brigade of midshipmen gather three times a day for hearty, shockingly high-quality meals.

The Naval Academy's official website describes King Hall's operation thusly: "Optimum efficiency is the only thing that can prevent utter chaos when more than 4,400 people sit down at one time for dinner at 392 tables spread over a 55,000-square-foot area. Hot meals are served to all within five minutes, reflecting the efficiency that exists in King Hall. The staff in the Academy's Midshipmen Food Service Division plan, prepare and serve more than 13,500 meals per day. Statistics of the operation are impressive, from the capacity of the automated food preparation equipment in the galley to the scullery which handles

Contemporary view of King Hall, U.S. Naval Academy, where Roosevelt Colbert once worked (MC3 Thomas Bonaparte, Jr., U.S. Navy).

more than 40,000 pieces of silver, dishes and glassware for an average meal." Roosevelt Colbert, one of the three men whose story frames this chapter, was a longtime member of that food service team, working diligently to satisfy the hunger of a horde of young White men, most of whom never would have dreamed of a world where they could and would have actually sat side by side with him to break bread, given the racial standards and norms of those times.

Countless other notable naval and Marine Corps heroes lie at the Academy's cemetery, nestled around a complex of shady hills north of the College Creek, alongside innumerable lesser-known alumni, family members, and midshipmen who died while at the Academy or in service to their nation in the years following their departures from the shores of the Severn; we will further explore this site and two side-by-side graves there in a subsequent chapter. It is a treasure trove for those interested in visiting the mortal remains of an impressive cohort of individuals who profoundly shaped American and global history. As a general rule, to experience a similarly grand collection of acclaimed military service members lying in such close quarters, one would have to visit one of the federally operated national cemeteries (or another service academy graveyard), the governance and establishment of which we will cover in more depth in a subsequent chapter. As it happens, Annapolis is also home to one of those federal facilities, where Gilford Weems, James Colbert, and Roosevelt Colbert lie in close familial proximity.

Annapolis National Cemetery was one of the original 14 national cemeteries established by President Abraham Lincoln in 1862 to accommodate the Union dead in the American Civil War. It is located on a 4.1-acre plot at the junction of Taylor Avenue and West Street, a stone's throw from the parking areas of Navy–Marine Corps Memorial Stadium, which are filled to overflowing half-a-dozen times each and every autumn for tailgate activities associated with the Naval Academy's beloved football team. Both of your authors attended the Naval Academy in the 1980s. Neither of us have any conscious memory of the importance of the graveyard we'd routinely pass on foot as we transitioned from game-time festivities to post-game debauchery at the bars and restaurants of downtown Annapolis. And we doubt that many of today's midshipmen would have any more idea than we did 40 years ago as to the historical significance of the site.

Part of Annapolis National Cemetery's low profile has to do with the fact that it is not home to the graves of any particularly prominent historical figures so that its pool of regular visitors tend to be limited to the relatives of the 3,100 decedents buried there; it has long been closed for new interments, except in cases of "one over one" burials of family members who wish to lie with veterans already buried there, or when the occasional disinterment results in a spot being freed up for those on its long waiting list for potential burials.

Although actual combat activity was limited in and around Annapolis during the Civil War, a large "parole camp" was located nearby (in the community now known as "Parole, Maryland"), where Union prisoners who had been exchanged for Confederate prisoners were held until they could be returned to their own units. Many of the Union soldiers barracked at the parole camp near Annapolis were grievously wounded upon their arrival, and for the parol-

Gate marker of Annapolis National Cemetery (James R. McNeal).

ees who arrived there healthy, local sanitation conditions were such that waves of smallpox, dysentery, and typhoid routinely took heavy tolls of the unfortunate soldiers, resulting in high mortality rates. Other nearby parole camps and field hospitals also stood as unhygienic meat grinders, and as a result, the vast majority of the early interments at Annapolis National Cemetery were of enlisted men (officers were not subjected to such conditions) who had died in parole camps and hospitals, and not on battlefields. That doesn't make their suffering and sacrifice any less profound, but it does tend to reduce the incentive of nonfamily members to make pilgrimages to such sites, and history almost always remembers the officers who lead men more than it remembers the men who serve under officers. Perhaps most tellingly, within the vast "FindAGrave" website's core database, which has become the web's most extensive repository of freely available cemetery information, when one searches for "notable graves" at Annapolis National Cemetery, the search engine returns a "None" result.

Side by Side in Eternity

The land on which Annapolis National Cemetery is located was originally leased to the federal government by Judge Nichols Brewer, whose family later sold the site outright after the judge's death in 1864 to ensure the continual operation of the cemetery under federal control. Immediately adjacent to the national cemetery is another graveyard that reflects Judge Brewer's one-time prominent influence in Annapolis: Brewer Hill Cemetery is a 4.5-acre parcel with over 7,000 interred souls, its oldest known marker dating to 1789. Why was this parcel separated from the land sold to the federal government for the national cemetery? Because it was originally the burial site for Judge Brewer's servants and slaves, along with other members of Annapolis's Black community, and the standards of the times dictated that Black and White Americans could not generally be buried in the same consecrated ground.

Brewer Hill Cemetery was purchased from Judge Brewer's son for $758 in 1884 by 11 men from nearby Mount Moriah African Episcopal Methodist Church and has been maintained and (in the 1990s) restored by Black Annapolitans ever since that time. Had James Colbert, Roosevelt Colbert, and Gilford Weems not been (begrudgingly) granted burial rights at Annapolis National Cemetery as small tokens of gratitude for their service to their nation (which included, in James Colbert's case, his death), they undoubtedly would have been buried just

View of Brewer Hill Cemetery (background) and Annapolis National Cemetery (foreground) (James R. McNeal).

up West Street alongside generations of Annapolis's Black citizenry. The most prominent marker (and the only obelisk) at Brewer Hill Cemetery belongs to Wiley H. Bates, a native North Carolinian who came to Annapolis in 1872, becoming a prominent businessman, civic leader, and (eventually) an elected alderman, from which position he worked diligently to create opportunities for Black children through his philanthropic and entrepreneurial activities. The Weems and Colbert families would have undoubtedly been familiar with him, even if the popular histories of Annapolis, recorded primarily by his White neighbors and their descendants, largely forget (at best) or ignore (more likely) his contributions to his community.

Roughly halfway as the crow flies between the Annapolis National Cemetery–Brewer Hill Cemetery complex and the Naval Academy Cemetery is another tiny, historical burial site with a marker honoring another forgotten hero of another forgotten conflict. U.S. Marine Corps private Hugh Purvis is buried at St. Anne's Cemetery, and visitors to his grave will usually find a small blue flag honoring him as a recipient of the congressional Medal of Honor, the highest acclamation given for distinguished service and conspicuous bravery in combat conditions. Purvis was awarded his Medal of Honor for his combat service in Korea, which might perplex casual visitors who note that he died in 1922, some three decades before the Korean War that most (though not all; more on that below) Americans can remember from their own family histories or from long-ago classroom experiences in studying 20th-century American history.

It will likely come as a surprise to most readers to learn that the United States had engaged in military action on the Korean Peninsula long before the Korean War and long before World War II, waging the Battle of Ganghwa (also known as Shinmiyangyo) on June 10, 1871, after the U.S. Navy sent an expedition to open relations with "Corea: The Hermit Nation" (as it was described in the title of a book written by William Elliott Griffis in 1882), and its commander decided that the Koreans might need a bit of forceful persuasion before they would allow Western mercantile interests into their isolated country. The United States had deployed a similar approach with Japan in 1854 when Commodore Matthew Perry sailed his fleet into Tokyo Bay, securing a commercial treaty with the Japanese government as its leaders considered their position at the business end of the American navy's most formidable naval armaments.

Although American interests largely turned inward during and immediately after the Civil War, by the early 1870s, businesses once again became interested in further engaging lucrative Asian markets or, perhaps more importantly, in exploiting lucrative Asian natural resources. In August 1866, a U.S. merchant ship, *The General Sherman*, attempted to sail up the Taedong River (which runs through modern-day Pyongyang), disregarded warnings (ostensibly friendly ones) to turn back before the tide receded, ran aground, then sent out raiding parties to provision their larders for however long it took them to free themselves from the sandbar on which they had beached themselves. The local Koreans even-

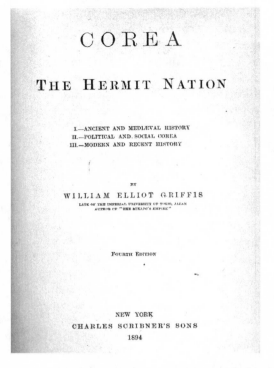

COREA

THE HERMIT NATION

I.—ANCIENT AND MEDIÆVAL HISTORY
II.—POLITICAL AND SOCIAL COREA
III.—MODERN AND RECENT HISTORY

BY

WILLIAM ELLIOT GRIFFIS
LATE OF THE IMPERIAL UNIVERSITY OF TOKIO, JAPAN
AUTHOR OF "THE MIKADO'S EMPIRE"

FOURTH EDITION

NEW YORK
CHARLES SCRIBNER'S SONS
1894

Title page of *Corea: The Hermit Kingdom* by William Elliot Griffis (1882) (Library of Congress).

tually had enough of such behavior, attacking the ship, and killing its crew. The mysterious disappearance of *The General Sherman* (the Koreans refused to divulge what had happened to the ship) eventually led to the deployment of the "Korean Expedition of 1871," which sailed under the command of Admiral John Rogers from Nagasaki with five warships and 1,200 soldiers, including Private Hugh Purvis, determined to find *The General Sherman* or avenge its loss, and to force the Korean government into the same type of commercial treaty that the Japanese had signed, under duress, nearly 20 years earlier.

The Koreans remained defiant. So on June 10, Admiral Rogers directed an attack on the Choji Garrison, a poorly defended position with limited armaments, on the island of Ganghwado. Private Purvis's Congressional Medal of Honor citation notes that "braving the enemy fire, Purvis was the first to scale the walls of the fort and capture the flag of the Korean forces." Nine sailors and five other marines received their own Medals of Honor for their valor that day, despite the historically questionable nature of their military endeavor. The Korean name for the battle, "Shinmiyangyo," translates to "Western disturbance in the Shinmi year," and the day marks the very first (but by no means the last) time that the Stars and Stripes were raised over an Asian territory by force. As it turned out, it was to be a short-lived occupation: the Koreans were not persuaded to sign a commercial treaty by the American action, instead sending massive reinforcements with then-modern weaponry to repel the American invaders. Deciding that discretion was the better part of valor, Admiral Rogers weighed anchor and set sail for China three weeks later. It took another 11 years before a commercial treaty, establishing "permanent relations of amity and friendship" was finally signed between Korea and the United States in 1882, this time without bloodshed.

Seven decades later, the United States again found itself embroiled in conflict on the Korean Peninsula, this time in a much more massive and tragic undertaking, the intensity and severity of which somehow seems to have faded in the historic rearview mirrors through which most Americans view our military history. In an admittedly unscientific poll conducted by one of your authors in an online forum that he frequents, contributors were asked to list the first five wars that came to mind when they considered American military history. The "winners" so recognized were the Civil War, the Revolutionary War, World War II, World War I, and the Vietnam War, in that order of mention frequency. At the time this little survey was being conducted, American forces were actively withdrawing from Afghanistan after 20 years of active warfare there, and yet that conflict had seemingly already slipped into a "second tier" ranking in terms of the wars that Americans actively remember and consider most important.

Although the Revolutionary War is certainly a crucial formative event in our nation's history, in terms of actual casualties, it was a relatively gentle affair in the ways that such tragedies are measured, resulting in approximately 50,000 soldiers being killed, wounded, or declared missing. When Confederate forces are counted, the Civil War remains America's bloodiest conflict, with approximately 1.1 million casualties. The escalation in carnage between the two wars bookmarking and largely defining the United States' first century was largely driven by advances in killing technology (e.g., machine guns, ironclad warships, more powerful ordnance, more lethal bullets, etc.). It was also the first

American war that was extensively photographed and that involved aerial reconnaissance and telegraphed news from battlefields, so civilian understanding of the horrors of war were greatly enhanced through that tumult. World War I (~325,000 American casualties) brough further technological advancements, with chemical warfare, military aviation, and tanks making their battlefield debuts. World War II (nearly as deadly for American combat forces as the Civil War, with another 1.1 million American service casualties) brought the dawn of nuclear warfare, devastating an enemy's homeland, even while it ostensibly saved the lives of countless American soldiers, sailors, airmen, and marines who would have been tasked with invading Japan. Korea sits in fifth place in the tally of American wartime military casualties with about 135,000 killed, wounded, or missing (it was the first war where jet airpower was widely deployed), while Vietnam stands fourth, with about 215,000 casualties.

The real-time carnage of the Korean conflict was severe, though, as it was easily the shortest of those major American wars, so the daily death and dismemberment rates were high, fostered by the ever rising efficacy of killing instruments and by brutally difficult geographic and climate conditions that strongly favored the defense of the region by its citizens over the invading forces of Americans and their allies. It was also unique in being one of the first "proxy war" hot eruptions of the Cold War era and in the fact that like Vietnam and Afghanistan after it, things ended essentially in stalemate conditions that led to Americans returning home without the imprint of a clear victory and with the modern borders between North and South Korea essentially representing the point at which the American forces and their allies could neither push forward nor be repelled farther. Its temporal proximity to World War II often makes it seem like a coda to that larger, longer conflict, and as the first of many engagements between the communist and capitalist worlds, where it can be framed as a particularly nasty chapter of the Cold War, rather than as a significant stand-alone conflict in its own right.

Such after-the-fact perspective and analysis would have been lost on or irrelevant to Private First Class (PFC) James Colbert, who died in Korea on April 24, 1951, becoming the first Korean War casualty to be buried at Annapolis National Cemetery. He lies at the feet of his grandfather, Gilford R. Weems, who had been a private in the 153rd Depot Brigade based at Camp Dix (now Fort Dix) in New Jersey during World War I, working to receive and organize recruits, outfit them with uniforms, equipment, and basic training, and prepare them for deployment to the front lines in France. The 153rd Depot Brigade also played a key role in receiving soldiers returning home at the end of the war, completing their outprocessing and discharges. PFC Colbert lies next to his own father and Gilford's son-in-law, Roosevelt Colbert, who had died in 1944 after diligent service as a mess attendant at the Naval Academy dining hall that now bears Fleet Admiral King's name.

James Colbert had graduated from Bates High School in Annapolis in 1945. He was awarded an athletic scholarship to North Carolina A&T State University, a historically Black land-grant research university in Greensboro, North Carolina. Following in his grandfather's footsteps, Colbert enlisted in the army after graduating from college, was deployed as part of the post–World War II occupying forces in Europe, before transferring to the 24th Infantry Regiment for his tragic final duties in Korea. In another example of that which is forgotten but should be remembered: It's notable that the 24th Infantry Regiment was comprised almost entirely of Black soldiers during its time in Korea, commanded by mostly White officers, despite the fact that President Harry S. Truman had formally desegregated the armed forces in 1948, two years before the Korean War began.

In this book's opening chapter, we told the story of the 54th Massachusetts Infantry Regiment, the second army unit opened for Black soldiers to serve their nation, following the slightly earlier First Kansas Colored Volunteers. In the aftermath of the Civil War, a second wave of Black units was organized, their servicemen known collectively as "the Buffalo Soldiers," a sobriquet originally bestowed on the Tenth Calvary Regiment by the Native Americans who fought against them in the Indian Wars, then expanded to describe all five units formed and mustered in 1866, including the 24th Infantry Regiment. All of the initial recruits for these new units were Black or of mixed-race descent, standing either as veterans of the various U.S. Colored Troops during the Civil War or freedmen seeking professional service opportunities upon having the shackles of slavery lifted from them.

From its formation until 1898, the 24th Infantry served primarily in the territories and emergent states of the American West, garrisoning frontier posts, engaging in the seemingly never-ending conflicts with the Native peoples of the region, providing security for the expanding networks of railroads and roadways, and protecting the border between Mexico and the United States. During the Spanish-American War, the 24th Infantry was deployed to Cuba, then a year later, they were transferred to the Philippines to suppress an emergent guerrilla movement there. After returning to the American mainland, the 24th Infantry spent most of the pre–World War I years along the Mexican border, ensuring that the Mexican Revolution did not spill onto U.S. soil, and occasionally crossing into Mexico itself on various campaigns, most notably under the command of General John J. Pershing in the so-called Punitive Exhibition against Francisco "Pancho" Villa's paramilitary forces.

In 1917, just after the United States entered as an active combatant into World War I, the 24th Infantry was deployed to Houston, Texas, to guard over the construction of Camp Logan, a new military facility. The local White civilians were actively hostile to the members of the 24th Infantry; that animosity boiling over after Private Alonso Edwards of the 24th attempted to intervene during the violent arrest of a local Black woman. Both Edwards and the woman, Sarah Travers, were jailed, and when a Black corporal from the 24th was dispatched to inquire as to the whereabouts of Private Edwards, he was pistol-whipped, shot at, chased, and eventually arrested.

When word of the treatment of their fellow soldiers reached Camp Logan (erroneously, as rumors were rampant that their corporal had been killed), Sergeant Vida Henry of the 24th led about 150 of his fellow soldiers on a legally mutinous and murderous march into Houston, killing 15 White civilians and policemen who attempted to stop their progress and seriously wounding another dozen. Four members of the 24th Infantry were killed on the march and in its violent aftermath (Sergeant Henry shot himself, distraught over having accidentally killed another service member), before the battalion fell into disarray, most of the soldiers making their way back to Camp Logan. The rioters were tried over a series of three mass courts-martial, with 19 men sentenced to death by hanging and 63 awarded life sentences in prison. It was one of the bloodiest single incidents of the era known as "the nadir of American race relations," but it was sadly eclipsed a mere four years later by the horrific Tulsa race massacre.

Following their most ignominious days in Houston, the 24th Infantry endured and were transferred to Fort Benning, Georgia, in the aftermath of the attack on Pearl Harbor. The unit deployed and served gallantly in the South Pacific theater through the entire duration of World War II, ending the war on Saipan and Tinian Island, serving garrison duty that included capturing and disarming (or killing) Japanese soldiers who had refused to surrender following Japan's defeat. In 1945,

Members of the 24th Infantry on trial for mutiny and murder (1917) (U.S. National Archives and Records Administration).

they were deployed to occupy Okinawa, then transferred to Gifu, Japan. On July 26, 1948, President Truman signed Executive Order 9981, which abolished discrimination on the basis of race, color, religion, or national origin in the armed forces. Ostensibly, E.O. 9981 should have resulted in the soldiers of the 24th Infantry being reintegrated into other White units, but as is often the case with such federal dictates, implementation significantly lagged intention. (It certainly didn't help that Secretary of the Army Kenneth C. Royall refused to implement Truman's executive order; he was eventually forced to resign in April 1949.) Most of the actual desegregation of the armed forces took place under President Dwight D. Eisenhower's administration, after the Korean War had ended; the last of the military's all-Black units were not dissolved until September 1954.

The 24th Infantry were active combatants throughout the entire Korean Peninsula, ebbing and flowing north and south in a variety of intense offensive and defensive engagements, including the defense of the Pusan perimeter in August and September 1950, for which they were awarded the Republic of Korea Presidential Unit Citation. Three members of the regiment were posthumously awarded congressional Medals of Honor. But the 24th Infantry Regiment also experienced extremely heavy casualties over the first year of the Korean War, suffered from a lack of supplies, and were victims of alleged atrocities committed by White officers, including the unit being inadvertently bombed by the U.S. Air Force, resulting in severe casualties. The continued segregation and discrimination experienced by their soldiers began to impact their morale and service, blossoming into a full-blown racial incident with the court-martial of Lieutenant Leon Gilbert, who refused a suicidal order to return with 12 of his men to a forward position that they had just been forced to abandon under withering machine-gun fire. Gilbert was arrested and tried on the spot and sentenced to death.

In his defense, Gilbert later noted, "I did not refuse to obey the order. I was trying to explain why it couldn't be carried out. There were twelve men in my command. Then I considered it my duty as an officer to show why the order meant certain death." When word of his sentence reached the public, a massive wave of protests erupted in the United States and beyond, and President Truman eventually commuted his sentence to hard labor, but not before mass courts-martial were staged against entire units of the 24th Infantry Regiment. Future Supreme Court justice Thurgood Marshall, then general counsel of the National Association for the Advancement of Colored People (NAACP) wrote at the time, "The letters we have received from convicted soldiers and the talks we have had with war correspondents strongly indicate that many of these men have been victimized by racial discrimination. It seems apparent that some of them are being made scapegoats for the failures of higher personnel."

In the aftermath of the Gilbert case, in September 1950, the Eighth Army Command ordered the 24th Infantry Regiment disbanded, but because the army was unable to mobilize a new regiment in its place, the 24th continued to serve as an active unit for over a year after they were ordered to disperse. Following a rout of the 24th Infantry Regiment's First Battalion after the crossing of the Han River in March 1951, troop morale continued to crater, and racially driven antipathy and hostility grew more evident and prominent among the White senior officers in the Korean theater, even though objective analysis by Colonel Thomas D. Gillis, who had become the regiment's commander, concluded that leadership had been the primary problem for the unit, and not troop capabilities or loyalty; he relieved a number of officers as a result of his review. Despite continued brave and faithful service through the waning days of the Korean War, the 24th Infantry Regiment was relieved of its frontline duties in October 1951 so that it could be unceremoniously dissolved. (A fully integrated 24th Infantry Regiment was reconstituted in 1995, serving in combat roles in both Iraq and Afghanistan. After a 2006 reorganization, a single battalion assigned to the 25th Infantry Division was granted the 24th Infantry Regiment designation and preserves the unit's legacy. At the time of this writing, they are based at Fort Wainwright, Alaska.)

PFC James Colbert was one of many members of the original 24th Infantry Regiment who did not live to see its demise, nor to be given the opportunity to serve in a properly desegregated unit, as he had been killed in action six months before its dissolution. His story, the story of the community within which he was raised, and the story of the cemetery where his remains lie with his military forebears, within eyesight of a cemetery filled with friends, family members, and ancestors who were not given the option to be buried wherever they wished simply because of the color of their skin, all remind us once again that history as an act of simple remembrance is often complicated by messy facts and considerations that have been forgotten (at best) or suppressed in the "official" crafting of various overarching narratives.

A 2020 editorial in Annapolis's *Capital Gazette* marked the 70th anniversary of the beginning of the Korean War by celebrating Colbert's life and sacrifice, along with the lives and sacrifices of PFC Charles Edward Kirby, Private Bernard Isaacs, and Sergeant Charles Wenn, three other Black soldiers who had died in the Korean War and been buried at Annapolis National Cemetery. That thoughtful article contained a final anecdote about how remembering important little things can often be as meaningful to those closest to historical events as attempting to remember or re-create the overarching narratives.

"When [Colbert]'s mother talked about her son to *The Evening Capital* just before his funeral at Asbury Methodist Church," the *Gazette*'s editorial writers recounted, "she pointed to the parakeets he'd brought her from Germany and his trophies from high school and college. But she wanted to make sure the reporter, who reported his status as the first Korean war casualty to be buried in the national cemetery, knew his name. The paper had called him James in its first story. 'You can just call him Mandy. His real name is James, but they all called him *Mandy*.'"

Let's remember that about him, even if we forget everything else.

CHAPTER NINE

Virgil I. "Gus" Grissom (1926–1967) and Roger B. Chaffee (1935–1967)

Arlington National Cemetery,
Arlington, Virginia

Edward H. White II (1930–1967)

West Point Cemetery, U.S. Military Academy,
West Point, New York

"All great and honorable actions are accompanied with great difficulties, and both must be enterprised and over-come with answerable courage."
—William Bradford

"Night brings out stars, as sorrow shows us truths."
—Philip James Bailey

On September 12, 1962, President John F. Kennedy gave one of the 20th century's most memorable speeches at Rice University in Houston, Texas. The key and most frequently cited quotation from his 33-minute address was the president's call to put American astronauts on the moon and return them safely to Earth before the end of the decade. The call to action was justified thusly in Kennedy's inimitable style: "We choose to go to the moon. We choose to go to the moon in this decade and do the other things, not because they are easy, but because they are hard, because that goal will serve to organize and measure the best of our energies and skills, because that challenge is one that we are willing to accept, one we are unwilling to postpone, and one which we intend to win, and the others, too."

As a historical footnote, "the other things" Kennedy refers to in that most famous quote allude to the preceding portion of his remarks, where he asked rhetorically why people climb the highest mountains, or why an American had flown solo across the Atlantic Ocean some 35 years earlier, or why tiny, erudite Rice University bothered to play the mighty juggernaut University of Texas in football. Kennedy went on to candidly acknowledge that compared to America's Cold War space race rivals in the Soviet Union, "We are behind, and will be behind for some time in manned flight. But we do not intend to stay behind, and in this decade, we shall make up and move ahead." (At the time of the Rice speech, the United States had amassed two suborbital and two orbital flights of the single-astronaut Mercury spacecraft, while the Soviets had followed Yuri Gagarin's first manned orbital flight in April 1961 with three longer orbital flights in the two-cosmonaut Vostok craft.) Before discussing the budgetary, scientific, engineering, and industrial aspects of his call for national greatness and glory, Kennedy also acknowledged the existence of various high-profile launch failures in the uncrewed components of the American space program, stating, "We have had our failures, but so have others, even if they do not admit them. And they may be less public."

In an era of federal bipartisanship that's likely incomprehensible in modern American political discourse, the financial spigots in Washington were opened to their fullest, and the American space program did indeed proceed with alacrity and intensity in the year following President Kennedy's inspirational call to action. Although his tragic assassination in November 1963 could well have been used by federal executives and legislators as a valid excuse to stand down from Kennedy's audacious (and expensive) goal, President Lyndon Baines Johnson was steadfast in his support for the space program, later noting, "We will not abandon our dream. We will never evacuate the frontiers of space to any other nation. I repeat that pledge, and I repeat that purpose, to you and to the Nation."

To his credit, Johnson did not hew to this position from a cold start after he became president: he had been instrumental as a Texas senator in writing, championing, and securing passage of the Space Act of 1958, which established the National Aeronautics and Space Administration (NASA), and he also chaired the National Space Council as Kennedy's vice president. Although JFK receives plentiful due historic credit for his public challenge to the nation to send a man to the moon, there's little doubt that LBJ was the key advisor in convincing Kennedy that such a massive federal space program could reap scientific, economic, and political benefits, all of which would have been deeply appealing to the White House and its core advisors in the aftermath of Yuri Gagarin's flight, the Bay of Pigs disaster, and just before the Cuban missile crisis added additional layers of menace to the intensifying Cold War between the United States and the Soviet Union.

With President Johnson's continuing commitment to putting Americans on the moon before the end of the 1960s, NASA, its vast industrial base, and the first groups of U.S. astronauts (the charismatic faces of the program) did indeed make rapid strides through the end of 1966. The single-seat Mercury program was completed in 1963 after six flights. (One of the famed original "Mercury Seven" astronauts, Donald K. "Deke" Slayton, was medically disqualified from flight due to atrial fibrillation.) Mercury's successor program, Project Gemini, had featured nine successful launches of two-man crews into low Earth orbit, testing and proving a variety of key concepts necessary for travel to the moon, most notably spacecraft docking, "extra-vehicular activities" (i.e., space walks), and physiological and psychological evaluations of how astronauts could and should thrive over long space missions in the closest of personal proximity. Gemini XII, the final flight of that program, had been a great success in November 1966, setting the stage in 1967 for the capstone element of the evolving moon-landing endeavor: Project Apollo.

The first crewed Apollo mission, designated by NASA as AS-204, was scheduled to launch on February 21, 1967, and was intended to test and prove the Apollo command and service modules in low Earth orbit. The command module was the conic capsule that housed the crew, atop the cylindrical service module, which held propulsion, communications, and life-support equipment, along with the fuel required to propel and maneuver the manned components of the spacecraft after the launch stages had been jettisoned; together, the unit was known as the CSM. In a fully configured moon flight, the CSM would be joined by the then-still-in-development Lunar Excursion Module (LEM), the delicate and iconic buglike craft that actually descended with two crew members to the surface of the moon from lunar orbit, then launched the moonwalkers back into lunar orbit for a reunion with their third crewmate, left orbiting in the CSM. AS-204 was to launch atop a Saturn IB launch vehicle, while the mighty Saturn V (the first rocket that could actually carry men to the moon) was also still in development and testing.

For the first launch of the (partial) spacecraft that would eventually ferry astronauts to the moon, NASA (with firm input from Deke Slayton, who had turned his post-grounding "desk job" as chief of the Astronaut Office into a formidable power position within the astronaut corps) selected an all-star trio of astronauts. The command pilot was Virgil I. "Gus" Grissom, one of the original Mercury Seven astronauts, the second American in space, and command pilot of the first crewed Gemini flight. AS-204's senior pilot was Edward H. White II, a veteran of Gemini IV, the second of the "next nine" astronauts after the original Mercury Seven to fly, and the first American to perform an EVA. Rounding out the crew was rookie Roger B. Chaffee, serving as the mission's pilot; Chaffee had replaced fellow rookie Donn Eisele on the AS-204 crew after Eisele had suffered two shoulder dislocations during weightlessness training aboard the KC-135 "vomit comet" reduced-gravity training plane.

Despite the successes of Projects Mercury and Gemini, the Apollo craft were fraught with technical difficulties, even as their production and delivery schedules grew tighter with the end of the decade approaching. The

Virgil I. "Gus" Grissom's official astronaut portrait (National Aeronautics and Space Administration).

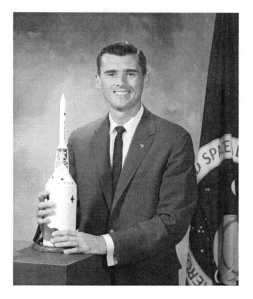

Roger Chaffee's official astronaut portrait (National Aeronautics and Space Administration).

161

Astronaut Ed White performs the first American extra-vehicular activity ("space walk"); photo by Commander James McDivitt (National Aeronautics and Space Administration).

CSM was larger and more complicated than any previous spacecraft, and it was undergoing rapid and frequent design changes throughout its final development and testing phases, leading to frustration from its first crew, as their simulators could not keep pace with the evolving configurations of the real craft they were to pilot into orbit. In August 1966, the crew raised concerns with the Apollo Spacecraft Program Office (ASPO) about the amount of flammable material in the crew cabin, eventually sending ASPO manager Joseph F. Shea a photo of the trio with their hands clasped and heads bowed in prayer over a model of their command module, with an inscription noting, "It isn't that we don't trust you, Joe, but this time we've decided to go over your head."

AS-204's CSM was assembled, modified, repaired, tweaked, and reassembled multiple times between those August meetings and the end of 1966, with the full spacecraft not completing its required altitude chamber tests successfully until December 30. Those tests were administered under the direction of the mission's backup crew, commanded by Grissom's fellow Mercury Seven veteran Walter Schirra, who was less than enthusiastic about his experiences aboard the new CSM. According to fellow astronaut Jim Lovell (who later commanded the ill-fated Apollo 13 mission), Schirra informed Grissom that "something about [the CSM] just doesn't ring right" and that Grissom should get out at the first signs of equipment or material failures and malfunctions.

The CSM was mounted atop its Saturn IB launch vehicle on Pad 34 at Cape Kennedy Air Force Station (now known as Cape Canaveral Space Force Station) on January 6, 1967. Testing and maintenance continued apace toward the planned February launch date. At 1:00 p.m. on January 27, the AS-204 crew entered their command module atop its launch vehicle for a "plugs-out" test designed to affirm that the spacecraft could operate while detached from gantry cables and umbilical cords, an essential milestone on the launch schedule. The test was

Grissom, White, and Chaffee standing before the AS-204 stack on its launch pad, ten days before their deaths (National Aeronautics and Space Administration).

considered to be "nonhazardous," as the launch vehicle was free of fuel and cryogenic coolant and all pyrotechnic bolts used to separate stages had been disabled. The tests did not proceed according to plan due to a variety of technical issues, including failures in the communications loops between the control center and the spacecraft. A peeved Grissom barked as the delays lengthened, "How are we going to get to the Moon if we can't talk between two or three buildings?" At 6:30 p.m., after the crew had already spent five and half hours sealed in the high-pressure, 100 percent oxygen atmosphere of the command module, the count-down clock still showed "T-minus 10 minutes" until the simulated "plugs-out" moment when power would be transferred to the rocket stack's internal systems.

Tragically, the countdown clock was never to advance past that mark. At 6:31 p.m., mission staff in the control blockhouse observed a power spike in one of the CSM's alternating current buses, followed by a voice (believed to be Grissom) shouting "Hey! Fire!" Sounds of scuffling ensued, along with a garbled transmission generally believed to be from Chaffee saying, "We've got a fire in the cockpit," followed by silence, a final garbled communication, and an audible cry of pain. The sudden intensity of the fire in the capsule's pure oxygen atmosphere caused a massive air pressure spike which ruptured the command module's inner wall, allowing flames to erupt into the launch pad support struc-tures. Heat and smoke held frantic pad workers at bay for nearly five minutes before they could access and open the hatch to the command module. But their efforts were to no avail: astronauts Grissom, Chaf-fee, and White were dead by the time their would-be rescuers reached them. It then took seven and a half hours for the ground crew to remove the astronauts from the capsule, and 27 crew members were treated for smoke inhalation and other injuries as a result of the fire and its aftermath.

The trio's tongue-in-cheek appeal to a higher power in August 1966 had been fruitless in large part because many of the predictable and preventable issues that they and their backup crew had raised were not given the serious consideration they deserved from those entrusted with their health, safety, and well-being. The CSM development program was grounded for 20 months while NASA and a variety of federal oversight boards attempted to understand how this tragedy had unfolded and how (or whether) the Apollo program could proceed in its aftermath. (Testing on the Lunar Module and Saturn V rocket continued in 1967.) The final investigation report concluded that the astronauts' primary

The Apollo I capsule after the fire that killed astronauts Grissom, Chaffee, and White (National Aeronautics and Space Administration).

cause of death was cardiac arrest caused by the lethal atmosphere of the cabin as various flammable materials (including the astronauts' own life-protecting suits) melted and off-gassed slews of toxins; although all three astronauts suffered severe third-degree burns, it was concluded that most of those burns had occurred after the trio had died.

The review ultimately identified five major causes for the fatal accident:

- A spacecraft power cable shorted to provide an ignition source, possibly caused by the leak of a combustible and corrosive coolant.
- The spacecraft's high-pressure, pure-oxygen environment rapidly fueled the emergent fire.
- The command module's cabin was sealed and could not be quickly removed by the astronauts or pad crew at high pressure.
- The cabin was still filled with combustible material.
- There were inadequate emergency preparedness policies for crew escape or rescue.

As the managers, politicians, and bureaucrats entrusted with oversight of NASA and its programs were going about their investigative work, the AS-204 astronauts' families were left with the grim task of memorializing and burying their loved ones, taken from them long before their due time. The astronauts' widows asked that their husbands' mission, AS-204, be redesignated as "Apollo 1" in recognition of the flight they never made. On April 24, 1967, NASA officially announced that AS-204 would be recorded as Apollo 1: "The first crewed Apollo Saturn flight, failed on ground test." Although the three astronauts had died shoulder to shoulder in their spacecraft, only Grissom and Chaffee were laid to rest side by side in Arlington National Cemetery. Their crewmate Ed White was interred some 250 miles to the northeast in the West Point Cemetery at the United States Military Academy; he lies a stone's throw away from Anna and Susan Warner, whose stories were recounted in Chapter Two of this book. Although political or public relations expediency and some degree of sentimentality might have pushed the families to lay their trio of fallen heroes together, there was no doubt among Ed White's family that the proud West Point alumnus wished to be buried at his alma mater.

"That was pretty much a decision made before the accident," White's son, Edward White III, recalled in a recent interview; he was 13 years old when his father was killed. "It was Dad's wish, someday, to be buried at West Point, and that's where his Dad was going to be buried as well. It was sort of the 'Long Gray Line,' so to speak. It wasn't any major issue for us, as my Mom was just carrying out Dad's wishes. NASA did try to pressure us a bit that they all be buried together at Arlington, but, you know, my Mom felt it was the right thing for it to be done at West Point, honoring his wishes that had been already expressed. And she made it clear to them, and then that was when they stopped bothering her."

The White family's decision to inter their fallen astronaut at West Point raises an interesting point with regard to decision making around burials in that not every cemetery is open to receiving the mortal remains of anyone who may wish to be buried in a particular site, especially in the military community. Although the U.S. Military Academy could conceivably have made an exception had Grissom's and Chaffee's families wished for their heroes to be buried with White, as a general rule, burials at the West Point Cemetery are restricted to graduates of the Academy and their immediate families, provided said graduates also served in the U.S. Corps of Cadets as U.S. citizens, were citizens at the time of death, served on active duty in the armed forces of the United States, and had such service terminated honorably.

The "Long Gray Line" referred to by White's son is a phrase used in the army to evoke the continuum of shared experiences common to all graduates from West Point and the sense of honor associated with army alumni and their families being buried on the grounds of their beloved campus is strongly inculcated in cadets as a part of their training. For Naval Academy graduates, "links in the chain" evokes a similar sense of continuity, the term being culled from a stanza of Royal Navy admiral R.A. Hopwood's "Laws of the Navy," which all navy plebes (freshman) are required to memorize, thusly: "On the strength of one link in the cable / Dependeth the might of the chain. / Who knows when thou mayest be tested? / So live that thou bearest the strain!"

The White family's own segment of "the Long Gray Line" actually has grown longer since Ed White was killed in 1967. "My Uncle Jim White, my Dad's younger brother, was killed in action in Vietnam and he's buried at West Point now, too," Ed White III explained. "He flew what they called 'Wild Weasels,' F-105s, over Laos, going after the surface-to-air missile sites. He was lost there and was MIA for a long time, until very recently. They recovered his plane up on this big mountain in Laos, and got a sample of his DNA there, and finally declared him killed in action. And he's now buried at West Point. To be buried there is very special. I've been up there many times and been able to see the graves and everything and it gives me a good feeling, every time I go to West Point and I see there the graves of my family. We've always been very positive about West Point, you know, as a family."

Grissom and Chaffee were both alumni of Purdue University and were undoubtedly proud of their alma mater, just as White was of his. But the culture inculcated at the typical land-grant university like Purdue does not usually feature the same level of mortality contemplation that military school cultures feature. Chaffee was a lieutenant commander in the navy at the time of his death, and Grissom was an air force lieutenant colonel. As veterans killed in the line of duty, burial at Arlington National Cemetery constituted a deeply meaningful military honor, as eligibility requirements for burial there are the most stringent of all U.S. national cemeteries. In-ground interments are restricted to those who die on active duty, have had 20 years of service, or earned certain military decorations, and their spouses and dependents. Other honorably discharged veterans and dependents may have their cremated remains inurned in Arlington's columbarium. Over 4 million visitors make pilgrimages to Arlington each year, making it the most widely visited site for "cemetery tourism" in the United States.

Although it is historically and properly referred to as a "national cemetery," Arlington is currently governed by the U.S. Army, and not the Department of Veterans Affairs, which oversees the vast majority of national cemeteries under the auspices of its National Cemetery Administration (NCA). The network of national cemeteries emerged in the early days of the Civil War, and the sites were originally intended solely for those who died during the war. In the ensuing years, though, Civil War veterans argued for the right to be buried next to their comrades in arms and criteria for burial in national cemeteries were expanded to recognize other forms of military service and to allow families to be buried together.

The first national cemeteries were established near military hospitals, prison camps, and recruitment and training centers, as more soldiers died of illness and injury than in combat on battlefields. In 1867, the National Cemetery Act was passed into law, providing financial resources to further develop national cemeteries. The U.S. Army's Office of the Quartermaster (AOQM) was tasked with recovering the remains of Union troops, and its agents set out to scour campaign routes, battlefields, hospitals, prisons, and shorelines in search of temporary graves. Unless relatives specifically claimed recovered bodies for burial elsewhere, remains were relocated to national cemeteries. By 1871, AOQM estimated that 300,000 veterans had been reinterred among 73 national cemeteries or in special soldiers' sections located within private cemeteries. Over 40 percent of the recovered Civil War remains could not be identified, and they remain the largest segment of unknown burials in cemeteries under the modern NCA's purview.

The NCA currently administers 155 national cemeteries in 42 states and Puerto Rico, along with an additional 34 soldiers' lots in private cemeteries and public monument sites. Although that's certainly a formidable real estate roster, options for military burials in such sites are actually a bit more limited than those numbers alone would imply, as 21 of the cemeteries are currently accepting only cremated remains, while 81 are categorized as "closed," meaning that the only interments that are being accepted are subsequent interments for veterans or eligible family members in an existing gravesite, or when burial spaces periodically become available when a disinterment has been completed.

Many states also own and operate veterans' cemeteries, which typically have similar eligibility requirements to the NCA and army-administered national cemeteries, though state residency requirements may also come into play. A majority of the established state veterans' cemeteries are considered "VA Grant–Funded Cemeteries," meaning that they receive federal funding to establish, expand, or improve designated burial sites for veterans and their dependents; such aid is only provided to states, and not to private organizations, counties, municipalities, or other government agencies. State cemeteries administered under the federal grant program must conform to the standards and guidelines pertaining to site selection, planning, and construction prescribed by the NCA, and they must be operated solely for the interment of service members who die on active duty, veterans (as defined by federal law), and their eligible spouses and dependent children.

The honors associated with being buried in such state facilities, and the experiences of those who visit them, are in no way hierarchically "lower" than those associated with their federal counterparts, and in many parts of the country, when residents refer to local military burial sites, they are actually more likely to be familiar with state facilities than with federal ones, that distinction being invisible to those who don't read the small print on plot contracts. At bottom line, geography, place of death, plot availability, and personal preferences all factor into the arithmetic of decision making surrounding the permanent resting places of fallen military members and their families, just as civilians may choose to "shop" their own burial sites while they have the wherewithal to do so.

Although astronauts Grissom, Chaffee, and White do not all lie together, they do lie in places of honor significant to them and to their loved ones, and both cemeteries are beautiful places to reflect on their sacrifices and on the causes on their untimely passing. As tragic and avoidable (with 20/20 hindsight) as the deaths of the Apollo 1 astronauts were, the general narrative at NASA and among the astronauts' peers and colleagues was that their deaths were not in vain, as the lessons learned from their on-pad accident fostered corrective paths that made spacecraft and space travel safer for those who followed them. The "Block 1" group of CSMs that Grissom, Chaffee, and White crewed never flew in space, as NASA and its contractors engineered complete redesigns in the "Block 2" group of Apollo spacecraft. NASA also implemented improved quality control provisions and new policies and practices for testing and emergency response.

After three uncrewed launches in late 1967 and early 1968, including the first two flights of the gargantuan Saturn V stack, Apollo 7 launched in October 1968 with a three-man crew for an Earth-orbiting test of the redesigned CSM. Two months later, Apollo 8 made the first round-trip to the moon, and seven months after that, Neil Armstrong and Edwin "Buzz" Aldrin put boots on the lunar ground for the first time, accompanied on their voyage by pilot Mike Collins, who orbited the moon in the CSM while Aldrin and Armstrong made the trip down to and up from the surface in the Lunar Module. It's become an accepted truism that although the lives of astronauts Grissom, Chaffee, and White were lost under some of the most tragic circumstances imaginable, the impact of their deaths profoundly altered NASA's culture for the better, perhaps saving the Apollo program that meant so much to its first crew.

That may be cold comfort at times to those who grew up without their fathers and those who lived without their husbands, brothers, and sons in the aftermath of the accident, but all of the astronauts understood the dangerous nature of their ventures and adventures, and their families have generally affirmed that they died doing work that they loved, for a cause that mattered to them. Grissom was eloquent in accepting the risks of his job, noting in a 1963 interview, "An awful lot of people have devoted more effort than I can describe to make Project Mercury and its successors, as safe as humanly possible. But we also recognize that there remains a great deal of risk, especially in initial operations, regardless of planning. You just can't forecast all the things that could happen, or when they could happen."

A month before his death, Grissom was further quoted thusly, in response to a media question about his fear of a potential space flight disaster: "You sort of have to put that out of your mind. There's always a possibility that you can have a catastrophic failure, of course; this can happen on any flight; it can happen on the last one as well as the first one. So, you just plan as best you can to take care of all these eventualities, and you get a well-trained crew and you go fly."

By all accounts, Apollo 1 had such a well-trained crew, and beyond the technical and safety improvements made by NASA after the astronauts' deaths, numerous other honors have been bestowed on them over the years (including the congressional Space Medal of Honor), with an equally large number of naming memorials in their honor, both on Earth and beyond. Astronauts Aldrin and Armstrong left an Apollo 1 mission patch on the moon's surface during mankind's first visit there, and the Apollo 15 crew left a small statue called "Fallen Astronaut" at their landing site, with a plaque citing the names of the Apollo 1 astronauts, other U.S. astronauts killed in terrestrial accidents, and the Soviet cosmonauts whose deaths had been disclosed internationally at the time. (Less than two months after the Apollo 1 disaster, cosmonaut

Chapter Nine. Grissom, Chaffee and White

Vladimir Komarov became the first person to die on a post-launch spacecraft when the parachutes on his Soyuz 1 capsule failed to deploy, and he was killed on reentry impact.) There are also craters on the moon and hills on Mars bearing the names of Grissom, Chaffee, and White.

As this book goes to print, planning for another Earth-based memorial to the Apollo 1 astronauts is moving forward, with the full engagement and support of the White family. "We're in the middle of working on a new monument at Arlington right now," Ed White III informed us. "For the whole Apollo 1 crew, so there'll be all three of them recognized on a nice memorial. We've got a planned location at Arlington and everything. It's pretty close to where the other two are buried, actually, so you could actually just walk from one spot to the other. My sister Bonnie's very much involved with it. We've just final-ized the design and we're submitting it for approval this week to the group at the cemetery that makes the final decisions on things like that. It's been a long time coming, we've been working on this for a while. I'll be happy when it's finally finished. Of course, we know how long it takes for anything to get done in Washington. So it could take a while, or maybe they'll move fast with it. You can just never know in advance how things are going to go, right?"

James Bond Stockdale (1923–2005) and William James Crowe, Jr. (1925–2007)

United States Naval Academy Cemetery, Annapolis, Maryland

"The language of friendship is not words but meanings."
—Henry David Thoreau

"Handcuffs weigh much more than gravestones."
—Visar Zhiti

The United States Naval Academy is situated on the southwestern shores of the Severn River, one of the many tidal waterways that feed and sustain the mighty Chesapeake Bay. Both the Severn River and the Naval Academy are integral, defining components of Maryland's historical capital city, Annapolis. "The Yard" (as the Academy campus is known) and the brigade of midshipmen (the student body of that academic institution) themselves provide cultural and tourism draws to Annapolis, with parades, formations, and marches around the Academy's imposing architecture providing generations' worth of photo opportunities and memories for families, friends, and other interested or curious parties. The Severn River provides a similarly iconic scenic setting, as midshipmen learn the sailors' skills, customs, and practices on its waters, crewing, piloting, sailing, or rowing armadas of watercraft, ranging from the miniature destroyers known as Yard Patrol craft through a plethora of wind- and muscle-powered craft of varying shapes, styles, and sizes. It's no accident that formal parades on Worden Field at the Academy are often backdropped by the varsity offshore sailing team running up the Severn with colorful spinnakers flying.

Chapter Ten. James B. Stockdale and William J. Crowe, Jr.

The Yard is bisected near Worden Field by a smaller tributary of the Severn known as College Creek, which is crossed within the Academy's secure territory by one vehicular bridge and one long pedestrian span. To the south of College Creek, casual visitors will find most of the things they likely preassociate with the Academy, e.g., the chapel, classroom buildings, the vast Bancroft Hall dormitory, Tecumseh Court formations, and various historical monuments and edifices. Midshipmen also spend the lion's share of their time on that side of College Creek, living, eating, studying, marching, running, and (on rare occasions) relaxing. It bustles, at bottom line. A busy place.

The area north of College Creek has a different character, largely defined by various athletic fields, staff and faculty housing, and administrative offices for ancillary organizations such as the U.S. Naval Institute and U.S. Naval Academy Foundation. Those northern reaches of the Yard draw fewer camera-toting tourists, and midshipmen tend to visit the area only when they have reason to do so, given its relative distance from the heart of their community and the foot time required to traverse the distances between those points while functioning in a highly regimented, tightly wound, "on time means five minutes early" environment.

There is one visually and geographically unique facet to that northern end of the Yard, as it is more forested and hillier than its immediate environs. It's not unusual to see sweat gear–clad midshipmen running up and down those hills, often hauling weights or other athletic gear, taking advantage of the rare opportunity to get an elevation training burn, with pleasant shade and maybe even a bit of breeze to mitigate the sting. In the day-to-day experience of the midshipmen, the ones who visit that hilly woodland may find themselves focused primarily on safely landing their next footfalls without twisting an ankle or knee or contemplating the immense array of required knowledge that they can be asked to disgorge at any time on command. But at some point, for those officers in training and for non–Academy visitors alike who find themselves on that tightly wound network of roads and paths, focus will likely shift outward, with eyes drawn inexorably toward the stones and markers that mark this as the hallowed ground of the Naval Academy Cemetery.

The cemetery's history is nearly as deep as the Academy's itself, its confines and those around it having been acquired by the navy in 1868, during a post–Civil War expansion period for the Yard. By the summer of 1869, the cemetery had been consecrated as the first remains were interred and earliest monuments erected. Today, the cemetery occupies just under seven acres, and space constraints limit burials primarily to those Naval Academy alumni who have achieved flag rank (i.e., rear admiral in the navy or brigadier general in the Marine Corps, army, or air force), or those service members who die while stationed on active duty at the Academy, along with their immediate families. In 1987, the Naval Academy built a columbarium to offer final resting spaces for all Academy alumni who wish to have their cremains sited in perpetuity on the shores of College Creek. The overall cemetery complex is historical and somewhat unique among military burial sites, as marker designs and layouts are not restricted to the fields of simple white marble headstones that define the vast majority of national cemetery vistas, thereby offering peeks into and perspective on the unique times and characters of the service members and their loved ones who are buried here.

Near the western edge of the Naval Academy Cemetery, a pair of similar, elegantly simple headstones mark the final act of affinity between two of the most storied figures in the history of the 20th-century navy. One stone reads "CROWE" on its obverse, with four stars below the name. The other, "STOCKDALE" above three stars. On the reverse of the "CROWE" stone is etched an image of the Presidential Medal of Freedom, while the "STOCKDALE" stone features a similarly carved replica of the Medal of Honor, recognizing the highest awards (of many) bestowed on the heroes buried beneath. Both stones serve as dual markers for the pair of Naval Academy classmates (they graduated in 1946 due to accelerated wartime schedules but were members of the Class of 1947) and their beloved spouses: Vice Admiral James Bond Stockdale (1923–2005) rests in peace with Sybil Elizabeth Bailey Stockdale (1924–2015), and Admiral William James Crowe, Jr. (1925–2007) shares his plot with Shirley Grennell Crowe (1928–2015). There were 111 years of married life experienced collectively between those two couples, their careers and stories winding and intersecting about each other over the decades on a globally significant basis.

By almost any objective reckoning, the combined accomplishments of Vice Admiral Stockdale and Admiral Crowe rival any other pairs of great public figures lying in perpetuity beside each other, and it was their active, direct choice to be interred as neighbors with their wives at the Naval Academy Cemetery. Both men have been recognized by the Academy, with no small amount of understatement, as "Notable Graduates," and their respective biographies there provide concise summaries

of their impressive public careers. Vice Admiral Stockdale was the elder
of the pair by two years, so we present his career overview first, adapted
by the Naval Academy's scribes from a biography on Stockdale's personal site at the time of his death:

> Admiral Stockdale was born on December 23, 1923 in Abingdon, Illinois.
> After graduating from the Naval Academy in 1946, he attended flight train-
> ing in Pensacola, Florida, and in 1954 was accepted to the Navy Test Pilot
> School where he served as an instructor for a brief time. Stockdale's flying
> career took him west, and in 1962 he earned a Master's Degree in Interna-
> tional Relations from Stanford University.
>
> On September 9, 1965 while returning from a mission, his A-4 Skyhawk
> was hit by anti-aircraft fire. Stockdale ejected, breaking a bone in his back
> and badly dislocating his knee. Stockdale wound up in Hỏa Lò Prison, the
> infamous "Hanoi Hilton," where he spent the next seven years. Despite
> being kept in solitary confinement for four years, in leg irons for two years,
> physically tortured more than 15 times, denied medical care and malnour-
> ished, Stockdale organized a system of communication and developed a
> cohesive set of rules governing prisoner behavior.
>
> In the Spring of 1969, he was told that he was to be taken "downtown"
> and paraded in front of foreign journalists. Stockdale slashed his scalp with
> a razor and beat himself in the face with a wooden stool knowing that his
> captors would not display a prisoner who was disfigured. Later, after dis-
> covering that some prisoners had died during torture, he slashed his wrists
> to demonstrate to his captors that he preferred death to submission. This
> act so convinced the Vietnamese of his determination to die rather than
> to cooperate that the Communists ceased the torture of American prison-
> ers and gradually improved their treatment of POWs. He was released from
> prison in 1973. He was awarded the Medal of Honor by President Gerald
> Ford in 1976. He was one of the most highly decorated officers in the his-
> tory of the Navy, wearing twenty-six personal combat decorations, includ-
> ing two Distinguished Flying Crosses, three Distinguished Service Medals,
> two Purple Hearts, and four Silver Star medals in addition to the Medal of
> Honor. He was the only three-star Admiral in the history of the Navy to
> wear both aviator wings and the Medal of Honor.
>
> After serving as the President of the Naval War College, Stockdale retired
> from the Navy in 1978. He published a number of books and articles and
> was awarded eleven honorary doctoral degrees. In 1992 he agreed to the
> request from H. Ross Perot to stand in as the Vice-Presidential candidate of
> the Reform Party. Upon his retirement in 1979, the Secretary of the Navy
> established the Vice Admiral Stockdale Award for the Inspirational Lead-
> ership presented annually in both the Pacific and Atlantic fleet. Admi-
> ral Stockdale was a member of the Navy's Carrier Hall of Fame and The
> National Aviation Hall of Fame, and he was an Honorary Fellow in the Soci-
> ety of Experimental Test Pilots.

Admiral Crowe's public career synopsis, also culled from his "Notable Graduates" entry at the Naval Academy website, supplemented by other public records, is as follows:

William Crowe was born in La Grange, Kentucky, and grew up in Oklahoma City, Oklahoma. After graduating from Classen High School, he attended the University of Oklahoma. Inspired in part by his father's experiences in the Navy during World War I, Crowe entered the United States Naval Academy, graduating in 1946 with the Class of 1947. He received a master's degree and a doctorate in politics from Princeton University. He taught political science at the Naval Academy, served as a trustee of Princeton University, and was Shapiro Visiting Professor of International Affairs at George Washington University.

His initial sea tour was aboard the USS Carmick (DMS-33). After completing submarine school in 1948, he qualified in submarines in March 1950 in the diesel submarine USS Flying Fish (SS-229). Almost all of his sea assignments over the next decade were on diesel submarines. In 1951 and 1952 Crowe served as Flag Lieutenant and Aide to the Commander of the US Atlantic Fleet's Submarine Force at New London, Connecticut. In 1970, at the age of forty-four, Crowe volunteered for service in Vietnam. He served first as an adviser and then as Senior Adviser to the Vietnamese Riverine Force in the Mekong Delta.

On July 10, 1985, Admiral Crowe was appointed by President Ronald Reagan to serve as Chairman of the Joint Chiefs of Staff (CJCS). When Chief of the Soviet General Staff Marshal Sergei Akhromeyev was in Washington in December 1987 for the signing of the Intermediate Nuclear Forces (INF) Treaty, a private Crowe-Akhromeyev meeting led to an agreement designed to prevent accidental armed conflict between US and Soviet armed forces and to a formal program of military-to-military dialogue between the services of the two countries. In the summer of 1988 Akhromeyev and the Soviet Service Vice Chiefs visited the United States at Crowe's invitation. When Crowe and the U.S. Service Vice Chiefs returned the visit in June 1989, he and Akhromeyev's successor, General Mikhail Moiseyev, signed the Agreement on the Prevention of Dangerous Military Activities and a military-to-military contacts agreement.

Admiral Crowe continued to serve as CJCS through the Bush administration until 1989, when he retired from active duty, returning to the University of Oklahoma and the William J. Crowe chair in geopolitics. President Bill Clinton named Crowe chairman of the President's Foreign Intelligence Advisory Board in 1993. In 1994, Clinton appointed Crowe the United States Ambassador to the United Kingdom, and he served in that capacity until 1997. In 1998–99 he chaired the State Department Review Boards that were appointed after the August 1998 bombings of U.S. embassies in Kenya and Tanzania. His awards include Defense Distinguished Service Medal (with three oak leaf clusters), Navy

176

Chapter Ten. James B. Stockdale and William J. Crowe, Jr.

Distinguished Service Medal (with two gold stars), Army Distinguished Service Medal, Air Force Distinguished Service Medal, Coast Guard Distinguished Service Medal, Legion of Merit (with two oak leaf clusters), Bronze Star (with combat "V"), and Air Medal.

The published accounts of the two admirals' careers are well documented and oft cited, though the true nature of their long personal relationship lies perhaps less in the public domain of heroic achievement and more in the bonds that bind friends who have experienced both the most grievous hurts and hysterical hijinks together. The friendship between Crowe and Stockdale actually originated on their very first day in Annapolis, just before they took their oath of office and began their plebe summer experience at the Naval Academy. In an oral history commissioned by the Naval Historical Foundation and conducted by Paul Stillwell in 2006 and 2007 (just after Stockdale's death in 2005), Admiral Crowe recalled their time in Annapolis thusly:

> Well, we actually met the first day we came to the Naval Academy. [Stockdale] was having breakfast with his father. It was in this small restaurant, and I was having breakfast by myself. I guess his father realized what I was doing and came over and asked me if I was entering the Naval Academy. [I] said I was, and he said, "Would you like to have breakfast with us?" ... So I met him there, and then he and I were in the same group in plebe summer, and I knew him then. But then when they went into companies for the academic year, we got split up. I was in the 14th Company, and I guess Jim must have been the 15th. But it wasn't near us. Then my youngster year Jim and his roommate ... lived right across the hall from me. They were in a different company, but this was on the company line, and I lived right across the hall from them. He and I became very, very friendly just from doing things together and lots of messing around. Then first-class year we were split up again, but by then he and I had become very good friends, and we decided to request the same ship together when we graduated. We did, and we got it, the USS Carmick in San Francisco. But he had only been aboard out there about two months when he got orders to go to another destroyer, and he and I never served together again. He went to the Rowan, and then he went to flight training, and I went to submarine training.

In their oral history interviews, Admiral Crowe regaled Stillwell with a variety of examples of that "lots of messing around" in which he and Stockdale engaged during their time in Annapolis. In Crowe's telling, Stockdale was more often the instigator, possessed as he was with "a lot of his father's gall, the traveling salesman," and "a lot of ego and a lot of vanity. He got that from his mother, that he's better than most people. You know, it got him through prison camp. A very important quality in a man ... he could try and bluff his way through anything." At Stockdale's funeral, Crowe shared what he called "his favorite story about Jim," about a trip the pair took to New York City.

"All the way up on the train to New York City [Stockdale] said, 'Now, look. We don't want anybody to think we're country bumpkins. When we get to New York City we're going to act like we know what the hell we're doing. They're never going to figure out we come from the Midwest, that we're city-ignorant,'" Crowe recalled. "Again, I didn't know how we were going to do this, but I was all for it. We strolled out of the Pennsylvania Station, got in a cab, and said, 'Pennsylvania Hotel.' The cab driver looked at us sort of funny, did a U-turn, and charged us 50 cents. The Pennsylvania Hotel was right across the street. When we got out and that guy was driving off, Jim and I started laughing, and Jim said, 'The least he could have done was drive around the block, for Christ's sake.'"

The adventures didn't end when the young officers went their separate ways after Stockdale disembarked from the *Carmick*, with the pair following their respective career arcs. As is often the case in the navy, their paths would cross in unexpected places and ways around the world over the years. Another of Admiral Crowe's conversations with Paul Stillwell included this choice anecdote about a European adventure:

Later on ... [Stockdale] was on a carrier, and I was on a submarine, and we both went to France. We were in Nice, about 15 miles outside of Monaco on the Riviera. We were anchored, and you could see the carrier from where I was. He and I went ashore together a lot there in Nice. He came aboard one night and said, "Well, I've fixed us up for tomorrow."

I said, "What are you talking about?"

He said, "We're going to go skiing."

I said, "Jim, have you ever been skiing?"

He said, "No, I've never been skiing."

I had never been on skis in my life. And I said, "What in the hell are you talking about?"

He said, "Well, sometime in your life you're going to be in a cocktail party, and there's going to be [someone] there talking about how he prefers to ski in the Swiss Alps. Well, we're going to go skiing in the French Alps, and you can butt in and say, 'Well, I personally prefer the French Alps.'"

I said, "Oh, really?"

We got up at 3:00 o'clock in the morning, caught this bus with a bunch of sailors on it about 4:00 or 5:00, and rode up into the mountains. This is a true story. We were dressed in blue—drill shirt, pants, dark socks. Not in uniform. We got out and went in a little place there and rented skis, never having been on them. Then we went over to the ski lift. I can hardly tell this story and believe it myself. We started up on the ski lift, and it had three stops. I said, "Think we ought to get off at this first stop?"

He said, "No, hell no, go to the top."

I said "Okay, we'll go to the top." That was Jim all the way. So we got off up at the top.

Then the problem came in getting the skis on. People were streaming by us, and Jim kept asking, "Do you speak English? Do you speak English?"

Finally one man says, "Yes, I speak English."

He said, "Can you help us? We've never had skis on before."

This guy's eyes got about that big. He helped us, but he kept saying, "Why are you up here? How are you going to go down this damn mountain?"

Jim said, "Carefully."

And that was Jim all the way. I mean, why we were at the very top? That was the last time either one of us ever went skiing. And, sure enough, I was at a party one time when somebody started talking about Swiss Alps, and I immediately informed him, "I ski in the French Alps."

Given the global significance of the conflicts and controversies that Crowe and Stockdale negotiated and navigated over their public lives and the utmost horror of Stockdale's time as a prisoner of war, it can be easy to imbue all of the admirals' actions and interactions with a degree of heft, severity, and import that renders their narratives heroic but also turn them into one-dimensional characters. But Crowe denied that flat sort of narrative, humanizing his friend by explaining to Stillwell that "he was really a gung-ho, practical, fun guy, and my memories of him are all sort of sweet."

Those affectionate bonds extended to the other members of the Stockdale and Crowe clans as their families grew. Stockdale was wed first, having met Sybil Bailey on a blind date in 1946 in Richmond, Virginia, where Sybil taught at the private St. Catherine's School after completing her degree at Mount Holyoke College. They married in the summer of 1947, and had four sons: Jim, Sid, Stan (who passed away in 2014), and Taylor. Crowe met his wife, Shirley Grinnell, in 1953 in their home state of Oklahoma. She was a flight attendant for American Airlines, and the sparks between them were such that Crowe proposed to her within three weeks of their first meeting, an offer which she accepted. Admiral and Mrs. Crowe had three children, sons Blake and Brent and daughter Mary, better known as "Bambi" to family and friends.

Bonds between families are forged across a network of multigenerational relationships, and the "little things" that might not have generated much attention in their time often turn out to generate the most affectionate and lasting memories, especially for the younger members of the families in question. In a 2020 interview with the authors, Admiral and Sybil Stockdale's son Jim recalled one fond early memory of his family's cross-connections with the Crowes as an example of the ways in which the Crowe family were present through various eras of his childhood.

"The first time I became aware of the closeness of the relationship between Dad and Bill Crowe was when we were living in Coronado, California," Jim recalled.

Seems to me it was 1963, maybe '64, or somewhere in there. We lived in Coronado and the Crowes were at Point Loma, where they used to park all of those diesel submarines. There were times then when we'd go back and forth and see one another. It wasn't like they were the family we got together with for holidays, but there was always this running thread, we would go over to their house and the Crowes would come over to ours.

One time when we visited the Crowes, Bill was throwing away a television set. It was an old, boxy kind, stood on legs, black and white, of course. We were driving a '55 station wagon at that point, and on our way out, I asked him, "Is that TV set by the curb meant for the trash guys to take?" And he said, "Yeah, it doesn't work anymore, hasn't worked a long time." So I said, "If we slipped it in the back of the station wagon, could I have it because I like to work on things like that?" He said, "Sure, take it," and kind of smiled, you know? I'm 12 or 13 years old or so at the time, and I used to get together with my friends and we would take broken stereos and different things and try to put them back together. If they didn't work, we would take the vacuum tubes out of them and go down to use these little panels they had at the Safeway and in grocery stores that would tell you whether it's a good or weak or bad tube. And then down below the testing thing, there were these rows of brand-new tubes you could buy to replace the old ones. It was pretty simple, pretty straightforward.

Well, two weeks later, he's over at our place in Coronado, and Mom says, "You know, Bill, Jimmy got that old TV set to work," and Bill came down and took a look. I had this old big wide family chair, and in front of it, there's the TV, working fine, three regular channels plus one from Tijuana. Bill was kind of beside himself that I had gotten his TV working and that he had given away a perfectly fine set just because it had some bad tubes in it. Finally, Mom came down and Dad came down and they were all kind of looking at Bill and at the TV and everyone's smiling. So that's probably my earliest respectable memory of the guy. He was always gentle, always fun. And I loved how he and Dad got along. On a very personal level, it was just lovely to see them together. Instead of a couple of naval officers, you'd just see a couple of guys just hanging out.

Chapter Ten. James B. Stockdale and William J. Crowe, Jr.

Jim's brother Sid Stockdale also appreciated the depth of his father's relationship with Bill Crowe, attributing it in part to shared aspects of their respective upbringings. In his own 2020 conversation with the authors, he noted,

> I think one thing that drew them together was that they both came from rural communities. Agricultural communities. My dad was from Abingdon, Illinois, a small town, and there was a Stockdale farm there that he worked on. And Bill Crowe of course came from Oklahoma. I think they connected because they were in this strange foreign place for both of them. But I also think they shared common values related to family and rural America, and that's what drew them together in a big way. That and I think that they both loved to have fun, and they were just comfortable with one another. As people grow older, their personalities obviously evolve, and my sense is that when my dad first started going to the Naval Academy, he didn't maybe have so much of that air of reverence about him that he did later. Maybe he was a little bit more naive than people would think and he just wanted to communicate that no, I'm not naive.

From the other side of the familial alliance, Admiral and Shirley Crowe's eldest son, Blake, also saw special shared facets of his father's relationship with Admiral Stockdale, his current impressions perhaps shaped by his own long career in the Marine Corps. Blake explained the following in a 2020 interview with the authors:

> I just think that they clicked in a way that most people probably don't, all the salty warts and all, they still liked each other. And they both became very successful, probably a surprise to each of them. They worked hard. They liked people. And I know that people wanted to work for my father and for Admiral Stockdale. I mean, people would go out of their ways to work for them: officers, enlisted, anyone, it didn't matter. And it wasn't because they were easy, you know? It's because they made their people feel appreciated, along with what they brought to the team. So it didn't matter if you were a mess specialists or if you were an admiral or a general in the NATO command, you got treated with the same respect. I think Admiral Stockdale did the same. I think everybody felt like they really cared about him. And he genuinely cared and would do anything to help them and lead them and make them successful and welcome. Everybody wants to be successful themselves. But Admiral Stockdale and my father wanted their people and their organizations to be successful. And if the organization was successful, then everyone in it was a success, and I think that they both believed in and shared that kind of message.

Those positive remembrances notwithstanding, two particular eras in the admirals' lives did place strains on their families' relationships. Most obviously and publicly was the period of Admiral Stockdale's imprisonment in Vietnam. Sybil Stockdale was an early champion for prisoners of war; soldiers, sailors, and aviators missing in action; and their families, cofounding and serving as first national coordinator for the National League of Families of American Prisoners Missing in Southeast Asia. She was a powerful and profound advocate, forcing the Nixon administration to abandon its "keep quiet" policy regarding prisoners of war in Vietnam and elsewhere and bringing the realities of their torture at their captors' hands into the public and policymaking spotlights.

In his interviews with Paul Stillwell, Admiral Crowe noted that her efforts took an increasing toll on her, and he believed she suffered from depression in the final years before her husband returned home. Crowe himself admitted he had suffered from depression and felt his own experiences allowed him to provide some modicum of understanding and support that otherwise might have been beyond his reach. "I recognized immediately what was happening," Crowe recalled. "You not only are sympathetic, but you can help some by encouraging them and

Hỏa Lò Prison, the notorious "Hanoi Hilton," where Admiral Stockdale was imprisoned in Vietnam (U.S. Air Force).

telling them: 'I've been through it, and I know how it feels, and I know how real it is.' And I have noticed that throughout the rest of my life I've had several brushes with people that had depression, some of whom didn't realize it."

Crowe also later learned that he'd accompanied Admiral Stockdale during his imprisonment in a most unexpected fashion. "He'd never say give up," Crowe said of his friend. "He'd never, never, never, he'd never give up. He talked to me a lot about his prison experience. He said that I'd taught him the Oklahoma fight song, 'Boomer Sooner.' And they piped music into the cells, patriotic music. And one of the songs was the same music. And he said he used to sit on his bunk singing in as loud a voice as he could, 'Boomer Sooner.' And the North Vietnamese had no idea what he was talking about. Little things become very important. Well, that colored his whole life."

"The Crowes were just incredibly gracious and warm to us, you know," remembered the youngest Stockdale son, Taylor. "It was such a crazy time period to be a kid during the whole thing. But I always felt like there was an element of being at home with them. Like they

Admiral Stockdale receives his Medal of Honor at a White House ceremony in 1976 (Dave Wilson, U.S. Navy).

were family to us, even though we didn't see them that often. I always felt like if there was anybody that could sort of be like my dad, it would be Admiral Crowe. When my dad came home from prison, we all went out to dinner in Washington, D.C., and my dad stood up and said, 'Bill Crowe, you're my best friend. You've always been my best friend.' And I remember thinking, wow, adults can have friends like that? It was very poignant. They really were best friends."

The second great trial in the long relationship between Admirals Stockdale and Crowe was, as is all too frequently the case, wrapped around an axle of politics. Businessman and fellow Naval Academy alumnus H. Ross Perot had worked with Sybil Stockdale on behalf of Vietnam POWs during Admiral Stockdale's imprisonment and had gotten to know and respect the admiral in the years that followed. In 1992, when Perot was in the early stages of formulating his third-party candidacy for the United States presidency, he asked Stockdale to serve as his provisional vice presidential nominee, with both parties expecting another candidate to assume that role should Perot's campaign advance. As it turned out, Perot dropped out of the race for several months, then redeclared his candidacy mere weeks before the scheduled vice presidential debate without having named a replacement for Admiral Stockdale, who was offered no formal preparation for that televised event and was not given any substantial guidance on political positions of interest to his own candidate. In one of the more egregious examples of modern American media focusing undue attention on out-of-context sound bites in presidential politics (see also the Howard Dean "scream" and Edmund Muskie's alleged tears as contemporaneous examples, among many others), Admiral Stockdale's debate performance was parsed and pilloried in an extravagantly unfair fashion, portraying a brilliant thinker and heroic warrior as an aged and out-of-touch figure of scorn. It deeply hurt the admiral, his family, his friends, and his many admirers.

Admiral Crowe was also actively involved in the 1992 presidential elections, offering an endorsement of Democrat Bill Clinton's campaign, a position that carried significant clout given Crowe's service as chairman of the Joint Chiefs of Staff under the Republican Reagan and Bush administrations; he went on to serve for five years in the Clinton administration. Admiral Stockdale could not stomach the idea of a commander in chief who had not served his country in a military capacity and had been outspoken in his opposition to the Vietnam War and, by perceptual extension, to those who fought, suffered, were lost, or died in Southeast Asia in the 1960s and 1970s. Crowe and

Stockdale endured a long estrangement as a result of their public participation in that 1992 electoral process.

"I think that Bill Crowe, perhaps unlike my dad, was politically very savvy," noted Taylor Stockdale.

And he, I think, was a statesman at heart. He probably knew that Bill Clinton was incredibly smart, and he could probably see that there were some really good elements to build his administration. He maybe didn't endorse everything that Bill Clinton did, but he had a pretty sophisticated view of Washington and how things really work. And he probably admired it. My sense is that Bill Crowe was more politically astute and a little bit more pragmatic. And my dad just, you know, he got hunkered down on a point of view, and he just couldn't shake himself out of it. At some point I said, "You know, I've got to tell you, it just breaks my heart that you're going to let this political bullshit ruin your friendship with this guy that you know, who I heard you say is your best friend. That's more important than this. So what do you say?" And, well, he said nothing. I couldn't get him off of it. So that was kind of an unfortunate wrinkle in the whole thing. But then, you know, after a while that subsided and he eventually got over it, which was really nice.

Admiral Crowe's Chairman of the Joint Chiefs of Staff portrait (U.S. Department of Defense).

Sid Stockdale concurs with the happiness between the families as the admirals rekindled their deep friendship. "I know that when they were back together, that Shirley and Mom were very happy about that," he noted. "I don't think that the wives were going to get in the way or try to strike out on their own to maintain their friendship if the guys were at loggerheads. So, they were very happy when it happened. I could tell by the way they were interacting and laughing with one another and telling stories. It was a very genuine engagement and really heartwarming to see that they were excited to get together and have fun and stay in contact."

Side by Side in Eternity

Presumably, it was after their rapprochement that Admirals Crowe and Stockdale decided that they would be buried side by side at the Naval Academy Cemetery, though the surviving family members remain somewhat vague on the details of how that decision came about. Taylor Stockdale believes that his father decided to be buried in Annapolis, rather than at Arlington National Cemetery, when he was serving as president of the Naval War College in the late 1970s. "He got somebody to start working on his grave, you know," Taylor remembered. "And he really liked it. And then he realized that the stone they were using was too soft so that a lawn mower could chip his tombstone. So he had to scrap that whole idea and go in a different direction. I don't remember any specific conversation about them being buried together when it was going on. I don't know when that all happened, but when I heard that the Crowes were going to be buried near my mom and dad, I thought that was awesome. How cool is that? Just perfect."

Jim Stockdale suspects that the admirals hatched their plan without extensive conversations with their spouses. "It was interesting, you know, especially for the surviving ones," he noted. "You kind of know where you're going to end up in a little bit. Kind of spooky, like 'That's where I'm going to be. Right *there*.' But there's another wrinkle to it. And that wrinkle is that Ross Perot paid for those headstones, that was something that Ross's generosity was involved with, after Dad and Bill decided they wanted to be together. I don't know exactly how that happened, but ultimately Dad's reputation was advanced by the guilty conscience of a wealthy patron."

Regardless of the way in which the lifelong friends' funerary pact may have actually been developed, Vice Admiral James Bond Stockdale was the first to go to his well-deserved rest on the hill at the Naval Academy Cemetery, passing away at the age of 81 on 5 July 2005. His funeral service was held at the Naval Academy Chapel, and eulogies were given by his four sons, Admiral Crowe, and Admiral Michael Mullen. Senator John McCain, Ross Perot, and U.S. Representative Sam Johnson were among the honorary pallbearers. Admiral William James Crowe, Jr., joined him just over two years later, dying at the age of 82 on 18 October 2007. Sybil Bailey Stockdale and Shirley Grennell Crowe both lived until 2015, with Mrs. Stockdale being the last of the four old friends laid to rest beneath those neighboring headstones.

In reflecting on the nature of the relationship between Admirals Stockdale and Crowe, the Naval Academy obviously looms large in the narrative, as they met there at the dawn of their professional careers,

The Stockdale-Crowe grave site at the U.S. Naval Academy Cemetery (James R. McNeal).

and they are now literally part of the fabric of the Naval Academy community, their grave sites accessible as reminders of their incomparable accomplishments and profound personal connections. In the scholarly components of the urban and regional planning discipline, there's a concept known as "sense of place" used to characterize the relationships between people and specific spatial settings. The term is often used to describe the essences or characteristics that make a place special or unique, thereby fostering authentic human attachment and sense of belonging. For lifelong professional nomads like Admirals Crowe and Stockdale, having a "sense of place" for the Naval Academy, around which their ambits always orbited, may have provided a subtle psychological anchor, tugging at their lives' lines, eventually reeling them back to the point where their friendship and their careers began.

There's certainly a fitting and lasting feeling of that "sense of place" associated with their decision to leave their mortal remains together in that particular location, rather than in Arlington or any other national cemetery, or even in their own respective historical family plots in Oklahoma and Illinois. It's just *right* that they rest there, together. And they knew it.

CHAPTER ELEVEN

Andrew Paul Britton (1981–2008) and Christopher Eoion Vine-Britton (1983–2010)

Glenwood Memorial Gardens, Raleigh, North Carolina (and Elsewhere)

"Where'er I roam, whatever realms to see, my heart untravell'd fondly turns to thee; still to my brother turns with ceaseless pain, and drags at each remove a lengthening chain."

—Oliver Goldsmith

"Great grief makes sacred those upon whom its hand is laid. Joy may elevate, ambition glorify, but only sorrow can consecrate."

—Horace Greeley

At the age of thirty-three, Ryan Kealey has achieved more in his military and CIA career than most men can dream of in a lifetime. He's seen the worst life has to offer and is lucky to have survived it. But being left alone with his demons is not an option, and the CIA needs him badly, as the enemy they're facing is former U.S. soldier Jason March. Ryan knows all about March—he trained him. He knows they're dealing with one of the most ruthless assassins in the world, a master of many languages, an explosives expert, a superb sharpshooter who can disappear like a shadow and who is capable of crimes they cannot begin to imagine. And now, March has resurfaced on the global stage, aligning himself with a powerful Middle East terror network whose goal is nothing less than the total destruction of the United States. Teaming up with the tenacious British-born agent Naomi Kharmai, with the clock ticking down, and the fate of the country resting uneasily on his shoulders, Ryan is caught in a desperate game of cat-and-mouse with the most cunning opponent he's ever faced, a man who is all the more deadly for being one of our own.

188

Chapter Eleven. Britton and Vine-Britton

If you'd happened to visit a brick-and-mortar bookstore (remember those?) or to browse one of the various online book repositories coming into their own around 2006, and if you were looking for a good read, with an interest in espionage-based fiction, then the odds are fairly good that you might have stumbled across the text contained in this chapter's first paragraph, describing and marketing its subject novel, *The American*, the first book published by author Andrew Britton. The author was but 24 years old at the time of its publication, and he quickly earned plaudits from readers and industry critics alike, comparing his smart, compelling, factually accurate narratives to the likes of the commercially titanic Tom Clancy and others who had followed in his creative footsteps. Like his protagonist, Ryan Kealey, Andrew Britton was an exceptionally accomplished and well-traveled young man, with a personal history anchored in military service. Britton's second Ryan Kealey book, *The Assassin*, was published in 2008, earning additional critical praise and commercial success, rising into the *New York Times* Best Sellers list.

A third book in the Kealey series, *The Invisible*, was published in February 2009. Sadly, its author did not survive to see its release: Andrew Paul Britton died at the age of 27 from an undiagnosed heart ailment in March 2008, leaving behind sufficient manuscripts and notes for his popular series to continue (with support from collaborating writers and editors) through another four titles to date at the time of this writing. His works have been translated into numerous languages and have featured

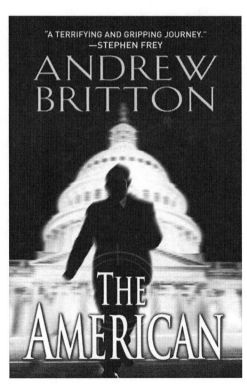

The cover of Andrew's first novel, *The American* (Kensington Books Publishing).

on bestseller lists both foreign and domestic, which was, all things considered, quite fitting, given the story arc of Andrew Britton's brief, bright life.

Andrew and his younger brother, Christopher, were born in Peterborough, Cambridgeshire, United Kingdom, and spent their earliest years in Eye Village, an ancient rural mill town, well removed from

The Britton family: Chris, Annie, Andrew, and Roxanne (Annie Britton-Nice Personal Collection).

the hustle and bustle of the important mercantile and transport hubs of Peterborough. Andrew and Christopher's parents, Paul and Annie Britton, divorced when the boys were young, with Annie later marrying Graham Nice, a native of London. Shortly after Annie and Graham discovered that Annie was expecting her third child, Graham received an offer to work in the United States for a year, with the family relocating when Annie was seven and a half months pregnant. Christopher and Andrew's sister, Roxanne, was born on American shores, mere weeks after the family had settled in Grand Rapids, Michigan, where they remained for nearly ten years.

Although the boys' time in Cambridgeshire was undoubtedly formative, Annie ensured that another part of her personal heritage carried with her family to the United States and was an ingrained element of her children's upbringing. "During the time that we were living in England, we spent an awful lot of time back at my home village of Camlough in Northern Ireland," she explained in a recent phone interview with your authors. "So the kids grew up a lot with my family around them, which was a huge influence, I think, especially on Andrew and his future as a writer. Northern Ireland is full of stories, and my family were great storytellers, and I think that definitely influenced him heavily."

The transition to Michigan wasn't particularly smooth for the family, especially for the introverted Andrew. During a 2011 radio interview on *Town Talk* on Dundalk FM, Annie described the situation thusly and candidly: "I hated it at the start, and I was very concerned for the boys more than anything else, because they had this kind of closeted upbringing and all of a sudden, the American boys are in their faces all the time. And they wanted them to say things over and over again. 'Say *trousers.*' They didn't know what trousers were. They didn't know what a *jumper* was. So, the boys felt awkward and everything, and as a matter of fact, I remember when Andrew was at middle school, the teachers sent for us and they said that they wanted to put him into speech therapy. We were just thinking 'What are they talking about?' But we went to the school and, of course, my husband was English, and I'm from Ireland, and they sat and listened to us for a moment and said 'Oh, we didn't realize!' It was just because he had an accent that they were going to put him through speech therapy. It's just typically American, I suppose, jump right in there and let's see if we can save them!"

Despite their deep closeness to each other and their shared early childhood experiences, the Britton boys were actually quite different one from the other, temperamentally speaking. "Andrew was extremely introverted; he was the quiet one in the house," Annie Britton told your authors. "He always had his nose in a book, no matter what was going on outside. One day when he about eleven, he said to me, 'I'm really, *really* bored.' And I told him he could go out and play, there was snow on the ground and kids were building forts and such, or he could stay inside and read a book. And he told me back, 'I've read all my books.' And I said, 'Okay, so read one of *my* books.'"

"We always had an area of the house that we considered to be our library, with bookshelves and lots of different books; no TV, no electronics, just for reading," Annie continued. "So I turned him around the corner to the library and I showed him what I considered to be *my* books, by people who I admired for their written works. One of my favorites was Jack Higgins, a Belfast author, and so I gave Andrew my copy of Higgins's *The Eagle Has Landed*. He took that away ... and then he didn't come back upstairs, I don't think, for two days, except to grab food and run back downstairs again. And then eventually he came up and left the book on the table and just looked at me and said, 'Brilliant!' And it went from there. He just *ate* books, really. Christmastime, birthdays: you knew exactly what to get him. You never bought him anything else except a collection of books, and Gerald Seymour was one of his favorite British authors; Stephen Leather, Tom Clancy. Those were some of his influences."

Christopher, on the other hand, was a much more tactile young fellow. "He was just one of those kids who was very mechanically minded, was constantly taking something apart, you know," Annie recalled. "You'd look around outside and see that an entire bike was spread across the yard, and then he moved from the bike situation up into cars. Just after he got his first vehicle, it was like the engine was out on the street immediately. And he eventually became a mechanic. That was his thing. He started off working at bikes, first of all, building bikes again, and then he moved up into the world of being a car mechanic. He was extremely handy and energetic, just a little action-packed guy."

When Andrew was 16 and Christopher was 14, the family relocated to Raleigh, North Carolina; the move was a challenging one for the reserved Andrew, who did not make friends easily and who had become a devoted and talented member of Rockford High School's band in Grand Rapids, a niche that he was unable or unwilling to fill again heading into his senior year in high school. His mother recalled that he worked part time at Sears, played soccer, and continued to read voraciously during his time in Raleigh before shocking everyone who knew him by announcing that he was enlisting in the United States Army immediately after graduating from Raleigh's Leesville Road High School.

Annie believes that Andrew's enlistment was, at least in part, one key step in a long-range plan that was not yet evident to those within his closest personal circles. "When Andrew decided to join the military, for the life of us, we could not work out at the time what possessed him to do that because he was just so introverted," Annie explained. "But we realized later, in retrospect, that he had already decided he was going to write and that his time in the army was really a research tool. In order to write about that type of life, he needed to experience it. He did an awful lot of research on everything he'd done. And he would only do something if he knew he was going to do it right. Give the best. Always."

After completing his basic training, Andrew was stationed at Fort Riley, Kansas, and trained as a combat engineer, a role that the U.S. Army's official recruiting website describes thusly: "As a Combat Engineer, you'll work quickly and skillfully to help Soldiers navigate while on combat missions by constructing bridges, clearing barriers with explosives, and detecting and avoiding mines and other environmental hazards. You'll provide expertise and come up with quick and creative engineering solutions, constructing fighting positions, fixed and floating bridges, and obstacles and defense positions." After leaving Kansas, Andrew was stationed in South Korea, eventually completing his three-year enlistment, then returning home to continue his education at the University of North Carolina at Chapel Hill, studying economics and psychology.

It was soon after his return from Korea that Andrew began writing seriously, though secretively. In a delightful interview conducted by D.G. Martin on PBS's *North Carolina Bookwatch* shortly after the publication of *The American* (which, for the record, was titled *The Heart of Betrayal* in his native England), Andrew explained the genesis of his process and the discipline he applied to his work. "Around 2003, I was reading this book and I wasn't completely satisfied when I finished it," he noted. "And so I just found myself wondering: 'Could I do this? Could I do something even better if I really tried?' And, of course, it was a kind of ludicrous idea, because I believe the book was by a world-renowned, best-selling author. But I wanted to do something like that, as I just love the written word. I love to read. I've always enjoyed reading. I read as often as I can. Elmore Leonard once said: 'If you can't read for four hours a day and write for four hours a day, you have no business being a writer.' And I manage to do both of those. I try as much as I can to get both of those things in every day: reading and writing."

His mother fleshed out the story in her interview with your authors. "Andrew was extremely secretive," Annie explained with a laugh. "So after he came home from the army, he started traveling up and down to Washington, D.C., and he would stop by and see me and say 'I'm heading off to D.C. this weekend. I won't be around for a few days.' And because he was such an intelligent young man and had spent that time in the military and was very military-minded, I honestly

Andrew Britton's press publicity photograph (Annie Britton-Nice Personal Collection).

thought he was probably joining the CIA or the FBI or something. That's where I was thinking that he was headed with those trips up and down to D.C., you know?"

"Then later, I had to go home to Ireland for a little bit, because my mom was sick," Annie continued. "And while I was at home, I was talking to Roxanne and I asked her about the boys, and she said that Christopher had been bitten by a dog. I tried calling him and there was no answer on his phone, so then I called their work, because at that time Andrew was also helping out part time at the garage where Christopher was working. I called there and I talked to the owner and he said, 'Oh my God, isn't Andrew, just like, an overnight success, blah, blah, blah!' and I asked him what he was talking about, and he said, 'Oh, right, sorry, I'm not supposed to tell you.' So I finally called and got hold of Andrew the next day and he said, 'Mom, I wanted to surprise you. I wanted to pick you up at the airport and surprise you: I got a contract for a three-book deal.' And so, the whole time he was in the military and when he came back home and the trips up and down to Washington, D.C., that was research, and he had taken that and made it all a part of his first book."

Chapter Eleven. Britton and Vine-Britton

In keeping with his secretive and self-sustaining personality, Andrew Britton also managed to achieve significant success as an author by essentially managing the entire front-end marketing and pitch aspects of his career on his own and in his own ways. In his PBS interview with D.G. Martin, Andrew walked his readers and listeners through his nontraditional approach after Martin had discussed how impressive it was that Andrew had moved his writing from a hobby to a livelihood so quickly, eventually directing inquiring, "So did this just happen easily and instantly?"

"Shockingly enough, it did, actually," Andrew answered with a laugh.

I never bought any books on how to write, how to structure a novel. I did buy every book I could find on how to get published, and I read them all cover to cover. Because I knew that when I was finished with the book that I would only get one chance to sell my work to any publisher. It had to be right the first time. So when I was finished with the book, I sent it to a private editor in Washington, D.C., and she helped me tremendously. She was very professional, and affordable, which was important to me at the time. And she managed to kind of tell me what I needed to cut out, what was working, as well as what was not working, and it's important to receive constructive criticism like that. And she told me both aspects: things I needed to change and things that were good, which was helpful. So I had some encouragement there and it helped me to move forward, make those corrections and perfect the book, at least to the best of my ability. And then I had to write a query letter, which is a one-page document that kind of outlines the book. Publishers and agents get thousands of them every month, so they have to be very brief, to the point, and have a hook, of course, that can capture their attention. I sent my query letter off cold to about sixteen or seventeen different publishers and agents with three chapters of the book, and just waited to see who would get back to me. And, fortunately, an agent got back to me very quickly, and it moved forward to the three-book deal from there.

Of course, that level of quick success, and the subsequent professional expectations that accompany it, can create challenges as well as opportunities for an emergent author, even one with Andrew Britton's work ethic and level of talent. "He'd give the writing his all, his everything," recalled Annie Britton-Nice.

For the first book, he had spent 14 months writing that, and he didn't tell anybody that he was writing it. That meant he was under nobody's shotgun of "You've got to get this done, I need a page, I need a page, I need a page." So in some ways, once you get published, that's when the *really* hard work starts. Because then you have a publisher, you have an editor, you have a team of people that work for you, but you're really working for them because they are on your back all the time, and you have a schedule, and you have deadlines. That means you can't just say, "I'm not going to bother doing anything today." You have to be on the ball every day. And you have to be switched on all the time to be in that mode of thinking.

So even when Andrew was out socially, he'd still be thinking about the work. I found so many wee notes in Andrew's stuff after he passed away, of receipts from restaurants and shops and stuff like that, where he would have bought something, and then he's sitting there making notes. Even out for a drink, he was sitting making all these scribbly wee notes. You could see that his mind was ticking all the time. But he got through the follow-up book, *The Assassin*, and it went to the *New York Times* Best Sellers list, which was brilliant. But Andrew then had to better himself. That's a tough one, and so during the whole writing of the third book, *The Invisible*, we really didn't see him much at all. And when we did see him, oh my God, he just looked tragic. The last pictures I have with him were taken when we were sitting in a bar doing a book signing, and my daughter ran in and "My God, you look like crap" to him. But ... he did. He did look very, very, *very* low.

Although Andrew's army physicals had not disclosed any underlying health issues, Annie did note that he'd developed worrying cardiac symptoms in his final years, no doubt exacerbated by the stress of his book contract and the obligations pursuant to it. "He'd been up to the hospital a couple of times for a stress test," Annie explained. "You'd be sitting talking to him, and then he'd sort of grab his chest a little bit, so I'd asked him many times if something was wrong, and he'd just say, 'I don't know. I just keep getting *this thing.*'"

Although the exact nature of Andrew Britton's underlying cardiac condition remains vague, his mother did note that he was essentially killed by an aneurysm and that his sudden passing in his sleep on March 18, 2008, was quick and painless but obviously no less shocking and devastating for those left behind. "I thank God for my belief in the afterlife, because if I didn't have that, I'd probably end up in a mental home somewhere," Annie told Padraig Quigley and Edel McMullin in their 2011 interview with her on Dundalk FM's *Town Talk*. "We're all here for a reason, I believe. And Andrew was so far ahead of the game in everything that he'd done, so I think that he had nearly finished what he was here for, you know what I mean? Except that he was about to move in with his girlfriend. They were going to buy a house and move in together, so my heart was broken for her as well as for anything else, because she lost the love of her life, and she was his first and only love."

Later, in that same *Town Talk* interview from 2011, Annie Britton-Nice described the aftermath of Andrew's death. "You know, if somebody had told me this was going to happen in advance, I would have probably topped myself, thinking 'I can't deal with this,'" she explained.

But you find within yourself an amazing strength, that you know you have to go on. And my big strength was that I would deal with it all with the same dignity and respect that Andrew would have given me. Andrew would have been at home and kicked the fridge a few times, and probably even thrown a few things at the window, but publicly he would have dealt with this with great respect, and so I just took it upon myself to deal with Andrew's passing as he would have dealt with mine. It's like my brother always said: "You'll find that there's people you carry, and people that need to be carried." And, you know, they really come to the forefront, the people that need to be carried, and I really had to carry a lot of them during those first few months, really. And that just made me go on. Plus, I had so many very good friends in Raleigh. The Irish community here is filled with amazing people, who turned out when I needed them. And that gave me strength in itself, because I knew that even though I was not being carried physically, mentally I was being carried.

Annie's beloved second son, Christopher, was tragically one of those who most needed carrying, so devastated was he by Andrew's death. "Watching Christopher after Andrew died was like looking at somebody who had cancer or some other serious disease that they would not take any medication for," Annie told your authors.

That's how bad it was for Christopher. And he would look at me and he would say, "Mom, it's going to be okay." And I knew in my heart it *wasn't* going to be okay. I'd look at him and I'd just want to cry because he looked like somebody who'd had his arms cut off. He was in really bad shape. Really bad shape. He went downhill very fast, then he started drinking heavily and he started smoking a lot of marijuana. And people would call me to tell me that he was lying on Andrew's grave and I would have to leave work and go get him. We took him in and out of rehab and we took him in and out of hospitals, but it was just a wound that was so deep that nothing, nothing could touch it. And we were all grieving, but my way of dealing with things is I just work very, very hard. I just push myself through things, and I work so hard that I'm tired and then I can sleep, and then I'll get up and I'll do the same thing the next day. That's just the way I deal with stuff. But Christopher couldn't. He just couldn't focus on anything else. That was just the big thing all the time, just that big gaping wound.

By the summer of 2010, two years after Andrew's death and following substance abuse and depression-related struggles that had made it difficult for him to maintain his mechanic's jobs and contributed to profound troubles in his relationship with his girlfriend, Christopher's mental health condition had deteriorated to a point where he was openly expressing suicidal ideations. In keeping with North Carolina laws that allow for an individual to be involuntarily committed for mental health treatment if he or she represents a physical threat to others or themselves, the Britton family obtained an involuntary committal order, and Christopher was taken by the Raleigh Police Department to the Wake Alcohol Treatment Center. In a largely inexplicable turn of events that seem from a distance (and to the family at the time) to have been anchored more in bureaucratic jurisdictional questions than in patient care considerations, Christopher was released from the alcohol treatment unit less than 12 hours after his admission. Later that morning, he hung himself.

Annie and Roxanne once again turned to Raleigh's regional Irish community for support during devastating times; both of them worked at the legendary Tír na nÓg Irish Pub, which held fundraisers to assist with burial and other expenses and provided a sense of community anchored in their cultural, spiritual, and familial history. As a meaningful act of comfort and consolation, Annie quickly arranged to have Christopher interred with Andrew, in both the community where they lived their final years and died and in their ancestral homeland. "That decision was instant for me," recalled Annie. "I mean, there was not much point in Christopher dying if he couldn't be put in with Andrew. So some of their ashes are buried together in the military plot at Glenwood Memorial Gardens in Raleigh, and the rest of the ashes are with my parents in Northern Ireland, in Camlough. It was absolutely important to me to have some of their ashes in Ireland, and really the only reason they're in a plot in Raleigh at all is because they both had girlfriends who were heavily mourning at the time and they needed somewhere to be so they could visit with them and sit with them afterwards. So really that was just a place for those girls to be, you know, to share *their* grief. I didn't want to take that away from them, but for me, the overall thing would be Ireland. Ireland was there from the start. And when it's my time to kick the bucket, I'll be home with my boys there. Reunited."

As helpful as Raleigh's Irish community had been to Annie and Roxanne following the loss of their sons and brothers, eventually Annie decided that a fresh start was in order, moving to Belgium for six months, then home to Ireland, then back to Raleigh, and then on

Roxanne Britton honored and remembered her brothers with an impressive tattoo (Annie Britton-Nice Personal Collection).

to Harper's Ferry, West Virginia, where Annie now manages the Ledge House Bed and Breakfast. (One of your authors met Annie during a stay there and can most enthusiastically recommend it as a wonderful getaway destination with a delightful host.)

"It's very heavy when other people can't move past your grief because it's *your* grief. Your own grief," Annie recalled.

And that's especially true working in a pub situation as I did, when you'd get people coming in, and after a couple of drinks, they'll go all maudlin: "Oh, my God, I can't believe you lost your boys! Oh, that's so sad! How do you get up every day?" Well, you *have* to get up every day. You have to get up and you have to move on. Otherwise, we're all going to do what Christopher did. We're just going to lay down and take our own lives. So there's no way that I couldn't get up. Even though in that first initial shock of knowing that your son, or your child, or any child is dead, and that all you want to do is just lay down in a corner and scream and cry. But something takes you over, or something certainly took *me* over. Some sense of *nobody else is going to be able to do this right except me*. And it's the last thing I can do for him is this. And I have got to make sure that he gets a good sendoff, that everything is

199

done with respect and honor, and that's what I did. And then when Christopher died, it was natural that I would do the same for him.

But people just keep coming up to you with it all, especially when I was at work. I used to stand there sometimes and I'd think: "I'm at work. You cannot do this to me. You cannot impose on me this way." And sometimes I had to just walk back to the office, take my purse and walk straight on out the back door. Because I just could not deal with it mentally. It's too heavy. And even when I went home to Ireland, I didn't stay at home with the family for a while. I moved down to a small village in County Down where I knew nobody. Absolutely nobody. But I did that because I felt that that was the right thing for me at the time. I didn't want to have to share my story every day. I didn't want to have to go over it every day. It was in the heart; it was in the head. I didn't want to talk about it verbally every day, too. And I also knew that at that time, it would have been very easy for me to become very reclusive, so I only would shop for enough food for one day, and that way I had to walk out to the far end of the village where the shop was, and I would have to exchange words with the shopkeeper, or somebody on the street. And it was my way of just like, just pop out every day, even if it was only for two minutes or five minutes, and talk to somebody every day and take a walk every day. But to be honest about it all? I couldn't have done any of that without the power of the relationship that I had with our Andrew to psych me up for it. I knew exactly what he would have wanted me to do. He would not have wanted me to fold. He would

Andrew's and Christopher's graves in North Carolina (Annie Britton-Nice Personal Collection).

not have wanted me to go down into a hole alongside him. He would have wanted me to do exactly what I did do.

Beyond serving as an emotional and spiritual navigation beacon for his mother during her darkest days, Annie is also proud of the ways in which Andrew's brief, shining success has touched the lives of others, both those who knew him in person and those who know him only through his published work. "He left a legacy of words and wisdom, I think," Annie told us. "Not just in his books but in his life, and the ways he showed that things can make perfect sense if you just keep moving forward, and if you are disciplined in the ways that you approach things. 'Get up, you have a job to do,' you know? He lived his life very much like that, focused, like he was a minimalist. Even after he passed, when I was in to clear out his apartment, it was the simplest thing to do because there was no clutter. There were just the basic needs in his life. He lived a very simple life. And so did Christopher. Christopher was the same. So I have tried to do the same, too. I do not want to leave a mess for anybody when I leave this world. I just hope, you know, to have it be, like, 'That's it. Thank you. That's the end of my chapter.'"

Epilogue: Personal Perspectives on Perpetual Proximity

BY J. ERIC SMITH

"There's a divinity that shapes our ends, rough-hew them how we will."

—William Shakespeare

"A grave, wherever found, preaches a short and pithy sermon to the soul."

—Nathaniel Hawthorne

Colonel Charles R. Smith, Jr. (July 29, 1939–September 10, 2002) was born and raised in the small Piedmont mill town of Albemarle, North Carolina. He attended and graduated from North Carolina State University before being commissioned in the United States Marine Corps in 1961. He served on active duty for 28 years, retiring as chief of staff at Marine Corps Recruit Depot, Parris Island, South Carolina, then going on to career in ministry as the station manager and on-air personality for the largest Christian radio station in South Carolina's Low Country.

Colonel Smith was a combat veteran of both Vietnam and Lebanon and was handsomely decorated for his service over the years, earning the Legion of Merit, the Bronze Star (with combat V), the Meritorious Service Medal (three awards), the Navy Commendation Medal (with Silver Star), the Marine Corps Expeditionary Medal (two awards), the National Defense Service Medal, the Vietnam Service Medal (with four stars), the Humanitarian Service Medal, the Vietnam Cross of Gallantry (two awards, with Silver Star and Palm and Frame), the Presidential Unit Commendation (one star), the Combat Action Ribbon (one star), the Republic of Vietnam Campaign Medal, and the Lebanese Order of the Cedar. He's one of a very small number of non–Lebanese citizens to receive that last honor, granted to him for his peace-making work as marine liaison to Ambassador Philip Habib, a crucial and meaningful side duty while he was serving as executive officer of the 32nd Marine Amphibious Unit in Beirut in 1982–83.

Colonel Smith is certainly less famous than many of the other folks we've profiled over the preceding pages, but he does hold a particular place of honor and respect in my own heart, simply because he was my father. And having disclosed that fact, I'll shift from the literary third-person to the more hands-on first-person tense for these final closing pages of this book.

Although the military biography that can be gleaned from my father's list of medals and ribbons was an important part of who and what he was, there was obviously more to his life than the details of his military accomplishments, as is, of course, the case for everyone

Young author to be J. Eric Smith (in the arms of Major Leonard Fahrni) and his mother, Linda Waters Smith, admire Colonel Charles R. Smith, Jr.'s, new Bronze Star Award (Linda Waters Smith Personal Collection).

Epilogue

we've written about in this book. My father was well educated with a pair of master's degrees, and he spent much of his life as an educator, either directly (as a schoolteacher, later in his life) or indirectly (as a mentor, storyteller, sage, and church elder). He was a man of great, deep faith, who touched countless lives through his ministries. He was also a "foodie" without pretense, who could just as easily appreciate a good chili dog as he could a fine meal at one of the world's great restaurants. He was a loving husband to my mom, a great dad to my sister and me, and a doting grandfather to my daughter, niece, and nephew.

But I think what I miss the most, when all's said and done, is the fact that he was really quite the goofball much of the time and was a lot of fun to spend time with. He had an infectious laugh and loved to tell tall tales and stories; the truth was malleable for him and did not necessarily have to correspond to reality. (The excellent Tim Burton movie *Big Fish* could have been his biography.) He also found humor in all sorts of places where most folks didn't look for it. I remember one time when my sister and I were young and our mom was away for some reason, so Dad was left with the responsibility of making dinner for us. He spent a long time in the kitchen that night making a very special dinner for us: a Spam lamb (for my sister) and a Spam ram (for me). Both of them were anatomically correct, ahem. We laughed and laughed and laughed through our dinner, and meat from a can never tasted as good as it did that night.

Like most military kids, the summers of my childhood were largely defined by long-haul family road trips, when my father, mother, sister, and I (along with an assortment of dogs, cats, and plants) would vacate one home, pile into the car, and set off on a long one-way trip to a new life with a new home in a new town. Summer was the season of change for us, and somewhere during each one of those trips—as my sister and I sat in the back seat, sticky with melted chocolate and potato chip grease, hypnotized by the power lines that appeared to oscillate up and down as you stared at them—there was a tangible crossover moment, a faint psychic "pop" as the last cord attaching us to our departure point snapped and we began to feel the gravitational pull of our new destination.

During years when my father didn't have a new assignment, we'd pile into the car anyway and drive down to visit relatives in North and South Carolina, just because it somehow wasn't really a summer if we didn't have that car time together. And if there were no necessary trips lined up, my father would often make some up anyway, just to go drive somewhere with us, to go see what a road on the map looked like when

Epilogue by J. Eric Smith

we were actually on it, to figure out the best way to get from here to there, even if we didn't need to go there for any particularly good reason.

Who knew what we might find if we just got in the car and drove? Maybe a great new place for chili dogs. Maybe a battlefield where one or more of our ancestors fought in the Civil War. Maybe a miniature golf course with great soft ice cream and a layout simple enough to allow the kids to be competitive with the adults. Maybe a town with a funny name. Maybe a mountain my father climbed when he was a boy himself. Maybe an old airplane. Maybe a stray cat that my mother would pick up and bring home and keep in our basement until she could find it a home. Or maybe nothing at all ... which was fine, really, because the chocolate still melted just the same way, and the potato chips were just as greasy, and the power lines oscillated up and down anyway, whether we got anywhere worthwhile at day's end or not.

My mother recently asked me about my earliest childhood memory, and of course it took place during the summer in the back seat of a car, which at the time I had to myself, since my sister hadn't been born yet. I had a pinwheel and was letting it spin in the breeze created by the open window in those pre-air-conditioning days. My mother turned to tell me to be careful not to let it blow out the window ... just moments before I lost my grip on it and it sailed away, gone almost before I realized it. What sticks with me to this day from that memory is the sense of shock I felt sitting there, realizing that something perfectly secure and happy—a summer road trip, no less—could change so suddenly, a whim of fate and physics taking something from me, just like that.

I relearned that lesson on a completely different scale nearly 40 years later, when I received a phone call at work telling me that my father had been critically injured in an auto accident. He was out running errands, preparing for yet another road trip to the beach, when another driver blacked out, crossed the median on a marsh causeway, and hit him square on, front bumper to front bumper at high speed, fate and physics in full force.

Once the full gravity of the situation became clear to us all, I hopped on a plane and flew down to South Carolina from Albany, New York, where I was living at the time. I was there, holding my father's head in my hands, with my mother and sister and a trusted family friend beside me, when he died from his injuries the next day, in the same hospital where I had been born some four-plus decades earlier. After my father's funeral (with full and moving military honors) at Beaufort National Cemetery, I didn't fly back home to Albany. I got behind the

205

wheel of a rented car and I *drove* that trip, taking a variety of routes that I'd never taken before, visiting some towns with funny names, passing a few battlefields and miniature golf courses, stopping along the way to have a chili dog or three in his honor. It was September, the end of summer. That was fitting and apt.

I returned to Beaufort a couple of months later after my father's gravestone had been completed and installed. It's a standard military marker, nothing special, though my father rests in a glorious spot, directly below a massive classic Carolina live oak, draped with Spanish moss, providing a perfect shady place to sit and reflect and visit, as one does. At the time of my father's death, Beaufort National Cemetery was close to capacity in terms of available burial spaces (they have since acquired adjacent acreage and added a large new section), so the cemetery's managers were squeezing new interments in and around a variety of much older graves.

My father's plot is at the end of a row, and the vast majority of the graves near him mark the mortal remains of scores of soldiers from the "United States Colored Troops" (USCT), who (as discussed at length in Chapter One, about "the Glory Soldiers") were members of regiments in the United States Army composed primarily of African American soldiers, although members of other minority groups also served within the units. Because my father's grave is at the end of a row, he has only one "side-by-side" neighbor. After my mother and I admired my father's new stone for the first

The grave of Colonel Charles R. Smith, Jr., USMC, Beaufort National Cemetery (J. Eric Smith).

206

time, I strolled over to investigate who lay in perpetual proximity to the most important soldier in my own life. My first reaction upon looking at the discolored, weathered stone was that its occupant was a private (PVT) in the USCT named "L. Harris." But later, as I was looking at photos I had snapped that day, I studied a contrast-enhanced close-up shot of his faded marker and realized that it actually said "_ Harris."

They didn't know his first name! He fought for his country and his freedom under the most harrowing circumstances imaginable (when Black soldiers were captured by Confederate troops, they weren't treated as prisoners of war but rather as escaped slaves, and it was a capital offense for escaped slaves to bear arms; atrocities were common), died, was buried in a national cemetery, and they still didn't know his first name. Wow!

I thought about PVT Harris a lot after realizing that he was buried without a first name, so I decided to do a little research to see what I could find about him. The official register of graves at the national cemetery did indeed list him without a first name as follows:

Harris, d. 11/11/1865, PVT 128 USCT, 11/11/1865, Plot: 32 3442

This told me that he died on November 11, 1865 (which half a century later would become Veteran's Day) and that he was a private in the 128th Infantry of the USCT.

The 128th was one of the last USCT regiments

The grave of Private Harris, USCT, Beaufort National Cemetery (J. Eric Smith).

Epilogue

formed: it was organized at Hilton Head, South Carolina, from April 23 to 29, 1865, served in the Department of the South, and was mustered out on October 20, 1865.

I found a roster of the 128th Infantry and was intrigued to note that there was no one with the surname "Harris" in the unit. It occurred to me that "Harris" might not have been a last name: if a soldier fell and his comrades could only identify him by one name, might it be a first name instead of a surname? I re-searched the roster of the 128th Infantry and, sure enough, found two records:

HARRIS DEPPEE: Company A (no incoming or outgoing rank listed)
HARRIS DEPPU: Company A, PVT in, PVT out

It seems hard to believe that "Harris Deppee" and "Harris Deppu," both in the same company, were different people. I suspect there was a record-keeping error here, and these records represent a single person. Could this have been PVT Harris, my father's perpetual posthumous neighbor?

Perhaps, though there was something that was bothering me about this information: if the 128th Infantry was mustered out on October 20, 1865, and PVT Harris died on November 11, 1865, then why was he buried in the national cemetery? Perhaps he had been injured before his unit was disenrolled, lingered, died, and then was buried. (As noted earlier in this book, many of the earliest national cemeteries were filled by casualties from hospitals and prisons, and not from the immediate aftermath of battles.) But if that were the case, it would seem that there would have been more information available about him, from those who cared for him during his terminal injury or illness, at least enough to provide a full name for a grave.

I began to wonder whether the national cemetery's records about PVT Harris were accurate with regard to his unit. There were only six infantry regiments of USCT troops enlisted from South Carolina—the 21st, 33rd, 34th, 103rd, 104th, and 128th—so it was relatively easy to look at the rosters and dates of service for each of those units to see if perhaps PVT Harris had been posthumously assigned to the wrong unit.

The 21st Infantry USCT was organized from earlier units of the South Carolina Colored Infantry (SCCI). They conducted garrison duty at Charleston and Mt. Pleasant, South Carolina, until August 1865, and at various points in South Carolina and Georgia until October 1866. They had four Harrises: Cato, George, Napoleon, and Simmons. It's

208

possible one of them is my father's neighbor, especially since Cato Harris of the 21st is also buried at Beaufort, having died July 29, 1864.

The 33rd Infantry USCT was also formed from earlier SCCI units. The 33rd was at Pocotaligo, South Carolina, until February 1865, then were involved in the occupation of Charleston until March 8. They moved to Savannah on March 8, and served there until June 6. They moved from there to Augusta, Georgia, and served there and at various points in the Department of the South until January 1866. They had six Harrises: Arthur, Edward, two Georges, Isaac, and William. It seems unlikely that any of them would have ended up at Beaufort National Cemetery either, since the unit had moved into Georgia by the time PVT Harris died.

The 34th Infantry was a heavily deployed combat unit also formed from the SCCI. Among many other engagements, they fought in the Battle of Honey Hill on November 30, 1864, in which the Confederate troops were commanded by my ancestor, Colonel Charles J. Colcock; that battle also featured in Chapter One of this book, as the remnants of Colonel Robert Gould Shaw's unit fought there. The 34th had been in Florida until November 25, 1864, when they were ordered to South Carolina, and they mustered out on February 28, 1866. So it is possible that one of their three Harrises (Andrew, Charles, and Harvey) was the one I'm seeking.

The 104th Infantry was organized at Beaufort, April 28 to June 25, 1865. They were attached to Department of the South and performed garrison and guard duty at various points in South Carolina until mustering out on February 5, 1866. Like the 128th, the 104th Infantry contained no one with the surname Harris.

That leaves the 103rd, with Jacob, Lewis, Ned, Samuel, and Stephen Harris listed on their roster. The 103rd was essentially a sister regiment to the 128th: it was organized at Hilton Head on March 10, 1865, from scratch (not from earlier SCCI regiments) and attached to District of Savannah, Department of the South, to June 1865, and then the Department of the South to April 1866. The 103rd served garrison and guard duty at Savannah and various points in Georgia and South Carolina for their entire term and were mustered out April 15–20, 1866.

That makes the 103rd the most likely unit in which the enigmatic PVT Harris might have served: it came from Hilton Head (like the 128th) and was still on active service at the time that PVT Harris died in November 1865 (unlike the 128th). If the two units were serving in similar capacities and both came from Hilton Head, record keepers at the national cemetery might not have been overly concerned with distinctions between the two groups.

Interestingly, the cemetery records list a grave for Isaac Harris of the 103rd Infantry, died May 28, 1865, though he is not listed on the 103rd roster. This somewhat confirms my hunch that the units listed for fallen USCT soldiers might have been handled in something of a casual estimated fashion. Other than the aforementioned Cato and Isaac, there are four other Harrises from the USCT at Beaufort: Benjamin of the 26th Infantry from Riker's Island, New York; Daniel of the 32nd Infantry from Camp William Penn, Pennsylvania; another Isaac of the Third Infantry, also from Camp William Penn; and Taylor, no unit listed.

At that point, my research avenues all reached dead ends, so to this day, I am not sure exactly who "_ Harris" was or which unit he served with. I still occasionally poke about in various archives, hoping for some new leads, but at the time that we put this book to bed, Harris's true identity remains a mystery to me. That being the case, though, I've come to count Harris as a sort of honorary member of our family, and whenever I visit Beaufort National Cemetery to pay respects to my father, I also spend time reflecting at Harris's grave.

My mother and I will usually take some flowers or other small objects of significance and remembrance to leave behind at my father's grave when we pay our respects, and I always make a point to leave some memorial atop Harris's remains as well, to clean the dust and dirt from his headstone as diligently as I tend to my father's, and to stomp down the ground mole hummocks that snake over both graves, laughing as I do so at the fact that my father was one of those classic lawn care–obsessed dads who would have pitched a fit had his own domestic sward in life been so marked and marred by burrowing critters. I know that those actions don't mean anything on one plane, but on another plane, it just feels *right* to me that someone cares for Harris's grave, wonders what his mother called him when he was a boy, how he came to enlist in the USCT, and how he ended his days. He deserves that, I think. So I do my part and will continue to do so as long as I'm able to visit his mortal remains and marker.

Those personal experiences with exploring "perpetual proximity" over the past two decades were at the forefront of my mind when Jim and I first formulated this book a few years ago. I've gleaned joy from researching and attempting to tell Harris's story in various outlets over the years, and I am happy to share his story again here to the best of my abilities given the sparse records of his life. I've also gleaned joy

Author J. Eric Smith stands between the graves of Private Harris and Colonel Smith, Beaufort National Cemetery (E. Paige Smith Duft).

from the process of researching and writing about the other examples of side-by-side burials documented in these pages. As we remarked in the introduction to this book, the subjects of the stories we have shared usually walked side by side in life before lying side by side in death.

Epilogue

We note the latter fact to celebrate the former, and we also note how easy and gratifying it can be to better understand the dynamic stories behind the static markers of those who passed before us. It is our hope that those who read these pages will follow our lead in your own lives, in your own times, and in your own sacred spaces. We honor those who came before us by doing so, and we gain a deeper appreciation about the subtleties and complexities of history when we knit together the stories told by neighboring graves and markers.

We thank you for treading among various markers and stones with us, we hope that the journey has been enriching, educational, and encouraging, and we celebrate your own walks down similar paths of exploration, curiosity, honor, remembrance, and respect.

Sources and Recommended Additional Reading

Note: The authors tried to deploy new interviews and primary source documents (including cemetery records, military records, contemporary newspaper and magazine coverage of then-current events, and books written in real time by or about our various subjects, etc.) as often as we could in telling the various stories contained in this book. In the bibliography that follows, we provide cites for a set of books that cover or expand on various aspects of our stories in broad or general terms (especially related to American funerary practice, national cemeteries, and modern "cemetery tourism"), then provide a chapter-by-chapter set of selected cites for key articles and pieces that either shaped our narrative or expand on it in depths deeper than we chose to document. The specific chapter cites represent the most significant ancillary resources adjacent to our research but do not represent the totality of sources consulted.

Selected Books Covering General Topics

American Battle Monuments Commission. *Normandy American Cemetery and Memorial.* Arlington, VA: American Battle Monuments Commission, 2010.

Dieterle, Lorraine Jacyno. *Arlington National Cemetery: A Nation's Story Carved in Stone.* San Francisco: Pomegranate Europe, 2001.

Edwards, Tryon, C. N. Catrevas, and Jonathan Edwards. *The New Dictionary of Thoughts: A Cyclopedia of Quotations.* New York: Standard Book, 1944.

Eggener, Keith L. *Cemeteries.* New York: Norton, 2010.

Fabre, Geneviève, and Robert G. O'Meally. *History and Memory in African-American Culture.* New York: Oxford University Press, 1994.

Faust, Drew Gilpin. *This Republic of Suffering: Death and the American Civil War.* New York: Knopf, 2012.

Finn, Terence T. *America at War: Concise Histories of U.S. Military Conflicts from Lexington to Afghanistan.* New York: Berkley Caliber, 2014.

Grant, John Thomas. *Final Thoughts: Eternal Beauty in Stone.* Atglen, PA: Schiffer, 2011.

Holt, Dean W. *American Military Cemeteries.* Jefferson, NC: McFarland, 2010.

Kerrigan, Michael. *History of Death.* London: Amber Books, 2017.

Lemay, Kate Clarke. *Triumph of the Dead: American World War II Cemeteries, Monuments, and Diplomacy in France.* Tuscaloosa: University of Alabama Press, 2018.

McElya, Micki. *The Politics of Mourning: Death and Honor in Arlington National Cemetery.* Cambridge, MA: Harvard University Press, 2016.

Mitford, Jessica. *The American Way of Death.* London: Quartet, 1980.

Poole, Robert M. *On Hallowed Ground: The Story of Arlington National Cemetery.* New York: Walker, 2009.

Rhoads, Loren. *199 Cemeteries to See before You Die.* New York: Running Press Book, 2017.

Rhoads, Loren. *Wish You Were Here:*

Sources and Recommended Additional Reading

Adventures in Cemetery Travel. San Francisco: Automatism Press, 2017.

Sloane, David Charles. *Last Great Necessity: Cemeteries in American History.* Baltimore: Johns Hopkins University Press, 1995.

Soldiers' National Cemetery Association. *Charter and Proceedings of the Board of Commissioners of the Soldiers' National Cemetery Association: Incorporated by the State of Pennsylvania.* Providence: Knowles, Anthony, 1864.

Williams, T. Harry. *The Selected Essays of T. Harry Williams.* Baton Rouge: Louisiana State University Press, 1983.

Yalom, Marilyn. *The American Resting Place: Four Hundred Years of History through Our Cemeteries and Burial Grounds.* Boston: Houghton Mifflin, 2008.

Prologue, Introduction, and Epilogue

Abercrombie, John J. *Battle of Honey Hill, S.C.* N.p., 1911.

Arbuthnot, Nancy Prothro. *Guiding Lights: United States Naval Academy Monuments and Memorials.* Annapolis: Naval Institute Press, 2009.

Beaufort County. *"From the Pages of History": Memorial Day, 29 May 1989, Beaufort, South Carolina.* Beaufort, SC: Beaufort County Department of Veterans Affairs, 1989.

Boykin, John. *Cursed Is the Peacemaker: The American Diplomat versus the Israeli General, Beirut 1982.* Belmont, CA: Applegate, 2002.

Brayton, Ellery M. *An Address Delivered on Decoration Day, May 30, 1890, at the National Cemetery, Beaufort, S.C.* N.p., 1890.

Gourdin, J. Raymond, and Marvin V. Greene. *104th Infantry Regiment, USCT: Colored Civil War Soldiers from South Carolina.* Westminster, MD: Heritage Books, 2007.

Jones, Charles C. 1885. "The Battle of Honey Hill." *Southern Historical Society Papers* 13: 355–367.

Josephson, Michael S., and Wes Hanson. *The Power of Character: Prominent*

Americans Talk about Life, Family, Work, Values, and More. Bloomington, IN: Unlimited Publishing, 2004.

McNeal, James R., and Scott Tomasheski. *The Herndon Climb: A History of the United States Naval Academy's Greatest Tradition.* Annapolis: Naval Institute Press, 2020.

United States. *Roll of Honor: Names of Soldiers Who Died in Defense of the American Union, Interred in the National [and Other] Cemeteries.* Washington, DC: Government Publishing Office, 1865.

Robert Gould Shaw and the Soldiers of the 54th Massachusetts Infantry Regiment

Alexander, Leslie M., and Walter C. Rucker. *Encyclopedia of African American History.* Santa Barbara: ABC-CLIO, 2010.

Baird, George William. *The 32nd Regiment, U.S.C.T. at the Battle of Honey Hill.* Bethesda: University Publications of America, 1994.

Duncan, Russell. *Where Death and Glory Meet: Colonel Robert Gould Shaw and the 54th Massachusetts Infantry.* Athens: University of Georgia Press, 1999.

Emilio, Luis Fenollosa. *The Assault on Fort Wagner, July 18, 1863: The Memorable Charge of the Fifty-Fourth Regiment of Massachusetts Volunteers, Written for "The Springfield Republican."* Bethesda: University Publications of America, 1991.

Greene, Robert Ewell. *Swamp Angels: A Biographical Study of the 54th Massachusetts Regiment: True Facts about the Black Defenders of the Civil War.* N.p.: BoMark/Greene Publishing, 1990.

Hargrove, Hondon B. *Black Union Soldiers in the Civil War.* Jefferson, NC: McFarland, 1988.

Mack-Williams, Kibibi. *African American History.* Ipswich, MA: Salem Press, 2017.

Morrill, Dan L. *The Civil War in the Carolinas.* Charleston: Nautical & Aviation Publishing Company of America, 2002.

Sources and Recommended Additional Reading

Reid, Mark A. *Spike Lee's* Do the Right Thing. Cambridge: Cambridge University Press, 2005.

Shaw, Robert Gould, and Russell Duncan. *Blue-Eyed Child of Fortune: The Civil War Letters of Colonel Robert Gould Shaw*. Athens: University of Georgia Press, 1992.

Susan Bogert Warner and Anna Bartlett Warner

Coffey, Ronnie Clark. *Constitution Island*. Charleston: Arcadia, 2008.

Davis, Christopher West. "An Island of American History." *New York Times*, July 21, 2002.

Hymnary. "Jesus Loves Me, This I Know, for the Bible Tells Me So." Accessed March 22, 2022. https://hymnary.org/text/jesus_loves_me_this_i_know_for_the_bible

Hymntime.com. "Anna Bartlett Warner." Accessed March 22, 2022. http://www.hymntime.com/tch/bio/w/a/r/n/warner_ab.htm

Sanderson, Dorothy Hurlbut. *They Wrote for a Living: A Bibliography of the Works of Susan Bogert Warner and Anna Bartlett Warner*. West Point, NY: The Constitution Island Association, 1976.

Stokes, Olivia Egleston Phelps. *Letters and Memories of Susan and Anna Bartlett Warner*. Tokyo: Athena Press, 2011.

United States. *Constitution Island*. Washington, DC: N.p., 1909.

Warner, Anna Bartlett. *Miss Tiller's Vegetable Garden and the Money She Made by It*. New York: A.D.F. Randolph, 1970.

Warner, Anna Bartlett. *Susan Warner ("Elizabeth Wetherell")*. Tokyo: Athena Press, 2011.

Warner, Susan. *The Wide, Wide World*. New York: Putnam, 1851.

The Virginia Military Institute Cadets and the Battle of New Market

American Battlefield Trust. "New Market." Accessed March 22, 2022. https://www.battlefields.org/learn/civil-war/battles/new-market

Davis, William C. *The Battle of New Market*. Harrisburg, PA: Stackpole Books, 1993.

Encyclopedia Virginia, Virginia Humanities. "New Market, Battle Of." Accessed March 22, 2022. https://encyclopediavirginia.org/entries/new-market-battle-of/

Gindlesperger, James. *Seed Corn of the Confederacy: The Story of the Cadets of the Virginia Military Institute at the Battle of New Market*. Shippensburg, PA: Burd Street Press, 1997.

Historynet. "Put the Boys In! The Battle of New Market, 1864." Accessed March 22, 2022. https://www.historynet.com/put-boys-battle-new-market-1864/

Shenandoah Valley Battlefields National Historic District. "The Battle of New Market: May 15, 1864." Accessed March 22, 2022. https://www.shenandoahatwar.org/battle-of-new-market

Virginia Military Institute. *Alphabetical List of Graduates of the Virginia Military Institute from 1839 to 1898, with Postoffice Address*. Baltimore: Williams & Wilkins, 1899.

VMI Alumni Association, John N. Upshur, Holmes Conrad, and John S. Wise. *New Market Day at V.M.I. Celebrating the Thirty-Ninth Anniversary of the Battle of New Market and Unveiling of Ezekiel's Statue: Virginia Mourning Her Dead*. 1903.

Whitehorne, Joseph W. A. *The Battle of New Market: Self-Guided Tour*. Washington, DC: Center of Military History, United States Army, 1988.

Wise, John S. *Battle of New Market, Va., May 15th, 1864: An Address Repeated by John S. Wise, Esq., a Cadet in the Corps of 1864, before the Professors, Officers and Cadets of the Virginia Military Institute, in the Hall of the Dialectic Society, May 18th, 1882*. [Lexington?, VA]: N.p., 1882.

Douglas Albert Munro and Edith Fairey Munro

Coast Guard News. "The Legend of the Heroes Mother." Accessed March

22, 2022. https://coastguardnews. com/the-legend-of-the-heroes-mother/2013/11/17/

Hoyt, Edwin P. *Guadalcanal*. Lanham, MD: Scarborough House, 1999.

Meyers, Donald W. "It Happened Here: South Cle Elum Man Became First Coast Guardsman to Win Medal of Honor." *Yakima Herald-Republic*, April 9, 2017.

National World War II Museum. "Signalman First Class Douglas A. Munro's Medal of Honor." Accessed March 22, 2022. https://www.national ww2museum.org/war/articles/-douglas-munro-coast-guard-medal-of-honor

Navsource Online: Destroyer Escort Photo Archive. "USS Douglas A. Munro (DE 422)." Accessed March 22, 2022. https://www.navsource.org/ archives/06/422.htm

Quann, C. James. "Douglas A. Munro: A World War II Hero from Cle Elum." *Columbia: The Magazine of Northwest History*, Fall 2000.

Scheina, Robert L. *Coast Guard History*. [Washington, DC]: U.S. Government Printing Office, 1989.

United States and John L. Zimmerman. *The Guadalcanal Campaign*. Washington, DC: Historical Division, Headquarters, U.S. Marine Corps, 1949.

U.S. Coast Guard Historian's Office. "The Gold Dust Twins: Commander Raymond Evans, USCG (Ret.) Remembers His Friend and Shipmate Douglas Munro." Accessed March 22, 2022. https://tinyurl.com/3573nfyv

Williams, Gary. *Guardian of Guadalcanal: The World War II Story of Coast Guard Medal of Honor Recipient Douglas Munro*. West Chester, OH: Lakota Press, 2014.

Leavenworth's German Prisoners of War

Doyle, Robert C. *The Enemy in Our Hands America's Treatment of Enemy Prisoners of War, from the Revolution to the War on Terror*. Lexington: University Press of Kentucky, 2010.

Farquhar, Michael. "Enemies among Us: German POWs in America." *Washington Post*, September 10, 1997.

Garcia, J. Malcolm. "German POWs on the American Homefront." *Smithsonian*, September 15, 2009.

Kansas City Star. "Mysterious Flowers Symbolize Questions over 14 Executed German POWs." *Baltimore Sun*, October 27, 1992.

Kansas Travel. "United States Disciplinary Barracks Cemetery." Accessed March 22, 2022. http://kansastravel. org/militaryprisoncemetery.htm

Krammer, Arnold. *Nazi Prisoners of War in America*. New York: Stein and Day, 1979.

Lamb, David. "Prisoners of Silence: In a Small Kansas Cemetery, the Graves of 14 German POWs Represent One of the Last Untold Stories of World War II." *Los Angeles Times*, November 30, 1990.

Manning, Carl. "Graves Recall Executed German POWs." *Los Angeles Times*, March 1, 1998.

Orona, Brittani and Online Archive of California. "Inventory of the Kenneth Knox Collection D-547." Accessed March 22, 2022. https://oac.cdlib. org/findaid/ark:/13030/c8qv3ks4/ entire_text/

U.S.D.B. History. [Fort Leavenworth? KS]: [U.S. Disciplinary Barracks?], 1950.

Quentin Roosevelt and Theodore Roosevelt, Jr.

Borja, Elizabeth, and National Air and Space Museum. "The Grave of Quentin Roosevelt." Accessed March 22, 2022. https://airandspace.si.edu/stories/ editorial/grave-quentin-roosevelt

Brady, Tim. *His Father's Son: The Life of General Ted Roosevelt, Jr.* New York: New American Library, 2017.

Burns, Eric. *The Golden Lad: The Haunting Story of Quentin and Theodore Roosevelt*. New York: Pegasus Books, 2016.

Congressional Medal of Honor Society: Stories of Sacrifice. "Theodore Roosevelt, Jr." Accessed March 22, 2022. https://www.cmohs.org/ recipients/theodore-roosevelt-jr

Fink, Jenny. "D-Day Anniversary: Only One Father Served with His Son at Normandy Invasion." *Newsweek*, June 6, 2019.

Jeffers, H. Paul. *In the Rough Rider's Shadow: The Story of a War Hero, Theodore Roosevelt, Jr.* New York: Ballantine Books, 2003.

National Guard. "Presidential Son Quentin Roosevelt Was a famous WWI Casualty." Accessed March 22, 2022. https://www.nationalguard.mil/News/Article/1564930/presidential-son-quentin-roosevelt-was-a-famous-wwi-casualty/

New Netherland Institute: Exploring America's Dutch Heritage. "Theodore Roosevelt, Jr. (1887–1944)" Accessed March 22, 2022. https://www.new netherlandinstitute.org/history-and-heritage/dutch_americans/theodore-roosevelt-jr/

Roosevelt, Quentin, and Kermit Roosevelt. *Quentin Roosevelt: A Sketch with Letters.* New York: Scribner's, 1922.

Walker, Robert W. *The Namesake: A Biography of Theodore Roosevelt, Jr.* New York: Brick Tower Press, 2014.

Hazel Ying Lee and Victor Ying Lee

Boule, Margie. "Hazel Ying Lee's Aerial Odyssey Wins Its Wings at Long Last." *Portland Oregonian*, April 2, 2003.

Chambers, Jennifer. *Remarkable Oregon Women: Revolutionaries & Visionaries.* Charleston: The History Press, 2015.

Cole, Jean Hascall. *Women Pilots of World War II.* Salt Lake City: University of Utah Press, 1995.

Kidd, Julie. *River View Cemetery Interments, Portland, Multnomah County, Oregon.* Portland: Genealogical Forum of Oregon, 1999.

Merry, Lois K. *Women Military Pilots of World War II: A History with Biographies of American, British, Russian, and German Aviators.* Jefferson, NC: McFarland, 2010.

Miller, William M. *To Live and Die a WASP: 38 Women Pilots Who Died in WWII.* Charleston: CreateSpace, 2016.

River View Cemetery Association. *By-Laws and Rules of the River View Cemetery Association. Organized 4th December, 1882.* Portland, OR: A. Anderson, 1883.

Steck, Em. "Women Airforce Service Pilots Aided American War Efforts with Help from These Women of Color." *Teen Vogue*, December 24, 2017.

Unander, Lee Sig. "Sky's the Limit." *1859: Oregon's Magazine*, November 10, 2016.

Williams, Vera S. *WASPs: Women Airforce Service Pilots of World War II.* Osceola, WI: Motorbooks International, 1994.

James Clifton "Mandy" Colbert, Roosevelt Colbert, and Gilford Weems

Bowers, William T. *Black Soldier—White Army: The 24th Infantry Regiment in Korea.* Washington, DC: Center of Military History, 1996.

Capital Gazette Editorial Board. "The Korean War Started 70 Years Ago. These Black Annapolis Men Never Came Home." *Capital Gazette*, June 25, 2020.

Griffis, William Elliot. *Corea, the Hermit Nation.* Cambridge: Cambridge University Press, 2015.

Morris, R. Rebecca. *A Low, Dirty Place: The Parole Camps of Annapolis, MD, 1862–1865.* Linthicum, MD: Ann Arundel County Historical Society, 2012.

Nishi, Dennis. *The Korean War.* San Diego: Greenhaven, 2003.

Rishell, Lyle. *With a Black Platoon in Combat: A Year in Korea.* College Station: Texas A&M University Press, 1993.

Scipio, L. Albert. *Last of the Black Regulars: A History of the 24th Infantry Regiment (1869–1951).* Silver Spring, MD: Roman Publications, 1983.

Taylor, Owen M. *The History of Annapolis, the Capital of Maryland: The State House, Its Various Public Buildings,*

Sources and Recommended Additional Reading

Together with a Full History and Description of the United States Naval Academy from Its Origin to the Present Time. Baltimore: Turnbull, 1900.

24th Infantry Association. *24th Infantry Division: The Victory Division*. Paducah, KY: Turner Pub., 1997.

United States. *List of Names of Men of the 24th Infantry Connected with the Houston, Texas Disturbance, Now in Confinement at El Paso, Texas, Whose Service Records Are Herewith*. 1917.

Virgil I. "Gus" Grissom, Roger B. Chaffee, and Edward H. White II

Associated Press Staff. "Lawyer Says Widows of *Apollo* Astronauts Quickly Forgotten with *PM-Challenger* Anniversary." *Associated Press*, January 28, 1988.

Chrysler, C. Donald, and Don L. Chaffee. *On Course to the Stars: The Roger B. Chaffee Story*. Grand Rapids: Kregel Publications, 1968.

Hollingham, Richard. "The Fire That May Have Saved the *Apollo* Programme." *BBC Future*, January 26, 2017.

Kranz, Gene, and Danny Campbell. *Failure Is Not an Option: [Mission Control from Mercury to* Apollo 13 *and Beyond]*. [Old Saybrook, CT]: Tantor Media, 2011.

Leopold, George. *Calculated Risk: The Supersonic Life and Times of Gus Grissom*. West Lafayette, IN: Purdue University Press, 2016.

Seamans, Robert C. *Project* Apollo: *The Tough Decisions*. Washington, DC: NASA, 2007.

Shayler, David J. *Gemini 4: An Astronaut Steps into the Void*. New York: Springer, 2018.

Walters, Ryan S. Apollo 1: *The Tragedy That Put Us on the Moon*. Washington, DC: Regnery History, 2021.

White, Mary C., and NASA History. "Detailed Biographies of *Apollo I* Crew: Ed White." Accessed March 22, 2022. https://history.nasa.gov/Apollo204/zorn/white.htm

Wired Staff. "January 27, 1967: 3 Astronauts Die in Capsule Fire." *Wired*, January 26, 2009.

James Bond Stockdale and William James Crowe, Jr.

Crowe, William J., and Julian Burns. *Selected Works of Admiral William J. Crowe, Jr., USN: Eleventh Chairman of the Joint Chiefs of Staff, 1 October 1985–30 September 1989*. Washington, DC: Joint History Office, Office of the Chairman of the Joint Chiefs of Staff, 2013.

Crowe, William J., and David Chanoff. *The Line of Fire: From Washington to the Gulf, the Politics and Battles of the New Military*. New York: Simon & Schuster, 1993.

Gunther, Marc. "Stockdale Happy to Do a Favor for His Friend: Retired Admiral Is a Man of Steel." *Baltimore Sun*, October 1, 1992.

Joint Chiefs of Staff. "11th Chairman of the Joint Chiefs of Staff: Admiral William James Crowe, Jr." Accessed March 22, 2022. https://www.jcs.mil/About/-The-Joint-Staff/Chairman/Admiral-William-James-Crowe-Jr/

Stillwell, Paul, and Naval Historical Foundation. "Oral History of Admiral William J. Crowe, Jr., U.S. Navy (Retired)." Accessed March 22, 2022. https://www.navyhistory.org/wp-content/uploads/2011/04/Crowe-Oral-History.pdf

Stockdale, James Bond. *Thoughts of a Philosophical Fighter Pilot*. Stanford: Hoover Institution Press, 1995.

Stockdale, James B., and Sybil Stockdale. *In Love and War: The Story of a Family's Ordeal and Sacrifice during the Vietnam Years*. Toronto: Bantam Books, 1985.

United States Naval Academy. "Notable Graduates: Admiral William J. Crowe." Accessed March 22, 2022. https://www.usna.edu/Notables/ambassadors/1947crowe.php

United States Naval Academy. "Notable Graduates: James B. Stockdale." Accessed March 22, 2022. https://

www.usna.edu/Notables/featured/10stockdale.php

Willbanks, James H. *America's Heroes: Medal of Honor Recipients from the Civil War to Afghanistan*. Santa Barbara: ABC-CLIO, 2011.

Andrew Paul Britton and Christopher Eoion Vine-Britton

"Andrew Britton." Accessed March 22, 2022. http://www.andrewbrittonbooks.com/

"Annie Britton Nice Interview on Dundalk FM." May 3, 2011. Accessed March 22, 2022, https://tinyurl.com/yckuaape

Britton, Andrew. *The American*. New York: Pinnacle Books, 2007.

Britton, Andrew. *The Assassin*. New York: Kensington Books, 2013.

Britton, Andrew. *The Invisible*. New York: Pinnacle Books, 2009.

"Famous Spy Novelist Dies Suddenly." *Raleigh Telegram*, [March?] 2008.

Gregg, R. "Young Man Hangs Himself after Being Released from Wake ATC Center." *Raleigh Telegram*, June 18, 2010.

Hanrahan, Kathy. "What's on Tap: Tir Na Nog Owner Keeps Irish Roots Alive in Raleigh." WRAL, March 16, 2017.

NC Bookwatch (via PBS), "Interview: Andrew Britton, The American." Accessed March 22, 2022. https://www.pbs.org/video/nc-bookwatch-andrew-britton-american/

Nice Britton, Annie. "Andrew Paul Britton (January 6, 1981—March 18, 2008). Accessed March 22, 2022, https://www.mem.com/Biography/2357006/6595986/6595989?title=Biography

Index

221

Index

Index

Index

Index

Index

Index

North Georgia College 54
Northern Ireland 191, 198
Norway 109, 142
Nunn, Bill 18
Nuremburg trials 87, 91

Oaklin Springs Baptist Cemetery 139
Obama, Pres. Barack 137
Oberlin, Louisiana 139
Office of Army Cemeteries 86
Ogden, Utah 132
Ohio River 8
Oise-Aisne American Cemetery, France 85–86, 93
Okinawa 155
Oklahoma 179, 181, 187
Oklahoma City, Oklahoma 176
Old Line State *see* Maryland
Old Porter's Lodge 59
Old Soldier's Home (cemetery) 85
Olustee (Civil War battle) 32
One Gallant Rush 20
103rd Infantry (USCT) 208–210
104th Infantry (USCT) 208–209
128th Infantry (USCT) 207–209
153rd Depot Brigade 152–153
162nd Regimental Combat Team 110
Oran, Algeria 111
Oregon 119
The Oregonian 129
"Ornithology of Egypt between Cairo and Assuan" 99
Ossining ("Sing Sing") 83

P-39 Airacobra 122, 125
P-51 Mustang 122
P-63 Kingcobra 122, 125–127
Pacific Northwest 116
Pad 34 (launch site) 163
Pakistan 95
Panama Canal Zone 72
Panic of 1837 41–42
Paris, France 82, 143
Parole, Maryland 147
Patton (film) 116
Patton, Gen. George S. 47, 111–112, 125
Pearl Harbor attack 72, 110, 116, 119, 154
Pearson, Richard 143
Pennsylvania Hotel 178
Pennsylvania Station 178
Pensacola, Florida 175
Perez, Rosie 18
Perl, France 125
Perot, H. Ross 175, 184, 186
Perry, Cmdr. Matthew 149
Pershing, Gen. John J. 154
Peterborough, Cambridgeshire 190–191
Philippines 110, 154

Philipsburg Manor 40
Philipse family 40
Phillips, Wendell 140
Plattsburgh, New York 104
Plot E *see* Oise-Aisne American Cemetery
Pocotaligo, South Carolina 209
Point Cruz, Guadalcanal 75
Point Loma, California 180
Poitier, Sidney 19
Ponton de Arce, L. 129
Port Angeles, Washington 72
Port Royal, South Carolina 26
Portland, Oregon 116–118, 129, 132, 135, 138; Commerce High School 117; H. Liebes and Company (store) 117
Presbyterian Church in America 42
Presidio (Monterrey, California) 119
Princeton University 176
prisoners of war (POWs): camps 88–90; Germans in WWII 86–96; Vietnam 2–3, 88
Progressive Party (1912 American election) 103–104
Project Apollo *see* Apollo (spacecraft)
Project Gemini *see* Gemini (spacecraft)
Providence, Maryland (settlement) 142
Public Broadcasting Service (PBS) 193, 195
Public Enemy 18
Puerto Rico 110, 168
Puller, Lewis B. "Chesty" 75, 77, 81
Pullman cars 89
Purdue University 167
Purvis, Hugh 149–151
Pusan, Korea 155
Putnam, George P. 43
Putnam, Col. Haldimand 30
Pyongyang, South Korea 150

Quantico, Virginia 50
Quasi-War with France 70
Quigley, Padraig 196
Quintus Horatius Flaccus (Horace) 36

Raheem, Radio (film character) 18, 20, 33
Raleigh, North Carolina 192–193, 197–198; Glenwood Memorial Gardens 198; Leesville Road High School 193; Police Department 198
Randall, Richard 143
Rawlins, Sgt. Maj. John (film character) 20
Reagan, Ronald W. 176, 184
Red Cross 105, 109
Reform Party 175
Register of the Officers and Cadets of the Virginia Military Institute 55
Reichl, Edward 84
Republic of Korea Presidential Unit Citation 155

228

Index

Index

Index

Index